USING YOUR IBM PERSONAL COMPUTER

by Lon Poole

Howard W. Sams & Co., Inc.

4300 WEST 62ND ST. INDIANAPOLIS, INDIANA 46268 USA

D0814006

International Standard Book Number: 0-672-22000-8
Library of Congress Catalog Card Number: 82-62203

Edited by: *Lou Keglovits*
Illustrated by: *T.R. Emrick*

Printed in the United States of America.

CONTENTS

ACKNOWLEDGMENTS

I wish to thank Nancy Fischer for helping with the music in Chapter 14, and Erfert Nielson for her invaluable last-minute assistance preparing the manuscript. Thanks to Janice Pascoe, director of marketing/product development for Howard W. Sams & Co., whose professionalism paved the path to publication. I am indebted to Dr. Osborne for his good advice and insistent optimism over the years, as well as for suggesting that I write this book. And I owe special thanks to Karin, who endured my monomania, auditioned my ideas, and kept things in perspective with her common sense.

Dan Rimes of AMDEK Corporation graciously provided an AMDEK Color II monitor; without it I could never have discovered the PC's full graphics potential.

Some of the material in Chapters 1 and 13 appeared previously in the magazine *PC: The Independent Guide to IBM Personal Computers*. The ideas for the animation sequences in Chapter 13 came from the book *Film Animation as a Hobby*, by Andrew and Mark Hobson (Sterling Publishing Co., New York, 1975).

IBM is a registered trademark of International Business Machines Corp.

Apple is a registered trademark of Apple Computer, Inc.

Radio Shack is a registered trademark of Tandy Corporation.

INTRODUCTION

This book is written for those who want to use an IBM Personal Computer (PC) with programs they buy off the shelf or find printed in magazines and books. It is also for everyone who wants to learn more about writing programs for the PC in BASIC, whether the desire stems from idle curiosity or from desperate need. You will learn:

- How to use the basic system components: the system unit, keyboard, display screen, printer, and disk drives.

- How to start packaged programs that you purchase on diskette or copy from books or magazines.

- How to write BASIC programs, from the fundamentals, to storing data on disk drives, to displaying graphics on the screen.

The best way to learn these operations is by doing, so you will get more out of this book if you can type in the examples yourself and see how the PC responds. The text also describes what happens during the operations, so you can check your results or read along even if you cannot use a PC at the time.

ORGANIZATION AND CONTENTS

This book is divided into two parts, plus several appendixes and an index. Those who only want to use packaged programs will find everything they need in Part 1. You will also need to know the material covered there before moving on to Part 2, which teaches BASIC programming to those who have never programmed a computer before. It contains many tables, illustrations, and annotated example programs which, along with the appendixes and index, provide the experienced BASIC programmer with an everyday reference to PC BASIC.

Chapter 1 briefly explains the function of each of the most popular components found on PC systems: the keyboard, display screen, system unit, disk drives, printers, and programs. Like the first chapter of a cookbook, it is there if you are unfamiliar with any of the ingredients or general terminology.

Chapter 2 tells you how to turn your system on, compares and contrasts the different choices of display screen, explains the use of the keys on the keyboard, and gives general directions for using a printer.

Chapter 3 discusses disks and disk drives. It covers diskette selection and handling, describes what the disk operating system is and what it does, explains what files are, and tells you how to use the most important disk commands.

Chapter 4 presents procedures for getting packaged programs started. It tells you how to deal with the several different formats that programs can have on disk, and includes complete instructions for transcribing programs from the printed page into the PC.

Chapter 5 continues where Chapter 3 left off, explaining additional disk commands and features that the advanced user or BASIC programmer will find useful. Topics include advanced command editing, command streaming, and automatic execution of command streams.

Chapter 6 starts the second part of the book with an introduction to BASIC fundamentals. You will learn how to start and end BASIC, how to write simple programs in immediate and programmed modes, how to type and edit program lines most effectively, and how to store and retrieve BASIC programs on disk.

Chapter 7 describes the different kinds of data a BASIC program can work with, including character strings and three kinds of numeric values. It explains the differences and similarities among constants, variables, and arrays, and introduces some commands that manipulate and combine them.

Chapter 8 continues the discussion of data manipulation. It describes the four different kinds of expressions and tells you how they are evaluated. It explains what functions are, and how you can develop your own.

Chapter 9 describes the BASIC commands that affect the order in which other program commands are executed. That includes decision-making, program loops, subroutines, and program overlays.

Chapter 10 explains how to print character strings and numeric values on the display screen and printer, and how to control where they appear and what they look like. It also tells you how to activate the special features and options available on most printers.

Chapter 11 discusses how to minimize keyboard entry errors through total control of the keyboard and careful design of a program's entry phase. It progressively develops a general keyboard entry routine that you will be able to use in everyday programming.

Chapter 12 covers storing and retrieving data on disk. It discusses general file structure as well as the two methods—sequential and random—available in BASIC for accessing data. All this is brought into focus by developing a simple but useful personal inventory program.

Chapter 13 describes all of the special BASIC commands that create graphics displays. You will learn how to draw lines, boxes, circles, arcs, ellipses, and how to use them to construct line graphs, bar graphs, pie charts, and more. There is a complete discussion of the PC's advanced graphics command, which greatly simplifies drawing complex shapes. The chapter concludes with a section on computer animation, including two working examples.

Chapter 14 covers sound. It tells you how to generate sound effects and music using the PC's own speaker.

Chapter 15 explains how to use BASIC's direct control commands to control the more obscure PC features. Specific topics include setting character color on graphics displays, selecting one display when two are attached to the system, and determining keyboard status.

The Appendixes provide summaries of all BASIC commands, disk commands, and error messages. They also list the standard PC characters and compare them to the characters available on most printers.

Within each chapter, material progresses from simple to more difficult. This does not mean that the material at the end of Chapter 4 is simpler than the material at the beginning of Chapter 6, however, because chapters are organized first and foremost by subject. Therefore, if you find the material you are reading getting too difficult, feel free to move on to another chapter. But if it also seems abstruse, you had best return to earlier chapters and practice some more with the material covered in them.

This book teaches you how to program the PC in BASIC to take full advantage of the machine's most popular features, but it does not attempt to explain every sordid detail of every BASIC instruction. Part 2 explains about 80 percent of the BASIC commands and command options that are available on the PC. The 20 percent not covered in depth includes commands and command options that deal with seldom used features, like the ability to store and retrieve programs and data on tape cassettes, and with advanced topics that relatively few BASIC programmers use, like machine language programming.

Part 1

USING THE PC

CHAPTER 1

ANATOMY OF THE PC

The IBM Personal Computer (the PC) is a system of many pieces, each designed to do a specific job. The nucleus of a PC system consists of three components: the keyboard, the system unit, and some kind of video display (Fig. 1-1). These three components handle all the fundamental chores

Fig. 1-1.   A PC system with a monochrome video monitor.

of a computer, namely entering, processing, and reporting information. A wide array of accessory components is available to enhance performance. These accessories can store vast quantities of information, produce printed reports, communicate with other computers, and more. This chapter introduces the most common components, both standard and optional, from IBM and other manufacturers.

KEYBOARD AND DISPLAY SCREEN

The keyboard is the standard device for entering commands. Much of the rest of the information that the computer uses comes originally from the keyboard as well. Using various combinations of its 83 keys, you can type any of the 256 characters which the PC recognizes.

The video display screen is the main device the computer uses for communicating with you. There can be up to 25 lines of text on the screen, although use of the bottom line is somewhat restricted. Lines can have a maximum length of either 40 or 80 characters. With most display screens, the characters on a 40-character line are twice the size of characters on an 80-character line. Naturally, the larger characters are easier to read.

The PC can use any one of several components as a video display screen. IBM makes a monochrome video monitor (Fig. 1-1) that displays text and limited graphics in green characters on a black background. Equivalent video monitors from other sources can also be used. Some of them display white on black, while others display green on black. Because monochrome monitors typically display sharp images, they are well suited for displaying text on either 40- or 80-character text lines.

The PC can also display text and full graphics in color, but this requires a different kind of display screen. A home television set will work, but it requires two special parts to transmit the computer's video output to the televison antenna terminals (Fig. 1-2). The first part, called an *RF modulator*, converts the PC's video signal to one the televison set can tune in. The second part is just a special switch that lets you choose whether the television set will use the computer signal or the regular antenna signal. Because home television sets are engineered for broadcast shows, they cannot match the PC's optical resolution. Even the best sets lose detail and are barely adequate for 80-character text lines.

Fortunately, high-quality color video monitors are available (Fig. 1-3). There are two types available, and they differ in price and picture quality. The less expensive color monitors, called *composite monitors*, offer optical resolution somewhat better than the best home televison sets. The more expensive color monitors, called *RGB monitors*, can display every bit of the detail the PC can generate. Neither type of color monitor uses an RF modulator or an antenna switch.

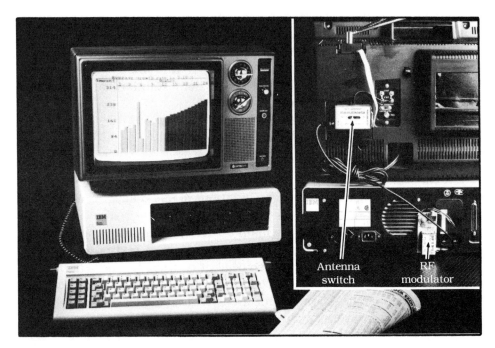

Fig. 1-2. A PC system with a home television as a video monitor.

Fig. 1-3. A PC system with an RGB color video monitor.

It is not possible to use an IBM-style monochrome monitor and a color monitor simultaneously. Your system can be set up to use both, but you will have to choose one or the other. For example, you can use an IBM monochrome monitor for text viewing and a home color television set for color graphics viewing, but the PC cannot display on both at the same time. The procedure for switching between the IBM monochrome monitor and a color monitor, a complicated maneuver, is described in Chapter 15.

SYSTEM UNIT

No component is as essential as the *system unit*, the kingpin of the PC system. It controls the flow of information between each and every component that plugs into it. The system unit can do more than shunt raw information from one device to another. It can process incoming information—extracting, combining, deleting, calculating—to come up with entirely new information all on its own.

You would expect the system unit to be a complex device, and one look inside it confirms that it is (Fig. 1-4). Fortunately, you need not understand the intricacies of all of its circuitry in order to use the PC. But unless you know which features your PC system has, you cannot make full use of them. In this respect, using a PC is like using an automobile. Under the hood of a car is an engine, a battery, probably a radiator, possibly an air conditioner, and many other parts. Chances are you don't know or care exactly how all of those parts work, but you know they are there. Well, a PC system unit has a power supply, a microprocessor, memory, probably a disk drive, possibly a second disk drive, and more.

Some internal parts are hard to spot unless the system unit is disassembled. The system board, for example, normally lies on the bottom of the system unit, hiding many of the small *integrated circuit chips* on it, including the microprocessor and memory chips.

The Power Supply

The main system on/off switch controls the flow of electricity through the system unit power supply. It in turn furnishes electricity of the correct voltage to the system unit electronic circuits, the diskette drives, and the keyboard. The power supply also contains the ventilation fan for the entire system unit, mounted on the underside of the power supply cover.

The Microprocessor

Located near the power supply on the system board is a large integrated circuit chip, the Intel 8088 microprocessor. It is the main brain of the whole system unit, since it coordinates all activities and performs general

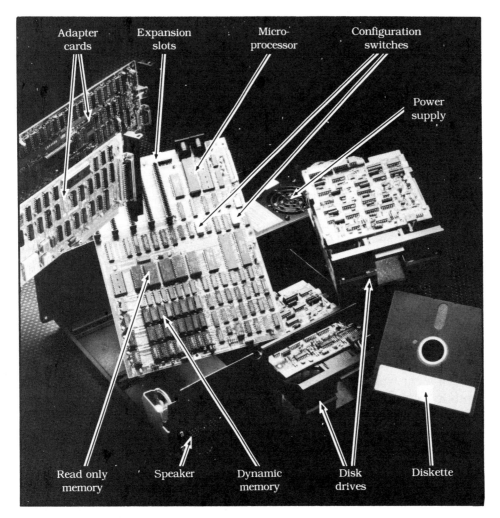

Fig. 1-4. Inside one system unit.

arithmetic calculations for the system. The 8088 microprocessor is fast, but someday its speed may be enhanced by the presence of a co-processor in the empty socket next to it. Candidates for co-processor include the Intel 8087 numeric data processor and the Intel 8089 high speed input/output processor.

Memory

A certain amount of memory is also present in every PC. Computer memory is measured in units called *bytes*. One byte of computer memory—one memory cell—can store one character, so you can think of bytes as characters, but computer memory stores information other than characters, including numeric values and programs. Because of certain facts about computer circuitry architecture, memory capacity is usually a multiple of 1024 bytes. That much memory is called *one K (1K)* bytes. A PC computer has between 60K (61,440) and 1024K (1,048,576) bytes of memory. Memory capacity is sometimes measured in *megabytes*—each megabyte being 1024K bytes.

Every PC has 40K of immutable memory, called *read-only memory (ROM)*, which has its contents indelibly set during its manufacture. The contents never change, even when the power is off. Crucial information that tells the PC how to interpret BASIC language commands and how to perform other basal chores resides in ROM.

Another kind of PC memory goes by several names, including *dynamic memory, read/write memory, and random-access memory (RAM)*. Information can be stored in it and recalled from it any time the PC is on. But turn the power off and its contents vanish. Dynamic memory's volatility is its main asset, because it allows the same memory to be used and reused for any purpose. The system board has at least 16K bytes of dynamic memory, and more chips can be added to increase this to 32K, 48K, or 64K bytes. Adapter cards can increase dynamic memory beyond that.

System Configuration Switches

Two sets of small switches lie near the 8088 microprocessor. The settings of these switches describe the configuration of the system—how much memory there is, what kind of display is in use, and more—so switch settings differ depending on the choice of options. The installation manuals for the optional equipment present on a particular PC depict the correct switch settings.

The Built-In Speaker

Diagonally opposite the power supply is a small speaker. The PC uses it to emit an audible signal in various circumstances, and also it can be programmed to play music and make sound effects.

Expansion Slots

Adapter cards plug into the five slots at the back of the system board. Because more than five cards exist, it is possible to run out of slots. A separate extension chassis that increases the number of slots solves the problem.

Adapter Cards

Adapter cards (Fig. 1-5) make the PC a versatile computer. Some support external equipment, like display screens, disk drives, printers, game controls, and communications with other computers. Other adapters are

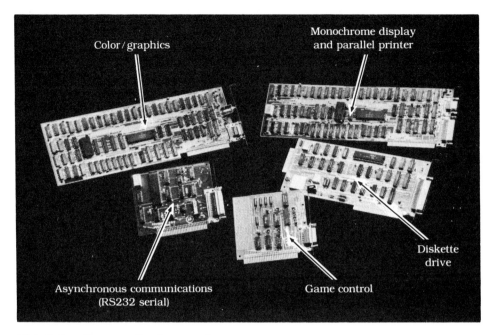

Fig. 1-5. Some adapter cards.

autonomous, including supplemental dynamic memory, battery-powered clocks, and experimental circuit testers. There are single adapter cards that combine several functions, thereby conserving slots in the system unit and making it possible to connect more optional equipment without using an extension chassis. The adapter cards your system needs will depend on how you plan to apply it and what external components you want to use with it. Table 1-1 enumerates some of the possibilities.

DISKS AND DRIVES

A disk is an auxiliary storage device, a kind of memory extension. Anything in memory can be stored on disk and subsequently recalled for reuse. This means the PC can switch from one task to another as fast as it can recall a program from disk. It also means program size and complexity are no longer limited by memory capacity, because now a program can store unneeded information on a disk and use the dynamic memory thus freed for other information recalled from disk.

The entire disk setup consists of three parts: an adapter card, a disk drive, and a disk (Fig. 1-6). The adapter fits in one of the expansion slots inside the system unit and coordinates the transfer of information between the microprocessor and dynamic memory on one hand and the disk drive on the other. The drive reads and writes information on a disk using tech-

Table 1-1. Optional Accessories and Adapters

Option	Adapter Card
Additional memory	Memory expansion
Continuous clock/calendar	Battery clock
Color monitor	Color/graphics
Diskettes	Diskette drive
Experimental circuit board	Prototype board and extender
Home television	Color/graphics
Joysticks	Game control
Light pen	Color/graphics
Modem	Asynchronous communications
Monochrome monitor	IBM monochrome display and parallel printer
Network communications	Asynchronous communications
Paddles	Game control
Printer	IBM monochrome display and parallel printer, parallel printer, or asynchronous communications
Telecommunications	Asynchronous communications
Videotext	Asynchronous communications
Winchester hard disk	Winchester hard disk drive

Fig. 1-6. Diskette drives and diskettes.

nology similar to sound or video tape recording. The disk itself is a platter that spins inside the drive and actually stores information on its magnetic coating.

Diskettes

By far the most common kind of disk on small computer systems like the PC is the flexible disk, usually called a *diskette* or *floppy disk*. Diskettes come in two sizes, 5¼-inch and 8-inch. Both sizes are similarly constructed. There is a ring-shaped piece of flexible plastic that is coated with a magnetic film and enclosed in a protective stiff plastic jacket (Fig. 1-7). The fragile flexible disk stores the information and is protected from physical indignities by the stiff plastic jacket. Individual diskette capacity ranges from about 90K bytes to more than one megabyte, depending on the drive.

Because the diskette is separate from the drive, it is possible to have several diskettes, each with different information on it, any of which will work with one drive. The diskette fits into a slot in a diskette drive. The drive grips the flexible plastic disk through the center hole and spins it inside the jacket. The drive uses the windows cut out of the protective jacket to access the information recorded on the surface of the magnetized flexible disk.

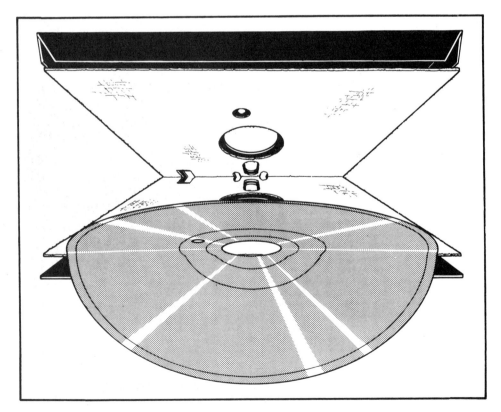

Fig. 1-7. Inside a diskette.

Winchester Disks

Another popular kind of disk drive has a rigid disk that uses a special technology to store 100 times more information on a single disk surface than conventional technology allows. This is called *Winchester technology*, and disk drives that use it are called *Winchester disks*. Because Winchester disks are extremely susceptible to even the tiniest particles of dust or smoke, they have no removable disk. The disk surface is sealed inside the drive and can be changed only by a service person. Storage capacities for Winchester disk drives available for the PC range upwards from five megabytes.

PRINTERS

With a printer, a PC can produce portable reports on paper. There are many different printers that will work with the PC (Fig. 1-8). Each provides a different combination of speed, print quality, number of character sets, types of paper that can be used, and other features.

Parallel and Serial Communications

Of all the methods that exist for communications between computers and printers, the two most popular are called *parallel* and *serial*. The exact

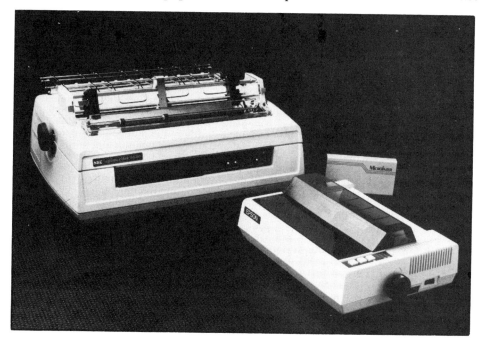

Fig. 1-8. Two printers and a printer buffer.

differences between them are rather technical and quite unimportant here. The PC can use either method, but parallel communications are standard.

The IBM 80CPS Matrix printer uses parallel communications. It plugs into either the IBM Monochrome Display and Parallel Printer adapter card or the IBM Parallel Printer adapter card. You should be able to substitute any other parallel printer for the IBM printer. Printers that use serial communications plug into either IBM's Asynchronous Communications adapter card or some other serial adapter card.

Printer Buffers

When printing, the PC stands idle much of the time, because its potential output rate far exceeds the print speed of even the fastest printer. You can plug in a device between the PC and the printer to act as a reservoir. Called a *printer buffer* or *print spooler*, this device (Fig. 1-8) contains dynamic memory like that found in the system unit, but dedicated to storing information destined for the printer. The printer buffer accepts information at a fast rate, stores it, and gradually releases it as the printer is ready. You can think of a printer buffer as a bucket with a hole in the bottom. The computer fills the buffer much like you might pour water into the bucket, and the buffer dribbles information to the printer much like the water leaks slowly out of the hole in the bucket.

A printer takes between two and five minutes to print 16K characters, but the PC can fill a 16K buffer in less than one minute. Once the buffer fills, the PC must slow back down to the printer's speed, adding more to the buffer as the printer empties it. The PC will eventually stop filling the buffer and go on to some other task, but printing will continue independently until the buffer is empty.

SOFTWARE

A PC without a program is like an orchestra without a musical score—dormant. Any computer needs instructions to bring it to life just as an orchestra needs sheet music. A program is an orderly collection of instructions that tells the computer how to do something, and that makes programs as important a part of the PC as any physical device. *Software* is a term coined to refer collectively to the repertoire of programs available to a computer.

Several kinds of programs co-exist in PC memory and cooperate to control the computer system. One type determines whether the computer is applied to word processing, accounting, financial analysis, videotext, entertainment, or something else. Such programs are called *application programs.*

Application programs may use instructions too advanced for the PC to understand without some help. In that case, a second kind of program translates the application program into instructions the PC understands. That may occur before the program is used, when a *compiler* prepares a translated version for subsequent use. Alternatively, an *interpreter* may extemporaneously translate an application program each time it is used. One interpreter for the BASIC programming language resides in part of the PC's read-only memory; others share dynamic memory with the application program.

Application programs usually rely on the co-existence of another kind of program to take care of fundamental communication with devices like the keyboard, display screen, and printer. That way the application program just says, ''Get a character from the keyboard'' or ''Display this,'' without knowing how to do it. Permanent programs in read-only memory handle communications with most system components, but a separate program in dynamic memory takes care of disk communications. The standard disk communications program is called the *PC disk operating system (PC DOS)*; others are also available.

SETTING UP

The computer system must be set up correctly before you can use it. All devices have a cable that attaches either directly to the back panel of the

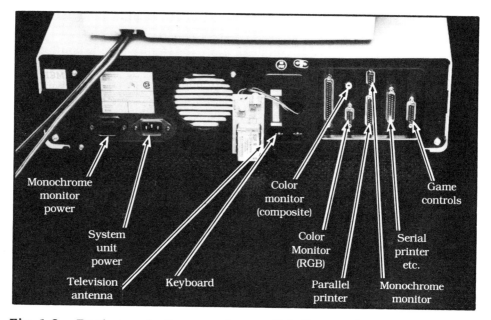

Fig. 1-9. **Back panel of one system unit (other socket arrangements are possible).**

Fig. 1-10.   A system cabling diagram.

system unit or to another device that in turn attaches to the system unit (Fig. 1-9). Most devices also have a power cord that must be plugged into a wall outlet.

   Because the PC can be configured so many different ways, it is impossible to illustrate specific cabling details here. Check the installation manual for each component to be sure it is correctly connected, then for future reference, draw a diagram that depicts proper cabling for your system (Fig. 1-10).

CHAPTER 2

THE MONITOR, KEYBOARD, AND PRINTER

The video display screen, keyboard, and system unit make up the core of any PC system. Most PC systems have a printer too. This chapter explains how to use those components.

POWER ON AND OFF

The simplest PC system, consisting of a system unit, monochrome monitor, and keyboard, is easy to turn on and off. The large red power switch on the side of the system unit energizes all three components. It also controls power to any disk drives installed in the system unit (more about that in later chapters). For the purposes of this chapter, you can ignore disk drives completely.

Turning the power of a more complex PC system on and off involves more switches, because each additional external component has its own power switch. The general rule for power on is, "Switch on external components in any order, but do it before switching on the system unit." Its complement is, "Switch off the system unit first, then switch off external components in any order." Of course if the manual for a specific external component recommends a different sequence, follow it.

USING A VIDEO DISPLAY SCREEN

The video display screen is vitally important to the PC system, and using it is a snap. A home television requires a little manipulation; a video monitor, virtually none.

But beware, for permanent display screen damage can occur through total neglect. Anything displayed without change for about ten minutes will start to burn permanently into the picture tube. The resulting ghost will haunt the display screen forever after. In fact, extensive use of a word processor, spread sheet program, or anything else that displays rows of text (as opposed to graphics) eventually streaks the screen with horizontal shadows evident even when the display is off. Take special care with a home television set, since the specters of computer displays may haunt broadcast viewing too.

A PC that has both a monochrome monitor and either a color monitor or television can only use one at a time. There is a way to switch from one to the other under program control, as described in Chapter 15.

Television Set

To use a television set as the video monitor with your PC, make sure it is connected correctly to the system unit via an RF modulator (Fig. 1-2). Tune the television to the proper channel, as specified in the instructions for the RF modulator. Usually this is channel 33. Set the antenna switch so it routes the computer video signal to the television (Fig. 2-1). Turn the set on, but leave the volume all the way down. The PC does not use the television speaker, just the picture.

If yours is a color set, start with the color controls adjusted for viewing broadcast shows, except set the red-green (hue) control all the way over to full green. If those settings produce unsatisfactory PC colors, go ahead and

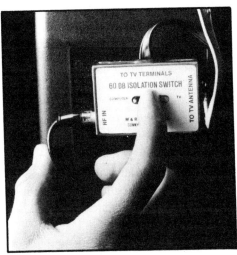

Fig. 2-1. Setting a television antenna slide switch.

readjust the controls until the picture is acceptable. Do not expect startling picture clarity from a television. Even the best sets look fuzzy next to a video monitor.

Home television sets do not show all of the picture they receive. They intentionally magnify the picture so the part around the edges gets lost, preventing the appearance of an ugly black border around a broadcast picture. This scheme is called *overscan*. It is more pronounced on some sets than others, but even the least bit of overscan can mean trouble if the computer tries to use the whole picture area, including the overscan area. Part of the display will be lost, just like a slide show or movie shown on too small a screen. While the PC cannot shrink its entire output to compensate for overscan, it can shift the picture it transmits either left or right. Chapter 4 explains one way to induce the picture shift.

Video Monitors

A video monitor is even easier to use than a television set, because there is no channel to select or antenna switch to set. Generally you can set the picture controls once and then leave them alone.

WHAT YOU SEE ON THE DISPLAY SCREEN

The PC puts something on the display screen within a few seconds after you turn on both pieces of equipment. The first thing you see is an underscore flashing on and off in the upper left-hand corner of the screen. (On television sets with excessive overscan the lone underscore may not be visible.) A short time later a message appears (Fig. 2-2).

The Cursor

The flashing underscore you see on the display screen is called the *cursor*. It marks the place where characters will next appear on the display screen.

```
The IBM Personal Computer Basic
Version C1.00 Copyright IBM Corp 1981
61404 Bytes free
Ok
_
```

Fig. 2-2. Typical screen display at power-on.

The cursor can assume shapes other than an underscore, including a rectangle or a square, and it can even be invisible. In that case, the computer still knows where the cursor is, even though you don't. Changing the cursor shape and visibility requires programming; Chapter 11 explains how it's done.

The Self-Test

In the first few seconds after you switch on the system unit, the PC performs a self-test. If it detects a problem, it puts a coded message on the display screen. Section 4 of the IBM manual *Guide to Operations* thoroughly explains the codes.

USING THE KEYBOARD

The keyboard bears a strong resemblance to a standard typewriter keyboard. Keys for all the letters of the alphabet, the numerals 0 through 9, and most punctuation marks are right where a typist would expect to find them. However, the 83 keys do include a few surprises.

All the keys on the keyboard belong to one of four groups (Fig. 2-3). Keys in the same group are clustered together and are the same color. The standard typewriter keys are the large block of light-colored keys right in the middle of the keyboard. Surrounding them on either side are two columns of dark-colored general control keys, many of which are also found on typewriters. At the right edge of the keyboard is a block of light-colored keys that serves two purposes. The keys can function as a numeric keypad like that of a calculator, or they can control the location of the cursor on

Fig. 2-3. Keyboard groups.

the display screen. On the far left edge of the keyboard are two columns of dark-colored keys called *function keys,* or *soft keys.* The effect and meaning of the function keys can be changed by programming.

Typewriter Keys

If you are used to a typewriter, the letter and numeral keys should pose no problem. Some of the punctuation keys may be in different places than you expect, but you will quickly acclimate to the new arrangement.

General Control Keys

The dark-colored keys bordering the typewriter keys perform general control functions as described below. Application programs may disable or even redefine some of these general control keys; check the program operating instructions.

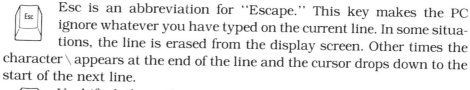 Esc is an abbreviation for "Escape." This key makes the PC ignore whatever you have typed on the current line. In some situations, the line is erased from the display screen. Other times the character \ appears at the end of the line and the cursor drops down to the start of the next line.

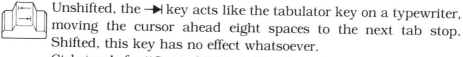 Unshifted, the ➝ key acts like the tabulator key on a typewriter, moving the cursor ahead eight spaces to the next tab stop. Shifted, this key has no effect whatsoever.

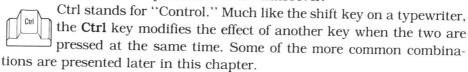 Ctrl stands for "Control." Much like the shift key on a typewriter, the **Ctrl** key modifies the effect of another key when the two are pressed at the same time. Some of the more common combinations are presented later in this chapter.

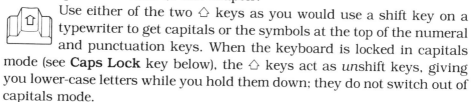 Use either of the two ⇧ keys as you would use a shift key on a typewriter to get capitals or the symbols at the top of the numeral and punctuation keys. When the keyboard is locked in capitals mode (see **Caps Lock** key below), the ⇧ keys act as *unshift* keys, giving you lower-case letters while you hold them down; they do not switch out of capitals mode.

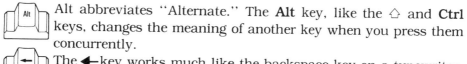 Alt abbreviates "Alternate." The **Alt** key, like the ⇧ and **Ctrl** keys, changes the meaning of another key when you press them concurrently.

The ⬅key works much like the backspace key on a typewriter. However, it not only moves the cursor back one space, but also erases the character that was there.

The nearest equivalent to the ⏎key on a typewriter is the power return key found on many electric typewriters. On other computers, the ⬅key is called *Return key* or *Enter key.* Its purpose is to end the line you are typing and advance to the next line.

PrtSc is an abbreviation for "Print Screen." Unless you simultaneously press the △ key, the **PrtSc** key generates an asterisk. Press the **PrtSc** and △ keys together and whatever is on the screen is reproduced on the printer. Of course, you must have a printer attached to your PC, and it must be ready to print. (Printer operations are discussed at the end of this chapter.)

The **Caps Lock** key locks the keyboard so it generates capital letters without using the △ key. In fact, when the keyboard is locked in capitals mode, using the △ key makes any letter key create a lower-case letter. The **Caps Lock** key differs from the shift lock key on a typewriter, because it affects only the 26 letters of the alphabet. For example, you must always press both the △ and / keys to get a question mark. Press **Caps Lock** once to set capitals mode; press it again to return to normal. There is no outward way to tell whether the caps lock mode is on or off, but Chapter 15 describes a short program that can tell.

By itself, the **Scroll Lock** key does nothing. But in most cases when you press the **Ctrl** key too, the computer stops whatever it may be doing and waits for a command from the keyboard.

The Dual-Mode Numeric Keypad

The group of light-colored keys at the right side of the keyboard is arranged much like the keypad of a standard office calculator. This makes it easy to enter numbers into the computer, especially for someone who can use a calculator by touch. The nearby **PrtSc**, **+**, and **−** keys produce the symbols for multiplication, addition, and subtraction, making this part of the keyboard even more like a calculator keypad.

 The **Num Lock** key determines which of two modes the keypad is in: numeric or nonnumeric. Each time you press the **Num Lock** key, the keypad switches mode. There is no outward way to tell which mode the keypad is in. The only way to tell is to press one of the keys and see what happens. However, Chapter 15 describes a short program that can determine which mode the keypad is in.

In the numeric mode, each of the light-colored keys in the numeric keypad generates one of the numerals 0 through 9, or a decimal point, as indicated on the top of the key.

The numeric keypad used in the nonnumeric mode usually controls the position of the cursor on the display screen, but not always. For example, the PC disk operating system (PC DOS) has its own interpretation of the nonnumeric mode (see Chapter 5 for details).

 The upper left-hand corner of the display screen is called the *home* position. The **Home** key moves the cursor there.

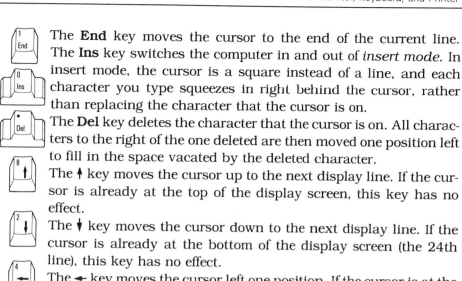

The **End** key moves the cursor to the end of the current line. The **Ins** key switches the computer in and out of *insert mode.* In insert mode, the cursor is a square instead of a line, and each character you type squeezes in right behind the cursor, rather than replacing the character that the cursor is on.

The **Del** key deletes the character that the cursor is on. All characters to the right of the one deleted are then moved one position left to fill in the space vacated by the deleted character.

The ↑ key moves the cursor up to the next display line. If the cursor is already at the top of the display screen, this key has no effect.

The ↓ key moves the cursor down to the next display line. If the cursor is already at the bottom of the display screen (the 24th line), this key has no effect.

The ← key moves the cursor left one position. If the cursor is at the left edge of the display, the ← key will move it to the right edge of the preceding display line. If the cursor is in the home position, this key has no effect.

The → key moves the cursor right one position. If the cursor is at the right edge of the display, the → key will move it to the left edge of the next lower display line. If the cursor is at the lower right-hand corner of the display screen, pressing the → key also inserts a blank line at the bottom of the screen. To make room for the new blank line, the former top line on the display screen disappears.

Function Keys

The two rows of dark-colored keys at the left edge of the keyboard can be programmed to generate different sequences of characters. Some application programs may use function keys for unique purposes; consult their operating instructions for specific details. Chapter 11 explains how to program the function keys yourself.

Combination Keystrokes

As described above, several of the keys do nothing in and of themselves. Instead, they change the effect of other keys. The ⇧, **Ctrl**, and **Alt** keys are all of this type. To use one of them, you press it, hold it down, and press another key. This book denotes such combination keystrokes by separating member keys with a vertical line. For example, **Ctrl│Scroll Lock** means, "Press the **Ctrl** and **Scroll Lock** keys simultaneously." There are many valid combination keystrokes that occur only while programming, especially with the **Alt** key.

Pressing the **Ctrl│Alt│Del** combination resets the computer much the same as turning the power off and back on again. However, the PC does not perform its complete self-test when reset with the **Ctrl|Alt|Del** combination.

You can freeze the screen display with the **Ctrl|Num Lock** combination keystroke. This puts the screen display in suspended animation; nothing new will display until you revive it by pressing any key except **Ctrl**, ⇧, **Alt**, **Caps Lock**, **Num Lock**, or **Scroll Lock**. The **Ctrl|Num Lock** combination works anytime.

The **Ctrl|Scroll Lock** combination keystroke will interrupt whatever the computer is doing and make it wait for a command from the keyboard. This process is called a *break*, and that is why the front of the **Scroll Lock** key is also labeled "Break."

Automatic Key Repeat

You may have discovered that when you hold down a key, it repeats automatically. This repeat feature works with all keys except **Ctrl**, ⇧, **Alt**, **Ins**, and **Num Lock** when they are pressed alone. However, combination keystrokes using the **Ctrl**, ⇧, or **Alt** keys will repeat.

TYPING COMMANDS

When there is no apparent system activity besides the flashing cursor, the PC is probably waiting for a command. You issue commands by typing some sequence of keys. The computer, directed by a program, examines what you typed and tries to determine what to do. Type everything correctly and the program directs the computer to carry out your command. Thus it is the program, not the computer itself, that determines the validity of the commands you type.

Each program has its own set of commands, and when it controls the PC, those are the only commands the PC understands. It may be an application program that is in control—word processing, for example. On the other hand, the disk operating system or the BASIC interpreter may be in control. This means you must know which program is in control of the PC as you prepare to type a command, and with experience that is easy to tell from the context of the display screen. Once you decide which program is in control, you can refer to its instruction or reference manual for a list of the commands it accepts. Chapters 3 and 5 explain the PC disk operating system (PC DOS) commands, and Chapters 6 through 15 cover BASIC commands.

A command may not be exclusive to one program. But be careful, because even though a command may look the same, its effect may differ according to the task at hand. In other words, a certain sequence of keystrokes may mean one thing to one program, the same thing to another program, something entirely different to a third program, and nothing at all to a fourth program.

Because command length varies, there is rarely a practical limit on the number of characters you can type. The controlling program does not act on a command until you signify that you are finished typing it. The almost universal terminator is the ←┘ key. So if you type a command and sit there waiting and waiting for something to happen, you probably forgot to press the ←┘ key. There are commands that don't need a terminator, and even a few that use a different terminator, but exceptions like that should be well documented in the program manual.

CORRECTING TYPING MISTAKES

Make a mistake and the computer does either the wrong thing or nothing at all. Few people never make mistakes, so the PC provides ways to correct errors. For errors you notice before pressing the ←┘ key, use the ← key to backspace until the error is erased. Then you can retype with more caution. Sometimes it's faster to erase the whole line and start over. To do this, press the **Esc** key. There are a number of other ways to correct errors, but they vary from program to program. Check the program operating instructions for details. Chapter 5 explains how to correct errors in PC DOS commands, and Chapter 6 explains how to edit BASIC commands.

Under some conditions it is possible to enter characters too fast for the PC to process them. If this happens, the PC beeps its speaker in warning. Stop typing for a few seconds, then cautiously try another character. If you hear no warning beep, go on with your typing. If the computer is still busy and unable to process more keystrokes at the moment, it will beep again.

USING A PRINTER

Printer operating procedures are remarkably similar in spite of the diversity of printer features. Most of the variety has to do with performance, not procedure. Some printers are fast and some are slow, character clarity and size varies, and so forth, but control of features like that is usually the province of programs. This chapter addresses operating procedures that apply to all printers. For specific details on your printer, refer to the printer operator's manual.

Printer Compatibility

Recall from Chapter 1 that both the PC and the printer must use t⊦ communications method, parallel or serial. There are separate s⊾

the back panel of the system unit for each method, but the PC cannot sense which one you have plugged a printer into, so it uses parallel communications by default. Every time you turn on the computer, you must change this assumption if you plan to use a serial printer. The PC disk operating system (PC DOS) has a special command, MODE, which resets the system so that it uses a serial printer instead of a parallel printer (see Chapter 3). Some PC systems shipped before June 1982 may have an early version of PC DOS, version 1.0, which does not have the MODE command for printers, but such systems can be retrofitted with a newer version of PC DOS.

Using serial communications, the PC can send information to a printer at any of 15 rates. They are called *baud rates*, and are sometimes expressed in *bits-per-second (BPS)*. (Each character comprises eight bits.) Printer baud rates are usually selectable too. For successful printing, the printer baud rate must match the PC baud rate. On the PC, the baud rate is under program control, while on the printer it is usually determined by internal switch settings. The standard PC rate is 2400 baud, but you can reset it with the MODE command described in Chapter 3, or the application program you use may reset it. Check with the program manual or dealer if problems arise.

A more complex compatibilty question exists, having to do with program-controlled printer features like subscripts, right margin justification, underlining, and type font selection. Programs control such features by sending the printer certain sequences of nonprinting characters. Unfortunately, different printer models may use dissimilar character sequences to control similar features. Fortunately, most programs that use these fea-

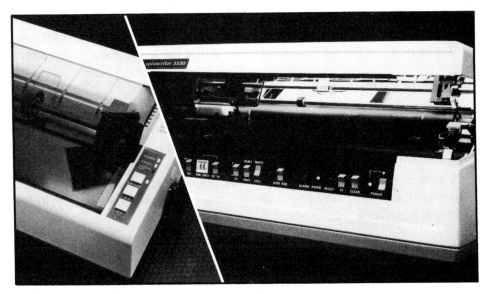

Fig. 2-4. Manual controls on two printers.

tures know the character sequences for several printers, and you can specify which to use. Consult the program manual for instructions on printer selection.

The Printer Controls

A typical printer has a power switch, a few buttons for manual control, and several status lights clustered on top or at the front of the printer in a control panel (Fig. 2-4). Sometimes the power switch is located on the side or at the back of the printer. Other control switches and levers may be located inside the printer. Table 2-1 lists the most common printer controls and status lights.

Most printers know how far the current print line is from the bottom of the page and will eject the page at the press of a button. With continuous paper, this advances the printer to the top of the next page. For this feature to work properly, you must align the paper before you turn the printer on, thereby giving the printer a place to start reckoning from. Some printers have a button you can push to establish the top of page at the current line.

Some printers have a switch labeled "auto line feed" or "local line feed." The switch may be on the front panel or it may be under the printer's top cover. Set it to the off position.

Getting Ready To Print

When preparing to print, the first order of business is selecting the right paper: continuous forms for uninterrupted printing, multiple-part for car-

Table 2-1. Common Printer Controls and Status Lights

Name*	Function
Switches and buttons	
Power	Turn the printer on and off
Online (Select)	Suspend/resume printing
Form Feed (FF)	Advance paper to next page
Line Feed (LF, Paper adv)	Advance paper one line
Clear (Reset)	Reset printer after error
Override	Acknowledge paper out; finish printing this page
Status lights (when lit)	
Power	Power on
Ready	Printer ready: interlocks and safety switches check ok
Select (Online)	Printing may proceed
Paper Out (Paper)	No more paper
Alarm (Error)	Ribbon out or internal error

*Some printers use different names.

bon copies, label stock for mailings, and so forth. For printing documents one page at a time, you can use single-sheet stationery if your printer accepts it. Once selected, put the paper in the printer, and align the paper vertically and horizontally.

Next, check the ribbon for alignment and wear; install a new one if needed. If your printer has interchangeable type elements (*daisy wheels* or *thimbles*), make sure the correct one is securely installed. Set any print density or forms thickness controls to accommodate the type of paper you are using.

Finally, close all the printer covers and guards. Open covers activate interlock switches that temporarily disable the printer. Turn the power switch on and set the "Select" or "Online" switch if there is one. The "Ready" and "Select" status lights must be lit for the printer to work.

CHAPTER 3

DISKS AND PC DOS

The most valuable PC accessory has got to be a disk drive, because with it the PC can handle a greater variety of tasks, and larger, more complex tasks at that. There is a lot you can do with a disk drive, so there is a lot to learn in order to use one. Since diskettes are the most common kind of drive found on PC systems, this chapter begins by explaining how to select and handle them. Later it introduces the PC disk operating system, and its commands. Chapter 5 contains more commands for the PC disk operating system, and Appendix B summarizes all of the commands.

DISKETTE SELECTION AND HANDLING

Being such fragile items, diskettes require special attention to ensure their longevity. It's important to select blank diskettes carefully, since there are so many apparently identical ones.

Choosing the Right Diskettes

Diskette design is standard, and all diskettes have basically the same parts (Fig. 3-1). But because diskette drive features differ, some diskette attributes do too. A few of the differences are easy to see, while others are invisible. Blank diskettes usually have a permanent label in the upper left-hand corner that lists attributes or at least a model number, from which the attributes can be determined. The wrong kind of diskette may simply fail to work or it may appear to work for awhile, only to fail later, destroying hours or days worth of work.

Fig. 3-1.   Diskette details: 8-inch (left) and 5¼-inch (right).

The IBM diskette drives packaged with PC systems require 5¼-inch double density, soft sectored diskettes. The IBM drives can use either dual sided diskettes or single sided diskettes. Only the 320K drives use both sides of a dual sided diskette, however. Never use single density diskettes in an IBM drive on the PC; you risk losing information sooner or later.

Diskette Care

Diskettes are precision equipment and cannot tolerate abuse. Insist on mistreating them, and they will eventually break down, possibly damaging the drive in the process. Sometimes it is possible to recover part of the information on a disabled diskette, but rarely all of it.

Diskettes are not the least bit rugged. Their jackets are only designed to protect them during the short trip from storage to the diskette drive. Observe the instructions for care that are printed on the backs of most diskette envelopes. Be especially careful when writing on a label affixed to a diskette, because pencils and ballpoint pens can exert enough pressure through the protective jacket to damage the magnetic coating on the disk inside. Keep diskettes away from television sets, video monitors, ringing telephones, and other sources of magnetic fields, which can disrupt information stored on diskettes.

Labeling

There is no way to tell diskettes apart by looking at them. Their contents change often, so use removable labels, not permanent ones, to identify them. An ambiguous label is little better than no label, so be sure to identify the diskette uniquely. It is also a good idea to keep a complete list of contents with the diskette.

Inserting Diskettes in Drives

To insert a diskette in a drive the drive door must be open. On a few drives you press a button or bar and the door springs open, but on most drives you lift the door up from the bottom. If there is a diskette in the drive, grasp it with your thumb and forefinger and pull it straight out. Be careful not to bend it as you pull it out.

Hold the diskette you want to insert with the label up. Slide it straight into the drive, taking care not to bend it (Fig. 3-2). Gently push the diskette all the way in. If it meets any resistance, stop. Remove it, check for obstructions, and try again. If it still sticks, try another diskette. If that sticks too, there is something wrong inside the drive; take it in for repairs.

Slowly close the drive door. If the door will only go down a fraction of an inch, the diskette is not in far enough.

Write-Protecting Diskettes

Diskettes can be physically protected against accidental erasure or overwriting. The presence or absence of a notch in a certain position on the

Fig. 3-2. Inserting a diskette.

diskette controls this. The notch is in a different place on 5¼-inch and 8-inch diskettes, and is interpreted differently as well.

On 8-inch diskettes, the existence of a notch on the right-hand side of the lower edge of the diskette protects the diskette against being written on by the drive (Fig. 3-1). Hence it is called a *write-protect notch*. Covering the notch with a special label or piece of opaque tape removes the protection. Some 8-inch diskettes have no notch and cannot be protected.

A notch at the top of the right-hand edge of a 5¼-inch diskette permits the drive to write on the diskette (Fig. 3-1). This notch is called a *write-enable* notch. To protect a 5¼-inch diskette, cover the notch with a small label or piece of opaque tape.

MULTIPLE DRIVE IDENTIFICATION

A PC system may have just one diskette drive, but it is likely to have two or more. The system unit has room for one or two 5¼-inch diskette drives or one 5¼-inch diskette drive and one Winchester drive; more drives can be added externally. A multiple drive system needs some way to distinguish drives, so it labels each with a letter: *A, B, C,* and so on.

To make the tremendous storage capacity of a Winchester drive easier to manage, it is often subdivided into several *volumes* or *partitions*, each with its own "drive" label. The PC cannot tell the difference between a Winchester partition and a diskette drive.

For reasons explained shortly, one drive (drive A) has special significance. On systems with two built-in drives, the left-hand drive is usually drive A. Systems with a Winchester drive may allow drive A to be one of the Winchester partitions.

THE DISK OPERATING SYSTEM

Accessing a disk drive is a complicated process, and it takes complex programming to do it. The *disk operating system*, or *DOS*, is a program that coordinates all disk activities. You might think of a disk operating system program as a file clerk, whom you would tell, "Get me the personnel file on Smithers," or "Put back this file on ABIG Holding Corporation," or "Get me the next name and address from our mailing list." Tasks like those, and others, are exactly what the disk operating system program does.

There are many different disk operating systems for the PC, each of which does the same job in a slightly different way. But functionally they are all the same. This book describes IBM's disk operating system for the PC, which is called *PC DOS*.

You must know how to use PC DOS because most application programs are kept on disk, and it takes PC DOS commands to get them started. Other PC DOS commands help keep the contents of your disks in order.

Versions of PC DOS

Prior to June 1982 IBM shipped version 1.0 of PC DOS. It does not support dual sided diskette drives, and it has no real provision for using a serial printer. In May 1982, IBM announced version 1.1, a replacement for the earlier version. It supports both single and dual sided diskette drives, and can use a serial printer effectively. Version 1.0 can be replaced at low cost by version 1.1 in almost all situations, so this book only describes PC DOS 1.1.

Starting PC DOS

For PC DOS to work properly, all drives must be on. All external drives have their own power switches, and they should be on before you turn on the system unit. Built-in drives have no separate power switch; their power comes on with the system unit. Unless otherwise instructed, you had best leave drive doors open when turning power on or off.

The disk operating system program does not reside permanently in PC read-only memory, but it is on disk. Somehow the system must transfer the PC DOS program from disk to dynamic memory, but how can it do that without the PC DOS program already in memory? Sounds like the PC needs to lift itself by its own bootstraps. A small program in PC read-only memory does just that. Called the *bootstrap program*, it can access drive A in order to transfer the disk operating system to memory, and that is all. The process of transferring the disk operating system to memory is called *loading DOS* or *booting DOS*.

The bootstrap program loads PC DOS when you turn the system unit on or reset the system with the **Ctrl**|**Alt**|**Del** combination keystroke. In both cases, drive A must contain the PC DOS program. The diskette labeled "DOS," which is packaged with the IBM manual *Disk Operating System*, has a copy of PC DOS, and other diskettes may have one also. If drive A is a Winchester partition, it must have a copy too. A disk that has the PC DOS program is called a *system disk*.

Within 10 seconds of the time you reset the system, or within two minutes of the time you turn on the system unit, the bootstrap program will load PC DOS. The display screen clears and a message appears asking you to enter the date (Fig. 3-3A). Type in the month, day, and year. Punctuate with hyphens or slashes, like this: 8-31-83 or 12/1/83. After you enter the date, another message appears, asking you to enter the time (Fig. 3-3B). Using 24-hour time, enter the hours, minutes, and seconds, and punctuate with colons, like this: 15:30:10 or 3:30:10. The seconds figure may be a whole number or it may include a decimal fraction. You may omit the seconds, or even minutes and seconds. In that case, the omitted numbers

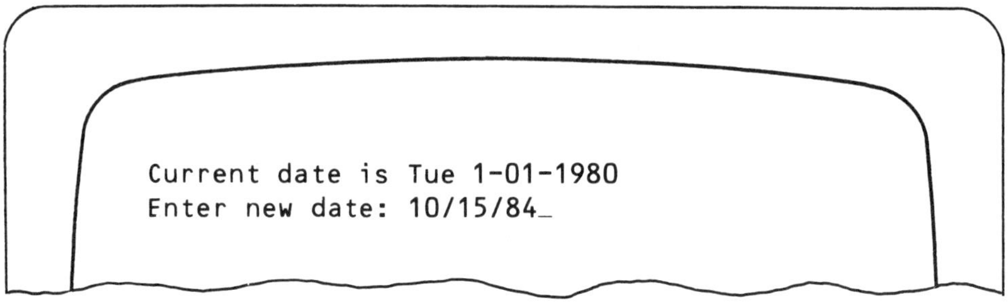

```
Current date is Tue 1-01-1980
Enter new date: 10/15/84_
```

(A) Enter the date.

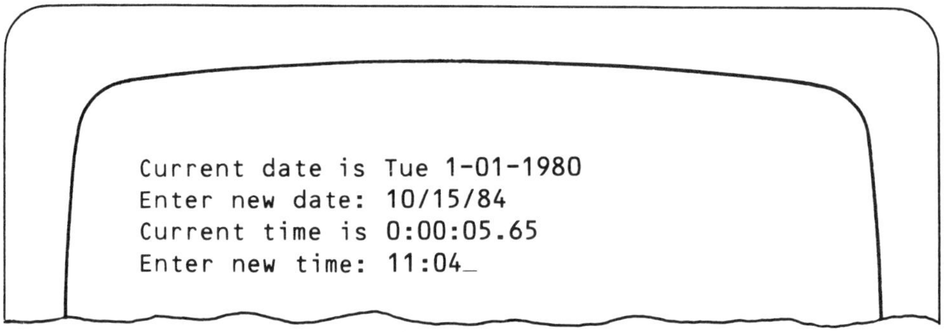

```
Current date is Tue 1-01-1980
Enter new date: 10/15/84
Current time is 0:00:05.65
Enter new time: 11:04_
```

(B) Then enter the time (24-hour clock).

Fig. 3-3. Just after successfully loading PC DOS.

are assumed to be 0. For example, you may enter 16:00:00 as 16:00 or even 16.

If something other than the date entry message appears, then there is a problem with the diskette you put in drive A. Should you see a message that begins "Non-System disk" (Fig. 3-4A), exchange the diskette in drive A with a system diskette and press the space bar to retry loading PC DOS. If the top line of the screen reads "The IBM Personal Computer Basic" (Fig. 3-4B), then the drive A door is not closed, the diskette is upside down, or the diskette was not set up for use with PC DOS. Correct the problem and try again. Other error messages can occur, or the diskette in drive A may be the kind that automatically starts an application program. In either case, try another diskette.

DOS Command Prompt

After you enter the time of day, PC DOS displays an identification and copyright message (Fig. 3-5). The characters A> next to the cursor are called the *command prompt*, because they cue you to enter a PC DOS command.

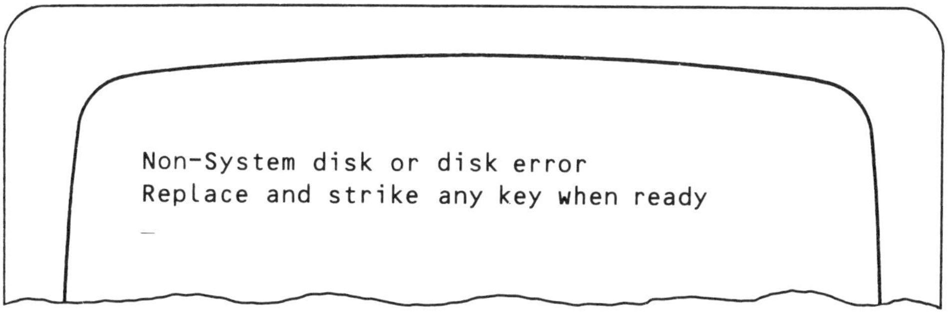

```
Non-System disk or disk error
Replace and strike any key when ready
_
```

(A)   Bad disk or wrong kind of disk.

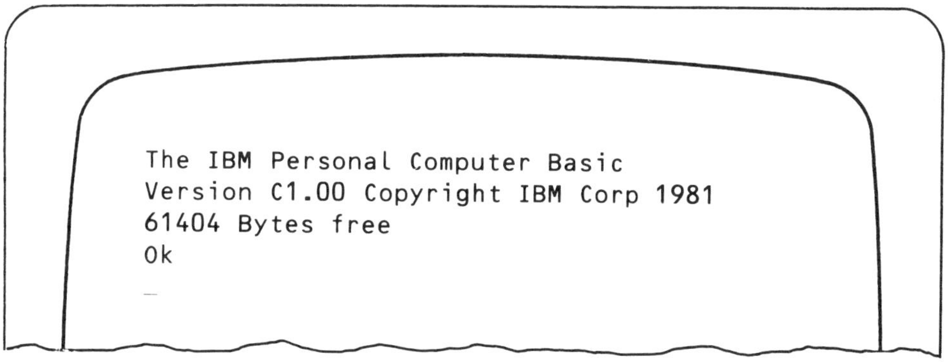

```
The IBM Personal Computer Basic
Version C1.00 Copyright IBM Corp 1981
61404 Bytes free
Ok
_
```

(B)   No disk or drive door open.

Fig. 3-4.   After an unsuccessful attempt to load PC DOS.

PC DOS FILES

Even the smallest diskette can store a large amount of information. Rarely is all this storage space used for one purpose, however. Usually, several small, independent blocks of information co-exist on a single disk. The higher the capacity of the disk, the more independent blocks there are likely to be; a Winchester disk may have several hundred.

PC DOS uses a sort of filing system to keep track of all the separate blocks of information. It treats each disk as a filing cabinet, and each block of information on it as a file drawer. In fact, blocks of information on a disk are called *files*.

Computer files are grouped into two classes according to the type of information they contain: program or data. A program file contains instructions that tell the computer how to do something. A data file contains an organized collection of facts and figures about something.

File Names

Each disk file has a unique name. A file can have any name not already in

```
Current date is Tue 1-01-1980
Enter new date: 10/15/84
Current time is 0:00:05.65
Enter new time: 11:04

The IBM Personal Computer DOS
Version 1.10 (C)Copyright IBM Corp 1981,
1982
A>_
```

Fig. 3-5. PC DOS identification message.

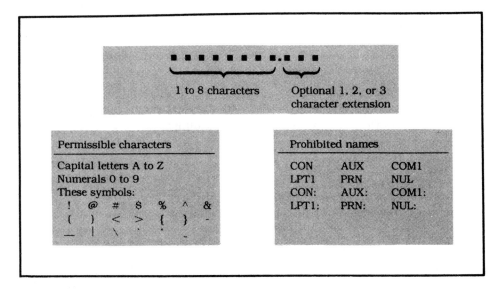

Fig. 3-6. PC DOS file name rules.

use, as long as it observes some rules (Fig. 3-6). The name must have at least one character, can have as many as eight, and can have a suffix. The optional suffix, called a *file name extension*, consists of a period followed by no more than three characters.

The term *file name* in precise usage just refers to the one-to-eight character root that precedes the file name extension, but common usage defines the term *file name* as both the root and the optional extension, and that is the definition this book will use.

Only some characters are allowed in file names and extensions (Fig. 3-6). PC DOS treats upper- and lower-case letters alike, so you can type a file name in any mixture of small letters and capitals.

If you specify a file name with more than eight characters and no extension, PC DOS automatically places a period after the eighth character, uses the next three characters as an extension, and disregards the rest. An error occurs if a name has more than eight characters ahead of an explicit extension. If an extension has more than three characters, PC DOS ignores the extra characters.

By convention the file name extension designates the file type. To maintain compatibility with other PC users, use the conventional extensions listed in Table 3-1.

Generic File Names

Most of the time you will want to specify file names specifically and uniquely so that there is no doubt about which file you mean. But at times it will be convenient to refer to a group of files all at once, rather than one at a time. You can use two special characters, ? and *, to specify generic file names. Generic file names are also called *global file names* and *ambiguous file names*.

A question mark represents a single ambiguous character within a file name. PC DOS tries to match unambiguous characters literally, but considers any *single* character a match to a question mark. Thus file names PHASE1.BAS, PHASE2.BAS, PHASE3.BAS, and PHASE4.BAS all match the generic file name PHASE?.BAS, but the file names PHASE10.BAS and PHASE153.BAS do not.

An asterisk represents any number of ambiguous characters. For example, PGM*.B* will match any file name that begins with PGM, as long as its extension starts with a B. However, an asterisk is only meaningful when used as the last character of a file name or extension. The generic file name *CALC.BAS is the same as *.BAS, which matches every file with a BAS extension. Similarly, *.*K is the same as *.*, which matches every file name.

Table 3-1. File Name Extensions and File Types

Extension	File type
.ASM	Assembly language program in source form
.BAK	Backup file; copy made of a file in case the original version is destroyed
.BAS	BASIC program
.BAT	Batch processing command file
.BIN	Intermediate file for compiler
.COB	COBOL program in source form
.COD	Assembly language version of .OBJ file (produced by compiler)
.COM	Command or program directly executable by PC DOS
.DAT	Data file
.DOC	Document (word processing) file
.EXE	Relocatable program executable by PC DOS
.FOR	FORTRAN program in source form
.HEX	Character-coded (ASCII) hexadecimal representation of binary data
.LIB	Library program
.MAC	Macro for assembly language program
.MAP	Link program listing
.OBJ	Machine language (object) version of a compiled program
.OVL	Application program overlay file
.OVR	Compiler program overlay file
.PAS	Pascal program in source form
.PIC	Screen display image
.PRN	Assembly language listing file
.SYM	Symbol table for compiler
.TER	Terminal description (IBM Asychronous Communications Support program)
.TMP	Temporary file
.TXT	Text file
.$$$	Temporary file, or an improperly saved but usable file

Drive Designations

All files on one disk must have different names, but the same file name can be used on different disks. Therefore it is possible for a multiple drive PC system to have two or more disks with the same file names. To resolve the ambiguity, you can prefix the file name with a two-character drive designation. The first character is the drive label (A, B, C, etc.) and the second character is a colon. Thus B:ADDRESS.DAT specifies a file on drive B.

On a single drive system, only drive A exists and there is no need to use a drive designation prefix with file names. PC DOS will automatically use the only available drive. If you do designate the drive, use only A:.

You can omit the drive designation on a multiple drive system too. This is possible because PC DOS keeps a log of which drive to use by default, called the *logged drive*, or the *default drive*. Initially, PC DOS logs drive A to use in case of default, as indicated by the command prompt, A>.

File Name Directory

Part of each disk is set aside to keep track of its contents. This area contains a list of all the files on the disk by name, and specifies their location on the disk as well. There is a limit of 64 files on each single sided diskette, and 112 files on each dual sided diskette. Winchester drive limits vary.

PC DOS COMMANDS

PC DOS has many commands to help you keep your disks in order. There are commands which work on whole disks, individual files, the disk directory, the system time and date, and more. The remainder of this chapter covers the most common ones, and Chapter 5 covers the rest.

Issuing Commands

You issue commands to PC DOS by typing certain words and symbols on the keyboard. What you type tells PC DOS what to do and what to do it to. As you type a PC DOS command on the keyboard, the display screen echoes what you type. Nothing else happens until you press the ◄┘ key to officially enter the command, and then PC DOS executes the displayed command. You can use any mixture of lower-case and upper-case letters in command words.

Resident and Transient Commands

The PC DOS program contains step-by-step instructions that tell it how to carry out many commands. These are called *resident* or *internal* commands, because the instructions for doing them are inside the PC DOS program itself. If you type a command that PC DOS cannot find among its set of resident commands, then it looks on disk for a file with the same name as the command, and with an extension of BAT, COM, or EXE. If it finds the right file, it transfers instructions from the file to dynamic memory and executes them. Such commands are called *transient* or *external* commands, because the instructions for performing them do not permanently reside within the PC DOS program. The PC DOS system diskette furnished by IBM includes a number of transient commands. Table 3-2 lists standard resident and transient commands.

It is possible to make up a new transient command by creating a file that contains instructions for carrying out the command. There is also a way to make up a new command that is a combination of existing commands; the procedure is described in Chapter 5.

Generally, PC DOS looks on the default drive for transient commands. However, you can prefix the command with a drive designation to specify which drive PC DOS should look on. If PC DOS cannot find instructions for

Table 3-2. Standard PC DOS Commands

Command	Resident	Transient
CHKDSK		•
COMP		•
COPY	•	
DATE*	•	
DIR	•	
DISKCOMP		•
DISKCOPY		•
ERASE	•	
EXE2BIN†		•
FORMAT		•
MODE		•
PAUSE	•	
REM	•	
RENAME	•	
SYS		•
TIME*	•	
TYPE	•	

*The DATE and TIME commands are transient in PC DOS 1.0.
†BASIC programmers rarely use command EXE2BIN and this book does not cover it.

the transient command, it displays the message "Bad command or file name." You must re-issue the command, making sure that the command file exists on the drive specified.

CAUTION—DOS 1.0 and 1.1 Command Mixing

If you possess more than one version of PC DOS, a hazardous situation exists. Commands with identical names may seem to do the same thing in either version, but the internal instructions for carrying out those apparently identical commands may differ significantly. You could, for example, load PC DOS version 1.1 from one diskette and then exchange it for a diskette that has version 1.0 transient command files on it. Don't do that! You risk ruining files by executing mismatched transient commands. Label every disk that contains transient command files with the file names and version number they go with, and then scrupulously avoid mismatching command files with the loaded version of PC DOS.

Correcting Typing Mistakes

Before you press the ← key to execute a command, look at the display screen and verify the accuracy of your typing. If you see mistakes, use the ←key to backspace to the start of the incorrect portion. Then retype the command from that point on. If the command is so botched it doesn't warrant correcting, use the **Esc** key to erase the whole line and start over. When you press the **Esc** key, PC DOS displays a \ character, ignores the line you were typing, and moves the cursor to the beginning of the next display line. It does not display another command prompt.

Activating the Printer

You can use the printer to make a permanent copy of the PC DOS commands you type. There are two ways to do it. Press the ⇧ and **PrtSc** keys at the same time, and PC DOS makes a single printed copy of the entire display screen. Or press the **Ctrl** and **PrtSc** keys in unison, and PC DOS echoes every line you type after that onto the printer, creating a running log of the dialogue. (Press **Ctrl|PrtSc** again to deactivate the printed log.)

Normally the **PrtSc** key only activates a parallel printer, but it can be changed to activate a serial printer instead. The MODE command, covered later in this chapter, makes the conversion.

Changing the Default Drive

Initially, PC DOS uses drive A whenever it needs a drive designation and none is supplied. To use a different drive in case of default, type the letter of the new drive, then a colon, and finally press the ◄┘ key. A new PC DOS command prompt appears on the display screen, indicating which drive is now logged for default use. Here is an example that switches from drive A to drive B:

```
A>b:
B>
```

Canceling a Command

Many PC DOS commands require you to specify drive designations or file names. If you accidentally specify the wrong one and wish to cancel the command, press the **Ctrl** and **Scroll Lock** keys in unison. The PC DOS command prompt (for example, A>) reappears.

VIEWING A DIRECTORY

To display a listing of the files present on the default drive, use the DIR command, like this:

```
A>dir
```

The example above displays the directory of the disk in drive A as soon as the ◄┘ key is pressed to execute the command.

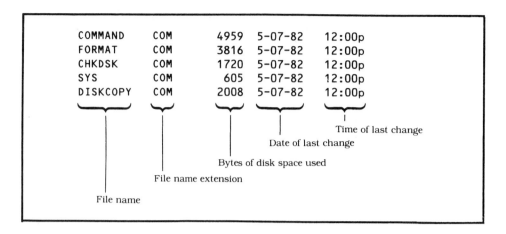

Fig. 3-7. Parts of a directory.

Directory Analysis

Each line of the directory listing has five parts: the file name, file name extension, file size, and the last date and time the file was altered (Fig. 3-7). Notice the directory omits the period between the file name and its extension. The file size quoted is the number of bytes the file occupies on the disk.

Lengthy Directories

There may be too many files in the directory to fit on the display screen at once. To make the directory display one page at a time, suffix the command with " /P," like this:

```
A>dir /p
```

Alternatively, you can condense the directory listing so that only the file names and extensions appear, in several columns across the screen. To do that, suffix the DIR command with " /W." Here is an example:

```
A>dir /w
```

Directory of Any Drive

Suppose you want to list the directory of a specific drive. Just add a drive designation to the end of the DIR command, like this:

```
A>dir b:
```

The command above lists the directory of the disk in drive B. Notice there is a blank space ahead of the drive designation. Without it, PC DOS would look for transient command DIRB: on the default drive.

Alternatively, you could change the default drive to be the one that holds the disk you wish the directory of. Here is an example:

```
A>b:
B>dir
```

Changing the default drive works because DIR is a resident command. PC DOS always knows how to execute a DIR instruction, no matter what the default drive is.

Selective Directory Listings

The DIR command will also look for a specific file. Just append the file name to the command, like this:

```
A>dir b:budget.bas
```

A DIR command like the one above searches the directory for the designated file name and lists it only if it exists. Of course the drive designation that prefixes the file name is optional if it is the same as the default drive.

The file name can be specific or generic. If generic, DIR lists all file names that match the pattern. For example, the following command will list all files on drive A with the extension COM:

```
A>dir *.com
```

PREPARING BLANK DISKS

A new blank disk will not work until its surface has been mapped out, analyzed for defects, and set up with a blank directory. This initialization process is called *formatting*. The FORMAT command initializes diskettes for IBM diskette drives. The following example formats the diskette in drive B:

```
A>format b:
```

When you press the ◀┘ key, this message appears:

```
Insert new diskette for drive B:
and strike any key when ready__
```

Place the diskette you want to format in drive B. Stop! Are you absolutely sure the diskette you just inserted is the one you truly want to format? Formatting erases everything on the diskette. Do not format your only copy of a valuable diskette!

Press the space bar or ◀┘ key to start formatting. On the display screen, several blank lines appear, followed by the message "Formatting. . ." At the same time, the light on the diskette drive comes on, and the drive starts making rhythmic sounds.

It takes about 20 seconds to format a single sided diskette. When the formatting is finished, a message like this appears:

```
Formatting...Format complete

160256 bytes total disk space
160256 bytes available on disk

Format another (Y/N)?_
```

When you answer the question posed by the message above, press the **Y** or **N** key but do *not* press the ← key. If you press **Y** and then ← (or any other key), PC DOS will not wait for you to put a new diskette in the designated drive. Instead it will go ahead and reformat the one it just did. This will not do any harm, but it will waste time.

The FORMAT command marks any defective tracks it encounters, preventing their future assignment to any file.

Single and Dual Sided Diskettes

The FORMAT command automatically senses the capacity of the diskette in the designated drive. It formats single sided diskettes on one side, for use in either 160K or 320K drives. A 160K drive always formats just one side of a diskette, even if the diskette has dual sided potential.

A 320K drive usually formats a dual sided diskette on both sides. However, adding "/1" to the end of a FORMAT command forces one-side formatting, regardless of diskette type:

```
A>format b:/1
```

A diskette's formatting, not its manufactured potential, determines how much it can store and what kind of drives it will work in. Any diskette formatted for single sided use will store 160K bytes maximum on any drive. If it is a dual sided diskette, reformatting it on a 320K drive will realize its full potential, at the expense of erasing existing contents, of course. Conversely, a diskette formatted for dual sided use will only work in a 320K drive. Any attempt to use it in a 160K drive incurs a message like "Disk error reading drive A:."

Creating System Disks

Recall that the bootstrap program can only load PC DOS from system disks. Add the suffix "/S" to a FORMAT command to create a system diskette, as follows:

```
A>format /s
```

The optional suffix stores the PC DOS program on the formatted diskette. That requires a total of three files, named IBMBIO.COM,

IBMDOS.COM, and COMMAND.COM. The first two files are written in such a way that they do not appear on the diskette directory listing. They are called *hidden files*.

Formatting on Any Drive

FORMAT is a transient command so you may need to prefix it with a drive designation. Consider this example:

```
B>a:format
```

Here the default drive is B, but knowing drive B did not have file FOR-MAT.COM, the user specified drive A for the transient command file. But the example above still formats drive B. Do you see why? Because no explicit drive designation appears *after* the command word, the FORMAT command uses the default drive, and that is drive B in this case.

Winchester Drive Formatting

Some Winchester drives have a modified FORMAT command that diagnoses the drive for faults and maps any bad spots so they will not be used to store information. Most Winchester drives have a separate command that partitions the disk surface into "drives" and creates blank directories for each one. However, none of the Winchester initialization programs is like another. For instructions, check your Winchester disk manual.

Format Errors

If PC DOS detects a problem with the diskette that prevents formatting, it displays a message that states the possible nature of the problem. The diskette may be upside down, write protected, defective, or of the wrong kind.

DUPLICATING DISKETTES

The single most important PC DOS command is DISKCOPY, because it makes duplicate copies of diskettes to use if the main diskette fails. The copies are called *backups*. The DISKCOPY command only works with diskette drives, but Winchester drives have a separate command capable of selectively duplicating the files that have changed since the last backup. Operating instructions vary too widely to include them here, so check your drive manual.

Duplicating With Two Drives

When you have two drives (both must be alike, 160K or 320K) you can copy the contents of one, called the *source*, to the other, called the *target* or *destination*. The following example will copy drive A to drive B:

```
A>diskcopy a: b:
```

The first drive specified is the source, the second is the target. Here drive A is the source and drive B is the target, but you can use any valid drive designations. When you press the ← key, the following appears on the display screen:

```
Insert source diskette in drive A
Insert target diskette in drive B
Strike any key when ready
```

Insert diskettes as the display screen instructions direct. Do not reverse the source and target diskettes! As an added precaution, place a write-protect label over the write-enable notch on the source diskette (review Fig. 3-1). That way, if you do inadvertently reverse the diskettes, the copy operation will not work.

By examining the source drive and diskette, PC DOS determines whether to do a single or dual sided copy, and displays a message announcing its choice. For a successful two-drive copy of a dual sided diskette, both source and target drives must be 320K drives, but any combination of 160K and 320K drives works when the source drive is single sided.

PC DOS copies the whole source diskette, unused parts included, onto the target diskette. Anything that was on the target diskette is erased in the process. It takes about 35 seconds to copy a single sided diskette. When the copy is finished, the message "Copy complete" appears on the display screen.

Next, a question appears asking if you want to copy another diskette. Answer by pressing the **Y** or **N** key alone; do *not* press the ← key. If you press **Y** and then ← (or any other key), PC DOS will not wait for you to put a new diskette in the target drive. Instead it will go ahead and recopy the one it just did. This will not do any harm, but it will waste time.

Single Drive Duplicating

The DISKCOPY command can make backup copies of diskettes using just one drive. The following example initiates a single drive copy on drive A:

```
A>diskcopy
```

Press the ← key and this message appears:

```
Insert source diskette in drive A:
Strike any key when ready
—
```

As a safety measure, place a write-protect label on the diskette you wish to copy before you put it in the drive. When you press any key, PC DOS reads as much of the source diskette as will fit in dynamic memory, then displays this:

```
Insert target diskette in drive A:
Strike any key when ready
```

Remove the source diskette and replace it with the target diskette. (Do not use a write-protect label on the target diskette.) This time when you press a key, PC DOS copies onto the target diskette the part of the source diskette it just read. The diskette-swapping cycle repeats as many times as necessary in order to duplicate the entire source diskette.

Alternate DISKCOPY Command Forms

You may omit one of the drive designations if you wish. In this case, the specified drive is the source drive and the default drive is used as the target drive. Here is an example:

```
A>diskcopy b:
```

For another method of disk duplication, see the section on file copying in Chapter 5.

Disk Duplication Errors

If PC DOS detects a problem with either diskette that prevents copying, it displays a message that describes the problem. A source diskette may be upside down, damaged, or the wrong type for the drive. A target diskette may be upside down, protected against writing, unformatted, defective, the wrong type for the drive, or incompatible with the source.

Nonfatal duplication errors are possible too. The absence of an error message does not guarantee a usable target diskette. You can formally compare the source and destination disks or check the status of the target drive after duplication.

COMPARING DISKS

The DISKCOMP command compares the contents of two diskettes using either one drive or two. Any combination of single and dual sided diskettes is allowed, subject to a couple of restrictions discussed shortly. The following example compares the diskette in drive A with the diskette in drive B:

```
A>diskcomp a: b:
```

The DISKCOMP command looks just like the DISKCOPY command. You specify two drives to be compared; they can be different or the same. If they are the same, PC DOS tells you when to swap diskettes. If you omit an explicit drive designation, the default drive is used.

When DISKCOMP finishes the comparison, it asks, "Compare more diskettes? (Y/N)" Answer in the affirmative to do another comparison using the same drive assignments.

Single and Dual Sided Comparisons

PC DOS examines the drives and diskettes, decides whether to compare one or two sides, and announces its choice on the display screen. One combination causes a problem: when the first diskette is dual sided and the second is single sided, the message "Incompatible diskette or drive types" appears. To force a single-sided comparision, append "/1" to the DISK-COMP command, like this:

```
A>diskcomp a: b: /1
```

REPORTING DISK STATUS

Use the CHKDSK command to analyze a diskette and its directory for internal integrity and agreement. Here is an example:

```
A>chkdsk b:
```

The example above checks drive B. Omit the drive designation, and the default drive is used.

The analysis begins as soon as you issue the command. There is no pause for you to switch diskettes. The result of the analysis is a report like this:

```
160256 bytes total disk space
  8704 bytes in 2 hidden  files
144384 bytes in 26 user files
  7168 bytes available on disk
 65536 bytes total  memory
 53136 bytes free
```

The report tells you the disk capacity (160256 is the same as 160K), the number of hidden files and the amount of space they use up (if any), the number of files and the amount of disk space they occupy, and amount of disk space unused. If there are bad tracks or sectors on the disk, the space they occupy is reported too. Finally, the report shows the total amount of dynamic memory in the computer and how much is left after the PC DOS program takes its share.

During the analysis, the CHKDSK command temporarily makes the drive it is checking the default drive. If you terminate the analysis early (for example, with the **Ctrl|Scroll Lock** multiple keystroke), the default drive is not reassigned.

ADJUSTING DISPLAY SCREEN MARGINS

When used as computer display screens, most home television sets cannot display each character position on every line. They magnify the picture in a way that puts the leftmost character positions, rightmost character positions, or both, off the screen. The MODE command will shift the display right or left to compensate for this overscan. The following example shifts right:

```
A>mode 40,r,t
```

In response to the command above, PC DOS displays a 40-character test pattern across the top of the display screen, like this:

```
0123456789012345678901234567890123456789
Do you see the leftmost 0? (Y/N)
—
```

If you can see the 0 at the left edge of the screen, type a "Y." Otherwise, type an "N" and the display will shift one character position to the right. Keep answering "N" until the leftmost 0 comes into view.

The MODE command has a number of options. Instead of shifting right, as the example above shows, it will shift left. Use this form of the command:

```
A>mode 40,l,t
```

The same test pattern appears as before, but if you respond "N," the screen moves left.

The sole number in the examples so far, 40, sets the display screen width at 40 characters. You can set the width at 80 characters by using 80 instead of 40, but most home televisions are not sharp enough to display 80 legible characters on the same line.

A MODE statement with only a screen width number will just set the width as indicated. The display will not shift. Conversely, you may leave off the first number in a MODE command (40 or 80), in which case the screen width remains unchanged. You may also omit both the first number and the last character (T) in order to suppress the test pattern and shift the display directly—one character position on a 40-character screen, two character positions on an 80-character screen. Here are examples:

```
A>mode 40
A>mode l,t
A>mode ,r
```

The MODE command has no effect on the monochrome display. It works only with displays attached to the color/graphics adapter.

SELECTING PRINTER ATTRIBUTES

Three variations of the MODE statement affect the printer instead of the display screen. With them you can alter the line width, set number of lines per page, and have the PC use serial instead of parallel communications with a printer.

Changing Printer Spacing

The variation of the MODE statement that changes the printer's horizontal and vertical spacing works with the IBM 80CPS Matrix printer, the Epson MX-80 printer, and any other printer compatible with those two. The printer must be on and ready to print when you issue the command, which looks like this:

```
A>mode lpt1:132,8
```

After pressing the ← key, a message appears confirming your entry. If the message "Printer error" appears, the printer is probably not ready to print.

The first component of this kind of MODE command, LPT1:, tells PC DOS the command pertains to the printer. The second component specifies

Table 3-3. RS232 Serial Communications Attributes Selectable by the MODE Command*

Attribute	Options	For MODE, type	Purpose
Baud rate	110	11	Data transmission speed
	150	15	
	300	30†	
	600	60	
	1200	12†	
	2400	24‡	
	4800	48	
	9600	96	
Parity	None	n†	Error checking
	Odd	o	
	Even	e‡	
Word length	7	7‡	Length of each data byte
	8	8†	
Stop bits	1	1†	Data byte terminator
	2	2	

*For serial printers, the general command is: MODE COM1: *Baud rate, Parity, Word length, Stop bits*, P. Omit the final ",P" for other serial devices.
†Common choices for serial printers.
‡Values preset when PC DOS is first loaded.

the number of characters per line. There are only two valid choices: 80 or 132. In either case the width of the line does not change; instead, the size of the characters changes. The third component of this kind of MODE statement determines the number of lines printed per inch. There are only two valid choices: 6 or 8. Each time the printer is turned on, it resets itself to print 80 characters per line and six lines per inch.

Using Serial Printers

PC DOS sends printer output to a parallel printer, but by issuing two MODE commands you can redirect it to a serial printer. The first command matches the PC to the printer attributes. The second command actually redirects the output. The changes remain in effect until you countermand them with another MODE command or reload PC DOS.

PC DOS uses the common *RS232* standard for serial communications. It is a flexible standard, not a rigid one, and the sender and receiver must agree on conventions that resolve certain ambiguities or they cannot communicate. The MODE command sets the PC DOS conventions to match those of the external serial device.

The first thing to do is determine the conventions of your serial printer. Table 3-3 lists the four variable attributes of serial communications and the alternatives PC DOS has for each one. Consult the manual for your serial printer to determine its baud rate, parity, word length, and number of stop bits. See if you need to set internal switches on the printer to select any of those attributes.

Use Table 3-3 to translate the printer's serial communication attributes into the symbols understood by the MODE statement. The following sample command sets up PC DOS to send characters at a baud rate of 300, with no parity, a word length of eight bits, and one stop bit:

```
A>mode com1:30,n,8,1,p
```

After pressing the ← key, a message appears confirming your entry.

The first component in this kind of MODE statement, COM1:, means the statement pertains to serial communications. The last component, the letter p, tells PC DOS that serial communications will be to a printer, not some other device.

The MODE command that actually redirects printed output to a serial printer looks like this:

```
A>mode lpt1:=com1
```

When you execute a command like the one above, the message ''LPT1: redirected to COM1:'' appears.

To switch back from serial to parallel, use this command:

```
A>mode lpt1:
```

COPYING FILES

Use the COPY command to copy individual files. Many different options are possible. You can copy a file using one or two drives of any kind: 160K diskette, 320K diskette, or Winchester partition. Names of the original and duplicate files can be different or, when two drives are used, the same. You might use the COPY command to transfer selected transient command files from the "DOS" diskette to another diskette. By copying only the files you want, you save room for other files.

Same Name, Different Drive

The simplest form of the COPY command uses only the name of the original file. The duplicate file gets the same name. The source and target drives must be different. The following example copies a file from drive A to drive B:

```
A>copy a:mode.com b:
```

The original file name always comes first in the COPY command; here it is A:MODE.COM. The A: part designates the source drive, of course. The second drive designation is the target drive, in this case, drive B.

The copy operation commences as soon as you press the ⬅ key. There is no message or pause to allow you to change diskettes, so have everything ready to go in advance. The COPY command is resident in PC DOS; no command file is required. When the copy operation finishes, a message appears on the display screen reporting the number of files copied.

When source and target file names are the same, you may omit either the source or target drive designation, but not both. The default drive will be used for the implicit drive designation, and the explicit drive designation must be different. The following example shows two instances of the COPY command, both of which copy from drive A to drive B, as the last example did. The first instance copies from the default drive to a specified drive. Then the default drive is changed to drive B. After that, the second instance copies from a specified drive to the new default drive.

```
A>copy mode.com b:
       1 File(s) copied
A>b:
B>copy a:mode.com
       1 File(s) copied
```

If a file by the same name already exists on the target drive, it is erased and replaced by the file on the source drive. If you inadvertently try to copy a file onto itself (same file name, same drive), the COPY command simply reports, "0 File(s) copied" and there is no harm done.

Different Name, Same Drive

In order to duplicate individual files on one drive, the source and target file names must be different. The following example makes a backup copy of file LETTER1.DOC on the same drive:

```
A>copy letter1.doc letter1.bak
```

This example uses the default drive, but you may explicitly designate any drive.

Different Name, Different Drives

To create a duplicate file with a different name and on a different drive from the original, you must specify both file names and at least one drive. Here is an example:

```
A>copy contract.doc b:contract.bak
```

The example above copies file CONTRACT.DOC from the default drive, A, to file CONTRACT.BAK on drive B. You could also explicitly state the source drive.

COPY With Generic File Names

You can use the ambiguous characters ? and * in file names with the COPY command. This can save you some typing when the source and target file names are the same except for their extensions. Here is an example:

```
A>copy amortize.bas *.bak
```

Using generic names, it is possible to copy all of the files from the source drive to the target drive. The following example copies all files from the default drive, A, to drive B:

```
A>copy *.* b:
```

Copying all files from one drive to another with the COPY command is similar to copying with the DISKCOPY command, but there are some important differences. For one thing, DISKCOPY leaves none of the previous files on the target drive, but the COPY command adds files to any already present on the target drive. If the target drive has too little space for all the source files, the COPY command will not copy them all.

If the target drive is empty before the COPY command begins, the directory is effectively reorganized as the COPY command proceeds. The reorganization improves the efficiency of disk access, especially on a disk that has been subject to lots of file creation and deletion. Because of the directory reorganization, the DISKCOMP command will most likely declare a diskette you copied using a COPY *.* command different from the original.

The DISKCOPY command does not reorganize the directory; it makes a literal carbon copy of the source drive.

Copy and Verify

If you want to have PC DOS read the target file, compare it to the source, and verify that the two are identical, suffix "/V" to the end of a COPY command, like this:

```
A>copy a:format.com b:/v
```

Errors during file copying are rare and can usually be attributed to a faulty target diskette. The COPY command operates more slowly with the "/V" option because it has to check the target file after writing it.

ERASING FILES

The ERASE command removes one or more files from a disk directory and frees the space they occupied on the disk for other files. It works with any kind of drive. Here is an example:

```
A>erase b:invntry.bak
```

As with other commands, the explicit drive designation is optional. If absent, the default drive is used.

Generic file names are allowed with the ERASE command, but use them with caution. They generally result in many files being deleted with one command, and a slight misstatement of the generic file name could erase the wrong group of files. The following example erases all files on drive B:

```
A>erase b:*.*
```

In this case only, the system asks, "Are you sure (Y/N)?" as a safeguard against accidental erasure of all files.

RENAMING FILES

The RENAME command changes the name of one or more files on any kind of drive. The new file name cannot already exist in the disk directory. Here is an example:

```
A>rename b:maillist.bas mail.bas
```

The first file name is the old file name, and the second file name is the new file name. An explicit drive designation prefix is optional with the first file name. If absent, the name change occurs on the default drive. The RENAME command ignores any explicit drive designation with the second file name.

You can use generic file names with the RENAME command. If the old file name is generic, all files that match it are renamed according to the new file name, which must be generic also. The following example renames all files that start with a 5 so that they start with a 4:

```
A>rename 5*.* 4*.*
```

A generic new file name used with a specific old file name can save typing, like this:

```
B>rename address1.dat *.bak
```

This effectively changes the file name extension of file ADDRESS1 from DAT to BAK.

CHAPTER 4

STARTING A PROGRAM

Many PC users figure they will never have to write computer programs themselves because they plan to use existing software. Chances are their plans will succeed, considering the diversity of well-written application programs now available. This chapter provides general instructions for starting up existing software, but it does not replace specific instructions that come with a program. Operating procedures vary so widely from one program to the next that this chapter cannot possibly cover them all in detail. Once started, most programs display specific operating instructions sufficient to get you going, and for details you can consult the program's printed manual or check with someone who already knows the program thoroughly.

Most application software for the PC comes recorded on diskette or printed in books and magazines. Before you can initiate a program stored on either medium you must transfer it into dynamic memory, where the PC can execute it. It takes just a few keystrokes to get a diskette program going, because a diskette drive can read a program off a diskette and transfer it to the PC quickly. But programs printed in books and magazines require relatively long and tedious manual transcribing from the page into the computer, since the computer cannot presently understand printing.

SOFTWARE ON DISKETTE

There are several different ways to start a diskette program. The method your program requires depends on several factors, and to some extent the only way to tell which method to use is to try each one until you find the one that works.

Duplicate It First

To avoid the inconvenience or disaster that may occur when a defective or damaged diskette prevents starting a program, be sure to make duplicate copies of every new software diskette you buy. Chapter 3 has instructions for copying whole diskettes or single programs. Note, however, that some packaged software is recorded on diskette in a way that prevents duplicating it. If you purchase a package like that, find out beforehand how you can get a replacement copy if one is needed.

The Disk Operating System's Role

The PC requires a disk operating system program of some kind to transfer an application program from diskette to dynamic memory. Several different disk operating systems work on the PC, including CP/M-86, UCSD Pascal (the p-system), and OASIS, but the most popular is PC DOS. Most software diskettes you buy will only work with one of the operating systems, although popular software packages come in several versions, each compatible with a different operating system. Be sure you only buy programs that work with the disk operating system you have. This chapter describes start-up procedures for application programs that use PC DOS; other disk operating systems are similar.

Because of licensing restrictions imposed by the owners of the operating systems, application software packages do not always include a copy of the disk operating system on the diskette you buy. Fortunately, a disk operating system can store a copy of itself on any diskette you designate. Chapter 5 has complete instructions for doing that with PC DOS. It's best to do this on a duplicate copy of the diskette you buy, not on the original, just in case anything should go wrong.

SELF-STARTING SOFTWARE

Some diskette software starts itself. All you have to do is place the diskette in drive A, close the drive door, and turn on the computer. If the system unit is already turned on, you can start the software by pressing **Ctrl|Alt|Del.** Either way, the procedure is the same as the one described in Chapter 3 for loading PC DOS, except here you use the self-starting program diskette in place of a plain system diskette.

Soon drive A starts to make noise and things start to appear on the display screen. At least one PC DOS command will flash by, maybe more. The commands come from a special file, named AUTOEXEC.BAT, that contains whatever PC DOS commands are necessary to automatically start the application program. (Chapter 5 has more on AUTOEXEC.BAT.) Eventually, the application program takes control of the PC and displays its first message. Consult the application program manual for specific operating instructions.

PROBLEMS ENCOUNTERED DURING SELF-STARTING

The PC may stop displaying new messages before it gets to the application program. It may be that the application program is simply not the self-starting kind. If the display screen looks the same as when you load PC DOS (see Fig. 3-5), then you must start the program manually, as described later in this chapter.

The message "Non-system disk or disk error" may mean you neglected to copy PC DOS onto the application diskette. You can either copy PC DOS on the application disk or start it manually as described below. The message just described or other messages, like "Disk error reading drive A," may also indicate a bad diskette. But before condemning the diskette, make sure you put the correct diskette in drive A, right-side up, and press **Ctrl|Alt|Del** to try self-starting again. If the error persists, try another copy of the application program diskette. Continued errors with more than one diskette suggest equipment malfunction. The IBM manual *Guide to Operations* contains a diagnostic diskette and instructions for using it to test your system.

MANUAL PROGRAM START-UP

Before you can start an application program manually, you must load the disk operating system, as described in Chapter 3. The PC DOS identification message, with the cursor waiting beside a command prompt, must be on the display screen (review Fig. 3-5).

Next you must determine what name the program has on the diskette. That name is probably not the full name of the program, but is some abbreviation or acronym. Check the package that the software came in; look for the "program name" or "file name." It will be eight characters or less, and may be suffixed with a period followed by three characters like COM, EXE, or BAS. The suffix indicates the type of file the program is stored in, and that determines the kind of command that will start the program. If you cannot find the program name and file type any other way, use the PC DOS command DIR, as explained in Chapter 3, to inspect the directory of file names on the application software diskette.

Starting Type COM and EXE Software

To start a program stored in a file with a suffix of COM or EXE, merely type the program's file name and press the ← key. No need to type the suffix itself, since PC DOS assumes the file has a suffix of COM or EXE. The following example starts the program in file WS.COM:

```
A>ws
```

A few seconds after you type in the file name correctly, the program's first message should appear on the display screen. If an error message appears instead, double check your typing to make sure you made no mistakes. If the error message is "Bad command or file name" and you made no typing errors, the program either is not on the drive, has a different name, or is not on a type COM or EXE file. Other error possibilities were discussed earlier in this chapter, in the section on self-starting.

The application program diskette need not be in drive A. To explicitly designate the drive, just prefix the program file name with a drive designation, like this:

```
B>a:ws
```

In this case, PC DOS looks for file WS.COM on drive A because it is explicitly designated, even though the default drive is drive B.

Starting Type BAS Software

Type BAS files contain BASIC language programs that require an interpreter to translate their instructions into the PC's machine language. The interpreter occupies part of the PC dynamic memory, sharing it with both PC DOS and the program it translates.

There are two versions of BASIC that work with PC DOS, Disk BASIC and Advanced BASIC. The Advanced BASIC interpreter has a larger repertory of commands than the Disk BASIC interpreter, but the former takes up more memory than the latter, leaving less for the application program. If you don't know which version a program requires, try the Advanced BASIC interpreter first. It lets you know right away if a program is too large to work with it. Trying the Disk BASIC interpreter with a program that might use an Advanced BASIC command flirts with danger. The program may work for a while and then fail when the Advanced BASIC command occurs, leaving things highly disrupted.

The interpreter itself is a program, and it must be transferred from disk to the PC memory. The Disk BASIC interpreter resides in a program file named BASIC.COM. The Advanced BASIC interpreter resides in a program file named BASICA.COM.

To start a type BAS application program, first type the file name of the interpreter you want, leave a blank space, and type the file name of the application program you want. Then press the ← key. Omit all file name suffixes; PC DOS assumes a COM suffix for the interpreter and a BAS suffix for the application program. The following example will start the program in file SAMPLES.BAS with the Disk BASIC interpreter:

```
A>basic samples
```

When you press the ← key, PC DOS transfers the interpreter from disk to the PC memory and clears the display screen. Then it transfers the application program from disk to memory and gives control to the interpreter, which starts interpreting the application program instructions.

In the example above, both the interpreter and application program files must be on the default drive. You can explicitly designate a drive for either or both. All you do is prefix the file name with the drive designation, like this:

```
B>a:basica samples
```

Here the default drive is drive B, but the prefix on the interpreter file name tells PC DOS to look on drive A for the Advanced BASIC interpreter. Because program file SAMPLES.BAS has no drive designation prefix, it must be on the default drive.

If PC DOS cannot find the BASIC interpreter on the specified drive, it displays the error message "Bad command or file name." If the application program is not on the designated drive, the message "File not found" appears after the interpreter displays its three-line identification message, and the PC DOS command prompt reappears below that.

Programs on Winchester Drives

Most application programs shipped on diskette can be copied to a Winchester drive and started from it the same as a diskette drive. Winchester drives often have room for several applications software packages. Chapter 3 explains how to copy a program from one drive to another, given the file name. The application program may use several files, so be sure to copy all files from the application program diskette to the Winchester drive.

If drive A on your system is a Winchester drive, one application program on it can be self-starting. Choose the AUTOEXEC.BAT file that goes with the application software package you want to be self-starting and copy it onto drive A. Because file names on one drive must be unique, only one AUTOEXEC.BAT file can exist on drive A, hence just one program can be self-starting when drive A is a Winchester partition.

TRANSCRIBING PRINTED SOFTWARE

Magazines and books contain printed BASIC programs that will work on the PC. At present the only way to get a printed program into the PC memory is to type it in from the keyboard. Someday you may be able to use an *optical scanner* to read the printed page into the PC, but not yet.

If you want to be sure a transcribed program will work, you must copy it verbatim. This is an exacting task but one that is not too onerous if the program is fairly short, say 300 lines or less.

A program not written specifically for the PC may or may not work even if you make a letter-perfect copy. There are differences, some subtle and some obvious, among the BASIC programming languages on different computers. You can never be sure if a program written in BASIC for another computer will work on the PC until you try it.

You type a BASIC program into the PC with the aid of one of the BASIC interpreters. The Disk BASIC interpreter will suffice for most programs not

```
The IBM Personal Computer Basic
Version D1.10 Copyright IBM Corp 1981,
1982
38907 Bytes free
Ok
_
```

(A)   Disk BASIC.

```
The IBM Personal Computer Basic
Version A1.10 Copyright IBM Corp 1981,
1982
33402 Bytes free
Ok
_
```

(B)   Advanced BASIC.

Fig. 4-1.   The BASIC interpreter identification messages.

written specifically for the PC. When in doubt, use the Advanced BASIC interpreter, since it knows the most BASIC commands.

To begin, type BASIC or BASICA, depending on which interpreter you want, and press the ← key. A message appears, identifying the interpreter in control (Fig. 4-1). On the fourth display line you will see the message "Ok" and on the fifth line, the cursor. Notice the PC DOS command prompt no longer appears, because PC DOS has handed control of the computer over to the interpreter. The interpreter has no true command prompt of its own, though the cursor often appears below the "Ok" message.

You can now type in the printed program lines. You may type any combination of capitals and small letters, even if the printed copy uses all capital letters. The PC automatically converts small letters to capitals as needed.

Each program line begins with a number, called the *line number*. Some program lines are long enough that they will not fit on one display line. In that case, just keep typing; do not press the ← key just because the cursor reaches the end of the display line. The program line will automatically wrap around to the next display line. Press the ← key only at the end of a program line, that is, just before you start a new program line with its line number. For example, Fig. 4-2 shows a program that alphabetizes a list of up to 100 items. If you transcribe it, you will have to press the ← key exactly 33 times, once at the end of each program line.

If you notice errors in your typing on a program line before pressing the ← key, you can use the ← or **Esc** keys to correct the problem. The ← key backspaces along the program line and the **Esc** key erases the program line, just as you would expect.

Checking for Transcription Errors

Because it is so very important that a transcription be accurate, you need to review it before attempting to start the program. With the computer still under the control of the interpreter (not PC DOS), press the **F1** key and the word "LIST" appears on display screen. Now press the ← key and your transcription of the printed program appears. If there are more than 22 program lines in the program, all but the last 22 will vanish off the top of the screen. If this happens, press the **F1** key again, but before you press the ← key, get ready to press the **Ctrl** and **Num Lock** keys simultaneously to freeze the display before the first screenful of program lines disappears.

Carefully compare the displayed program listing with the printed one. Make sure you did not confuse capital letter O's and numeral 0's, small l's and numeral 1's, or Z's and 2's. If you spot any typographical errors, jot down the number of the erroneous program line. When you have reviewed all the program lines visible on the display screen, you can proceed to the

```
10 DIM ITEM$(100)
20 CLS
30 PRINT ,"ALPHABETIZE"
40 PRINT
50 INPUT "How many items";NBR
60 FOR J=1 TO NBR
70 PRINT "What is item";J
80 INPUT ITEM$(J)
90 NEXT J
100 N=NBR
110 N=INT(N/2)
120 IF N=0 THEN 240
130 J=1
140 K=NBR-N
150 L=J
160 M=L+N
170 IF ITEM$(L)<=ITEM$(M) THEN 210
180 SWAP ITEM$(L),ITEM$(M)
190 L=L-N
200 IF L>=1 THEN 160
210 J=J+1
220 IF J>K THEN 110
230 GOTO 150
240 CLS
250 FOR J=1 TO NBR
260 PRINT ITEM$(J)
270 NEXT J
280 INPUT "Reprint (Y/N)";A$
290 IF LEFT$(A$,1)="Y" OR LEFT$(A$,1)="y" THEN 240
300 END
```

Fig. 4-2. The alphabetize program.

next screenful, if any. Get ready to press **Ctrl|Num Lock** again, and press the space bar or ◄─┘ key. Immediately more lines appear on the screen. Quickly press **Ctrl|Num Lock.** Starting where you left off, review the next segment of transcribed program lines. Continue the cycle, noting the line numbers of program lines where errors appear, until you have checked the whole program.

Most people find it easier to check a transcription if it is printed instead of displayed. If you have a printer, you can print a copy by pressing the **F1** key, then the **F6** key; no need to press the ◄─┘ key. The message 'LIST ,"LPT1:" ' appears on the display screen and printing begins. Of course the printer must be ready to print before you do this.

Table 4-1. Cursor Movement and Editing Keys
(For Use With BASIC Programs)

Key(s)	Effect
↑	Move cursor up one display line
↓	Move cursor down one display line
→	Move cursor right one character
←	Move cursor left one character
Ctrl →	Move cursor right one word*
Ctrl ←	Move cursor left one word*
Home	Move cursor to upper left corner
End	Move cursor to end of program line
→⊦	Move cursor to next tab stop†
Esc	Erase the program line from the screen
←	Delete the last character that was typed
Ctrl ←	Same as **Del**
Del	Delete the character at the current cursor position
Ins	Switch into or out of insert mode‡
Ctrl Home	Clear screen and move cursor to upper left corner
Ctrl End	Erase remainder of program line
←	Make changes to current program line permanent

*A *word* is a character or group of characters that begins with a letter or numeral. Blank spaces, punctuation, and special characters separate words.

†Tab stops are preset eight spaces apart, at character positions 1, 9, 17, etc.

‡All of the keys listed here switch out of insert mode except →⊦ and ←

Recalling Incorrect Program Lines

With a list of the line numbers of erroneous program lines in hand, you are ready to begin making corrections. The computer must still be under the control of the interpreter. Any program line visible on the display screen can be edited. In nonnumeric mode, several of the keys on the dual-purpose keypad can move the cursor around on the display screen, and others facilitate inserting and deleting characters.

It doesn't matter how a program line gets on the display screen; once it's there, you can change it. You can use the **F1** key to start listing program lines and press **Ctrl Scroll Lock** to halt the listing instantly. There is another simple way to recall a program line for correction: type the command EDIT, leave a blank space, type the line number of the program line you want, and press the ← key. The program line you requested appears on the next display line, with the cursor flashing underneath its first character.

Making Changes

In order to correct an error on a displayed program line, you must move the cursor to the mistake. Chapter 2 describes the many keys that move the cursor; Table 4-1 recapitulates those and mentions a few new ones.

With the cursor in position beneath the error, any characters you type will replace characters on the display (Fig. 4-3). To delete characters, use either the **Del** or ←key (Fig. 4-4). To insert characters, press the **Ins** key, type the new characters, and press the **Ins** key again (Fig. 4-5).

The changes you make to a program line only affect the picture on the display screen at first. If you simply move the cursor to another program line with the ↟ or ↡ keys, the changes will not take effect. To make the

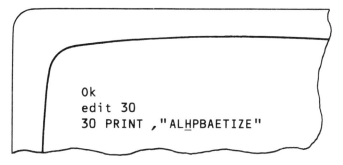

(**A**) Position cursor under the character to replace.

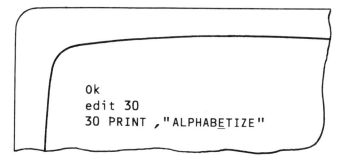

(**B**) Type the correct characters.

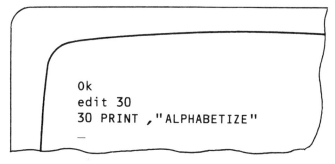

(**C**) Press the ← key.

Fig. 4-3. Replacing characters in a program line.

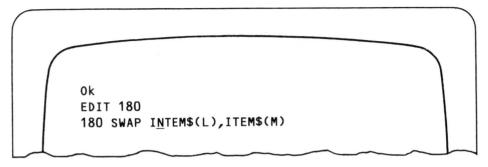

(A) Position cursor under the character to delete.

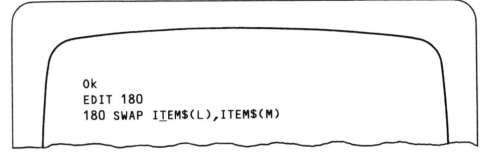

(B) Press the **Del** key to delete a character.

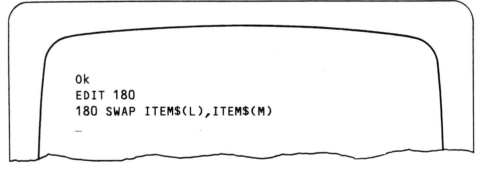

(C) Press the ← key.

Fig. 4-4. Deleting characters in a program line.

changes permanent, you must press the ← key while the cursor is still on the edited program line. The cursor can be anywhere on the program line when you press the ← key.

Incorrect Line Numbers

The line number at the beginning of each BASIC program line is very important, because it determines the sequence of command execution.

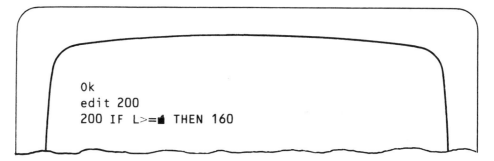

(A) Position cursor under the character to insert ahead of; press the **Ins** key.

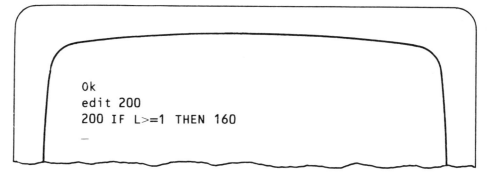

(B) Type the character(s) to be inserted.

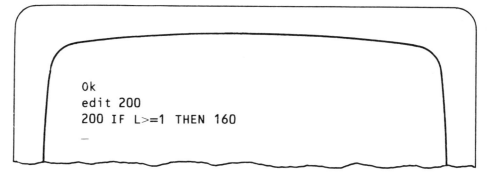

(C) Press the ◄┘ key.

Fig. 4-5. Inserting characters in a program line.

Mixed up line numbers disorganize the program and can be confusing to fix, so make every effort to type them in correctly the first time.

Correcting a program line that you typed with an incorrect line number is a two-step process. First, correct the line number using the techniques just described. Now the line is in the computer twice, once with the right number and once with the wrong number. To delete the spurious line, simply type its line number and press the ◄┘ key.

Storing a Transcribed Program

Although it is possible to use the program as soon as it is typed in correctly, it's best to store a copy of it on a disk for future use. In fact, you can store a program as often as you like while you are transcribing and correcting it. That lets you break up the work into small sessions and protects your past work in case something happens to erase the program from PC memory while you are working on it. The procedure for retrieving a program that you store on disk appears in the next section.

You must choose a file name for the program. Review the rules presented in Chapter 3 for assigning file names (Fig. 3-6). Do not worry about a file name extension, because the computer will automatically suffix your file name with .BAS.

Place a properly formatted diskette in an available drive, or choose a Winchester drive partition with space available. Press the **F4** key and the message "SAVE" appears. Type the drive designation and the name of the program file, and then press the ← key. The cursor disappears for a few seconds as the drive becomes active. Eventually the cursor reappears along with the message "Ok." Should some kind of error message also appear, the program was not completely stored. Try again, possibly with a different diskette, drive, or file name.

Retrieving a Transcribed Program

You can transfer a program from disk to PC memory without first executing the program. The incoming program replaces any program currently in PC memory, so if you want to save the existing program, be sure to store it before retrieving another from disk.

Make sure the correct diskette is in the drive you plan to use. Press the **F3** key and the message 'LOAD" ' appears. Type the drive designation and the name of the program file, and then press the ← key. The cursor disappears for a few seconds as the drive becomes active. When the cursor reappears along with the message "Ok," the transfer is complete. If an error message also appears, the program was not retrieved. Try again: check your typing, use a different drive, or try the backup diskette.

Starting a Transcribed Program

After transcribing or retrieving a program you can initiate it with the **F2** key. The word "RUN" appears, followed by the application program's first message. Alternatively you can store the program on diskette, return control of the computer to PC DOS, and start the transcribed program like any diskette-based program. Type the command SYSTEM to return control of the PC to PC DOS, as follows:

```
Ok
system
A>
```

CHAPTER 5

ADVANCED PC DOS FEATURES

This chapter continues the coverage of the IBM PC disk operating system, describing new commands, new variations of old commands, and some advanced command editing techniques. It also explains how you can combine existing commands to create your own custom commands, and tells you how to automatically execute any sequence of commands when PC DOS is started. Those who plan to use only packaged software on the PC can skip this chapter. Though they may find some of the material here useful, none of it is essential.

FILE CONCATENATION

The COPY command can concatenate the contents of several text files. This requires two or more explicit source file names, joined by plus signs (+), and one target file name, as follows:

```
A>copy ch1.txt+ch2.txt+ch3.txt b:book.txt
```

Contents of the first source file are copied into the target file immediately followed by the contents of the second source file, the contents of the third source file (if any), and so on until all are copied into the target file. When the concatenation finishes, the message "1 File(s) copied" appears.

Drive designations are optional on all source file names and on the target file name; the default drive is used in the absence of an explicit drive designation. You may omit the target file name. The COPY command will use the first source file as the target file, effectively appending the contents of all subsequent source files to it.

Generic File Names

Concatenated source file names can be generic and so can the target file name. The following example concatenates all files on drive B with TXT extensions and puts the result in file BOOK.DOC on drive A:

```
A>copy b:*.txt book.doc
```

When concatenation is through, the display screen reports the number of target files that were copied to.

Generic names let you append one file to many others with a single COPY command, like this:

```
A>copy *.doc+advert.txt b:*.txt
```

In the example above, every file on drive A with a DOC extension has file ADVERT.TXT appended to it, and each combination is copied with a TXT extension to drive B.

If there is room enough on the disk, you can combine all files of one type into a single file. For example:

```
A>copy all.txt+*.txt
```

Here all files with TXT extensions are appended to file ALL.TXT. The first file name, ALL.TXT in this case, must exist for this operation to work.

Generic file names do not work in all concatenation situations. The COPY command prohibits an explicitly stated target file also being listed among the source files, but it cannot always tell when that will happen. Consider this:

```
A>copy *.txt all.txt
```

The command above tries to do the same thing as the previous example, but it will err if file ALL.TXT already exists. The error occurs when the time comes to copy file ALL.TXT (onto itself), because by then file ALL.TXT has probably changed. The message "Content of destination lost before copy" appears but concatenation continues with the next file. The resultant ALL.TXT file contains the contents of all TXT files except the *former* contents of ALL.TXT itself.

Another potential error situation exists when several source files and the destination file all are generic. Although the IBM manual *Disk Operating System, 2nd Ed.* claims such combinations work, experiments show otherwise. Before concatenating with more than one generic source file *and* a generic destination file, be sure to back up all participating files. After attempting such a concatenation, check destination files for accuracy.

DISPLAYING FILE CONTENTS

The TYPE command displays the contents of any file. Here is an example:

```
A>type b:address.dat
```

The drive designation prefix is optional if the file is on the default drive. You can use the **PrtSc** key together with the **Ctrl** or ⇧ keys to send displayed output to the printer, as described in Chapter 4.

You will only be able to read files that contain text, like word processing files, some data files, and parts of some program files. That is because program instructions are usually stored on disk in a condensed form where each instruction is represented by a special one- or two-byte code. The TYPE command decodes the instruction bytes as if they were regular single characters, so encoded instructions will appear unintelligible.

COMPARING FILES

To compare one file with another, use the COMP command. The files may be on the same drive or different drives. To begin, type the command and the names of the two files to compare. Here is an example:

```
A>comp b:program.bas b:program.bak
```

Be sure to prefix the file names with drive designations if they are not on the default drive. Press the ◄─┘ key and the following message appears, advising you to get the diskettes ready:

```
Insert diskette(s) with files to compare
and strike any key when ready
```

First the file sizes are compared. If they are different, the compare operation ends. Otherwise, the files are compared one byte (character) at a time. One or more messages appear announcing the success of the compare. Discrepancies are reported by citing the location of the discrepant byte (relative to the file beginning) and the discrepant values, but the actual numbers reported are less important than the fact that a compare error has occurred. More than ten discrepancies end the compare. Here is a sample report:

```
Compare error at offset E
File 1 = 64
File 2 = 67
Compare error at offset 13
File 1 = 6B
File 2 = 65
Eof mark not found
Compare more files (Y/N)?_
```

The message "Eof mark not found" does not necessarily indicate an error. It is normal when comparing program files and many data files too. The message "Files compare ok" means the files are identical.

If the second file to compare has the same name as the first, it must be on a different drive, and in that case you need only enter the drive designation for the second file. If the file names are different, enter the second file name. Prefix the file name with a drive designation unless it is on the default drive.

The COMP command allows generic file names, but only the first file that matches each generic name will be used. In other words, each command compares only two files.

SETTING THE CLOCK AND CALENDAR

The PC has an internal 24-hour clock that keeps track of time in hours, minutes, seconds, and hundredths of seconds. The clock is tied to a calendar. As long as you leave the computer on, the clock continues to run. At midnight, the date changes, including the month and year when the time comes. But reloading PC DOS clears the time and date and you must enter a new date and time to be used on disk directories.

You can examine and set the date and time whenever you wish with the DATE and TIME commands. To use either command, simply type it in and press the ⬅ key. The computer displays the current date or time and asks you for a new date or time. You may enter nothing and just press the ⬅ key to keep the current date or time unchanged.

To change the date, enter the new month, day, and year; punctuate with hyphens or slashes. To change the time, enter the new hours, minutes, and seconds punctuated by colons. The seconds figure may be a whole number or it may include a decimal fraction. You may omit the new seconds, or even minutes and seconds, entering just the new hour. In that case, the omitted numbers are set to 0. The following example shows how to use the DATE and TIME commands:

```
A>date
Current date is Sun 4-01-1984
Enter new date: 4/2/84

A>time
Current time is 10:43:38.70
Enter new time: 17:15
A>__
```

COPYING THE PC DOS PROGRAM

You may occasionally acquire packaged software that needs PC DOS and does not have it. The SYS command will copy the PC DOS program from the computer memory onto a designated drive. Here is an example:

```
A>sys b:
```

The drive designation is optional if it is the same as the default drive. The SYS command works only on diskettes formatted with the "/S" option. On other diskettes, the message "No room for system on destination disk" appears and PC DOS is not stored.

EDITING PC DOS COMMANDS

Though PC DOS recognizes most of the keyboard conventions described in Chapter 2, it does redefine the group of light-colored keys at the right side of the keyboard, the dual-mode keypad in its nonnumeric mode. PC DOS also has special definitions for all of the function keys. The new meanings facilitate entering, changing, and re-entering PC DOS commands.

Displayed Versus Stored Command

When you press the ← key to officially enter a PC DOS command, two things happen. First, PC DOS executes the displayed command. Second, it copies the command from the display screen into an earmarked part of dynamic memory. This duplicate copy of the command you just entered is called the *stored command* or *command template*.

The Stored Command Pointer

PC DOS maintains a character pointer for the stored command. The pointer is very much like a second, invisible cursor. As you type a command, the display screen cursor moves ahead on the display line. At the same time, the stored command pointer moves ahead in the stored command. Using some of the redefined keys, you can move the pointer and cursor independently. You can also recall the stored command to the display screen, where you can edit and re-execute it.

Numeric Keypad

PC DOS does not use the dual-purpose numeric keypad for cursor control. So if you press the **Num Lock** key to put the keypad in nonnumeric mode and then press any of the **Home, End,** ↑, ↓, →, or ← keys, do not expect to see simple cursor movement on the display screen. The ←, →, **Ins**, and **Del** keys have new definitions, but none of the other keypad keys do anything. Table 5-1 lists the keypad functions.

Table 5-1. PC DOS Numeric Keypad Summary (Nonnumeric Mode)

Key	Effect on displayed command	Effect on stored command
←	Backspace—delete next character to the left	Move pointer one character to the left
→	Recall the next character from the stored command	Move pointer one character to the right
Ins*	None; characters typed subsequently are appended whether insert mode is on or off	Insert mode *on*: typed characters do not move pointer Insert mode *off*: typed characters move pointer
Del	None	Move pointer one character to the right
All other keypad keys	None	None

*If insert mode is off, the **Ins** key switches it on. If insert mode is on, the **Ins** key switches it off.

Function Key Uses

PC DOS defines seven of the ten function keys at the left edge of the keyboard; the other three do nothing. This section describes how keys **F1** through **F5** are used for editing. Later in this chapter, the section on batch processing describes one way to use key **F6**. Keys **F6** and **F7** can also be used with programs EDLIN and DEBUG, as described in the IBM manual *Disk Operating System*. Table 5-2 summarizes function key definitions in PC DOS.

Table 5-2. PC DOS Function Keys Summary

Key	Function
F1	Recall the next character from the stored command; advances the stored command pointer
F2	Take the next typed character; recall the segment of the stored command that ends at its next occurrence
F3	Recall the remainder of the stored command
F4	Take the next typed character; skip over the segment of the stored command that ends at its next occurrence
F5	Make the displayed command the stored command but do not execute it
F6	Same as typing **Ctrl|Z**
F7	Same as typing **Ctrl|@**
F8	None
F9	None
F10	None

Reusing a Stored Command

The **F1** key recalls the stored command to the display screen one character at a time. Suppose you just listed a partial directory with the following command:

A>dir b:*.com

At the same time the command was executed, it was made the stored command. Therefore, if you press the **F1** key once, the letter d will appear on the display screen (Fig. 5-1A). Press the **F1** key ten times more, and the whole command is redisplayed (Fig. 5-1B). You could then press the ◄┘ key to execute the redisplayed command. Instead, press the **Esc** key to cancel it. Pressing the **Esc** key clears the displayed command, but does not erase the stored command; it only resets the pointer to the beginning (Fig. 5-1C).

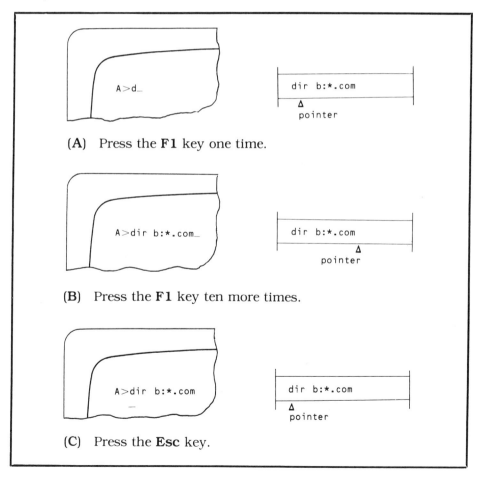

(**A**)   Press the **F1** key one time.

(**B**)   Press the **F1** key ten more times.

(**C**)   Press the **Esc** key.

Fig. 5-1.   **Recalling the stored command and canceling the recall.**

In PC DOS, the → key does the same thing as the **F1** key, so you could press it to redisplay the stored command too. Both the → key and the **F1** key recall one character from the stored command to the display screen and advance the stored command pointer by one at the same time.

Changing a Stored Command

At any point, you can type characters instead of pressing the **F1** or → keys, thereby changing the displayed command. Each character you type advances the stored command pointer too. The typed characters replace stored characters, but only in the displayed command, not in the stored command. Suppose you want to enter the same DIR command as in the last example, but for drive A instead of drive B. Press → (or **F1**) four times, and the first four characters of the stored command will appear on the display screen (Fig. 5-2A). The stored command pointer is now on the drive designation character, B.

Type the new drive designation. At this point, the stored command pointer has moved ahead one character to the colon (Fig. 5-2B). You could now press the → or **F1** key six times to recall the rest of the stored command, but there is an easier way. The **F3** key recalls the remainder of the stored command all at once (Fig. 5-2C). When you press the ← key, the current displayed command becomes the stored command, and PC DOS lists a partial directory for drive A (Fig. 5-2D).

Skipping Stored Command Characters

The **Del** key moves the stored command pointer ahead without recalling characters to the display screen. In a way, it deletes characters from the stored command. But this is only partly true, because the characters are not actually removed from the stored command—the pointer just moves past them.

You can use the **Del** key on the last example to remove the drive designation so that the DIR command will use the default drive. First, use the **F1** or → key to recall the first four characters of the stored command (Fig. 5-3A). Now press the **Del** key. The stored command pointer moves ahead but nothing new appears on the display screen (Fig. 5-3B). Recall the rest of the stored command with the **F3** key (Fig. 5-3C). Press the ← key to execute the displayed command, or the **Esc** key to cancel it.

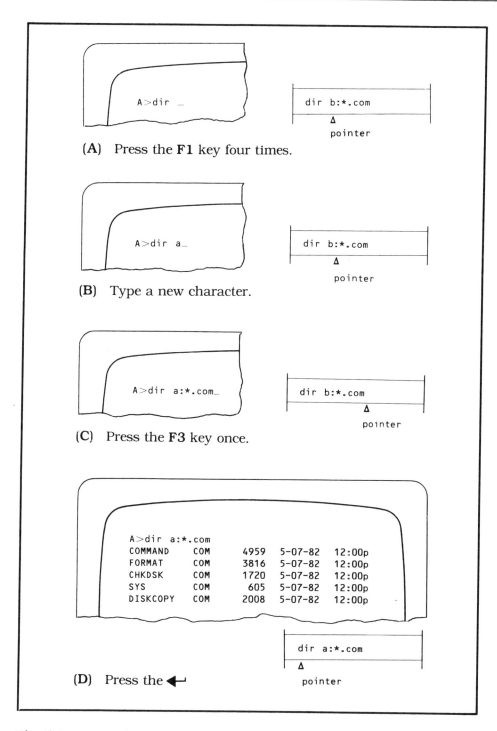

(A) Press the **F1** key four times.

(B) Type a new character.

(C) Press the **F3** key once.

(D) Press the ⏎

Fig. 5-2. **Recalling and changing the stored command.**

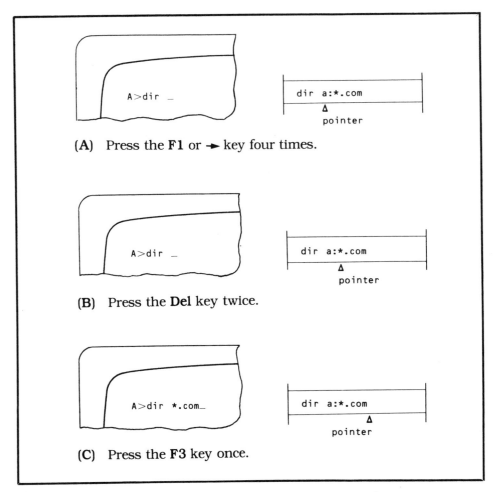

(A) Press the **F1** or ➡ key four times.

(B) Press the **Del** key twice.

(C) Press the **F3** key once.

Fig. 5-3. Skipping characters in the stored command.

Recalling Sections of the Stored Command

Suppose you have just executed the following command to copy all files with COM extensions from drive A to drive B:

        A>copy a:*.com b:*.com

Now you want to copy all files with BAS extensions from drive A to drive B. You could recall the stored command and edit it with just the **F1** and **F3** keys, but that involves pressing the **F1** key 14 times. The **F2** key can relieve some of the drudgery, because it can recall a whole section of the stored command.

To use the **F2** key, you must determine the next character in the stored command that you want to change. In the example just cited that is the letter c. Press the **F2** key, followed by the **C** key and all the characters of the stored command up to the next letter c are recalled to the display (Fig. 5-4A). Now type the new file extension for the source files (Fig. 5-4B). Once again press the **F2** key followed by the **C** key, this time to recall the

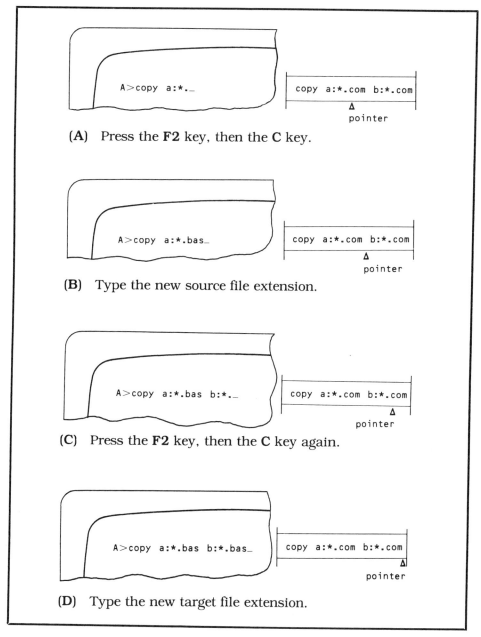

(A) Press the **F2** key, then the **C** key.

(B) Type the new source file extension.

(C) Press the **F2** key, then the **C** key again.

(D) Type the new target file extension.

Fig. 5-4. **Recalling segments of the stored command.**

unchanged section of the stored command up to the next letter c (Fig. 5-4C). Finally, type the new file extension for the target files (Fig. 5-4D). When you press the ← key, the COPY command will copy all files with BAS extensions from drive A to drive B, and the displayed command will become the stored command.

The **F2** key recalls a section of the stored command to the display screen. The section begins where the pointer is and ends just ahead of the first instance of the character you type right after pressing the **F2** key. In looking for the first instance of the character, the character that the pointer is on is not considered. If the character does not exist in the stored command (starting at the current pointer position), no recall occurs.

Inserting and Replacing Stored Command Sections

With the **F4** and **Ins** keys you can delete a section from the middle of a stored command and replace it with any number of characters. Suppose you want to compare several pairs of files which have the same extensions. Your first command might look like this:

```
A>comp a:roosevelt.doc b:*.bak
```

In this case, the ambiguous character in the second file name means the COMP command will compare the file named on drive A with the file by the same name, but with the file name extension of BAK, in drive B.

If the next files to compare are TRUMAN.DOC and TRUMAN.BAK, you need only replace "roosevelt" in the stored command with "truman" and the command will be ready to go. One way to make the substitution is to start by recalling the first section of the displayed command with the **F2** and **R** keys (Fig. 5-5A). At this point, you can delete all of the old file name at once by using the **F4** key. Press **F4** and then type a decimal point to skip over all the characters between the current pointer position and the next decimal point in the stored command (Fig. 5-5B). Now press the **Ins** key. That switches the keyboard to insert mode. Type the new file name; the characters appear in the displayed command, but the stored command and its pointer are unchanged (Fig. 5-5C). Finally, recall the remainder of the stored command with the **F3** key (Fig. 5-5D). When you press the ← key, the new files will be compared.

The **F4** key works like a super-**Del** key, skipping over a whole section of the stored command at once. The section begins at the current position of the pointer and ends just ahead of the first instance of the character you type right after pressing the **F4** key. In looking for the first instance of the character, the character that the the pointer is on is not considered. If the character does not exist in the stored command (starting at the current pointer position), the pointer does not move.

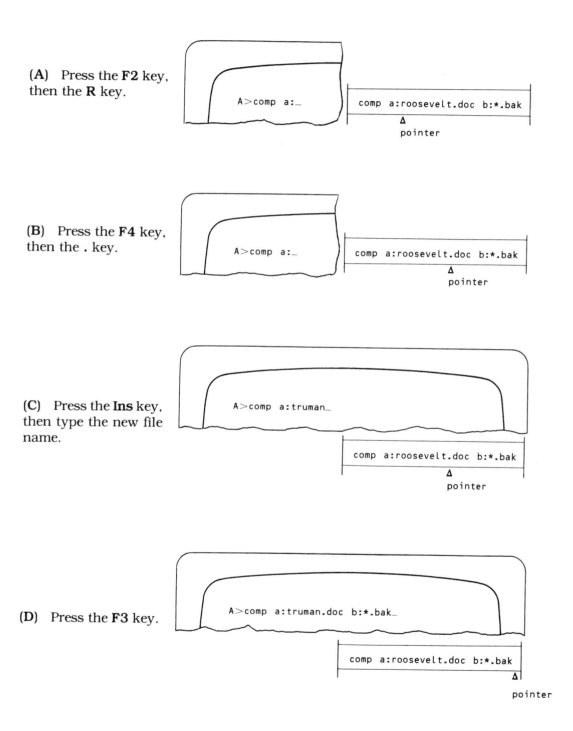

(A) Press the **F2** key, then the **R** key.

A>comp a:_

comp a:roosevelt.doc b:*.bak
△
pointer

(B) Press the **F4** key, then the **.** key.

A>comp a:_

comp a:roosevelt.doc b:*.bak
△
pointer

(C) Press the **Ins** key, then type the new file name.

A>comp a:truman_

comp a:roosevelt.doc b:*.bak
△
pointer

(D) Press the **F3** key.

A>comp a:truman.doc b:*.bak_

comp a:roosevelt.doc b:*.bak
△
pointer

Fig. 5-5. Replacing a section of the stored command.

The **Ins** key switches PC DOS in and out of insert mode. There is no visible difference between insert mode and normal mode in PC DOS; the cursor does not change shape as it does when typing a BASIC program. In insert mode, the display screen cursor continues to advance as you type, but the stored command pointer stays put. The following keys end insert mode: **Ins**, **Esc**, ➡, **F1**, **F2**, **F3**, **F5**, and ⬅.

Storing a Command Without Execution

Pressing the **F5** key causes the current displayed command to become the stored command but suppresses its execution. The character @ appears at the current cursor position to indicate the transfer took place, and the cursor moves down to the start of the next display line. If there is no command currently displayed, pressing the **F5** key effectively clears the stored command.

DEVICE NAMES

Some PC DOS commands can send and receive information between not only disk files but other parts of the system too. The other accessible devices include serial devices, the printer, and the keyboard and display screen. There is also a dummy device available for testing purposes. Each device has a standard name, which you use just like a disk file name. Table 5-3 lists the recognized devices and their names.

Device names are most often used with the COPY command. You can copy the contents of a disk file to the display screen with a command like this:

```
A>copy chap3a.doc con:
```

Of course, this does the same thing as a TYPE command.

Table 5-3. Device Names

Device name*	Input device	Output device
AUX:†	Serial device	Serial device
COM1:	Serial device	Serial device
CON:	Display screen	Keyboard
LPT1:	None	Main printer
NUL:	Dummy for testing	Dummy for testing
PRN:†	None	Printer

*The colon at the end of the device name is optional.
†Device names AUX: and PRN: do not work with the MODE command.

The COPY command also lets you copy from the keyboard to a disk file. Just specify device CON: as the primary "file" (Fig. 5-6A). When you press the ← key to execute such a command, the cursor drops down to the beginning of the next display line. Everything you type from that point on appears on the display screen and will also go out to the specified disk file (Fig. 5-6B). However, the combination keystrokes **Ctrl|Alt|Del** and **Ctrl|Scroll Lock** are not copied—they interrupt normal processing as usual.

Typing a special character sequence ends the copy operation and returns the keyboard to command mode. The sequence is easiest to create by pressing first the **F6** key, then the ← key. When you do that, the characters ∧Z appear (Fig. 5-6C). However, these characters only work if you type them at the beginning of a line, that is, right after having pressed the ← key. You can verify the copy operation visually with the TYPE command (Fig. 5-6D).

When copying from device CON:, the **Esc** key displays the character \ and cancels everything you typed since the last time you pressed the ← key. Also, the ← key backspaces on the line you are typing, but it cannot back up past the point where you last pressed the ← key.

You cannot type more than 127 characters without pressing the ← key. If you try to, the computer just beeps each time you press a key and nothing appears on the display screen. You must press the ← key and start a new line.

Characters do not go to the disk one at a time as you type them. Instead, they accumulate in a dedicated area of dynamic memory, called a *buffer*, until it is full. Then the whole group is transferred to disk and the next typed characters start to accumulate in the buffer. When you use the **F6** key to end the copy operation, the leftover characters in the buffer are sent to the disk to complete the file.

BATCH PROCESSING

The PC, like most small computers, responds immediately to each command you give it. Because the computer interacts continually with you, this method is called *interactive processing*. It is convenient for word processing, small business accounting, and personal computing, but sometimes an easier method is to give the computer a batch of commands to execute automatically, one after the other. PC DOS has this feature, called *batch processing*.

```
A>copy con: othello.txt
_
```

(A) Use device CON: as the first "file" name.

```
A>copy con: othello.txt
O, beware, my lord, of jealousy!
It is the green-ey'd monster which doth
mock
The meat it feeds on.
_
```

(B) Type text to be copied.

```
A>copy con: othello.txt
O, beware, my lord, of jealousy!
It is the green-ey'd monster which doth
mock
The meat it feeds on.
^Z
                1 File(s) copied
A>_
```

(C) Conclude copy by pressing the **F6** key, then the ← key.

```
A>type othello.txt
O, beware, my lord, of jealousy!
It is the green-ey'd monster which doth
mock
The meat it feeds on.

A>_
```

(D) Verify the copy with the TYPE command.

Fig. 5-6.   Copying directly from the keyboard to a disk file.

Creating a Batch File

To use batch processing, you must first create a disk file that contains the sequence of commands you want executed. Files like this are called *batch files*. Essentially, the batch file name becomes a new command that you defined in advance as a particular combination of existing commands.

You can use the COPY command to create a batch file. Simply copy from the keyboard (device CON:) to the batch file, as described earlier in this chapter. Type each command on a separate line, and conclude the file by pressing the **F6** key followed by the ◄┘ key. One useful batch file copies drive A to drive B, and then compares the two drives to verify the copy accuracy (Fig. 5-7).

Using the COPY command is the most straightforward way to create a batch file, but there are other ways. You can use a word processor to do it—just be sure to create a "nondocument" type file, one without any text formatting. The PC line editor EDLIN, described in the IBM manual *Disk Operating System*, will also work. It is even possible to write a program in BASIC or some other programming language to create a batch file.

Executing Batch File Commands

To start the sequence of commands contained in a batch file, type the name of the appropriate batch file exactly as you would type a PC DOS command. You may type the BAT file name extension, but it is not required. For example, you can initiate the batch file COPYAB.BAT (Fig. 5-7) by typing this:

```
A>copyab
```

When you press the ◄┘ key, the following appears without any further entry on your part:

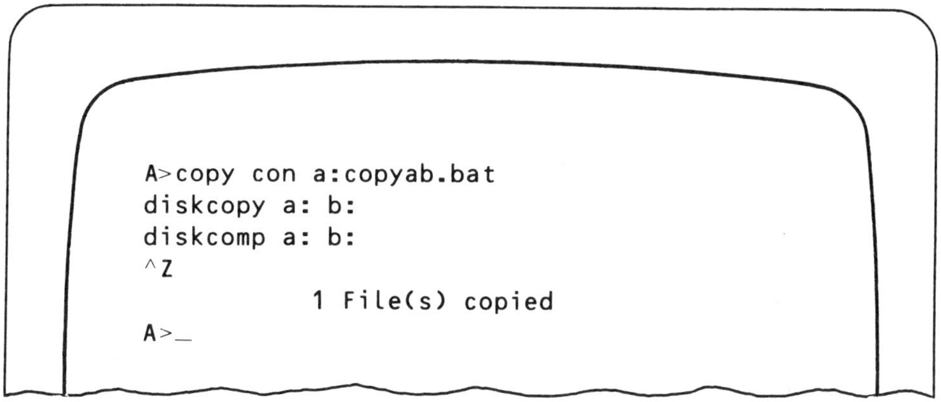

```
A>copy con a:copyab.bat
diskcopy a: b:
diskcomp a: b:
^Z
            1 File(s) copied

A>_
```

Fig. 5-7. Creating a batch file.

```
A>diskcopy a: b:
Insert source diskette in drive A
Insert target diskette in drive B
Strike any key when ready
—
```

Even in batch mode, PC DOS still waits for you to start the actual diskette copy operation by pressing some key. When the copy finishes, the following message "Copy another? (Y/N)" appears. You must answer at the keyboard again, even though commands are coming from a batch file. Respond negatively, and the batch operation proceeds without any further keyboard entry:

```
A>diskcomp a: b:
Insert first diskette in drive A
Insert second diskette in drive B
Strike any key when ready
—
```

Once more, you must press a key to signify the diskettes are ready. After finishing the compare, PC DOS asks, "Compare more diskettes? (Y/N)." Answer negatively and the command sequence from batch file COPYAB.BAT ends like this:

```
A>
A>_
```

Batch File Variables

The commands in a batch file can contain dummy characters that are replaced by real characters when batch processing starts. The dummy characters are called *variables* or *parameters*. Each variable consists of two characters. The first character is always a percent symbol (%) and the second character is a numeral between 0 and 9. Thus there are ten variables available to each batch file: %0, %1, %2, etc. You can use the variables wherever you like in a batch file, and you can use them more than once in the same batch file. For example, you can create a batch file to copy one file to another and then compare the file contents like this:

```
A>copy con copycomp.bat
copy %1 %2
comp %1 %2
∧Z
        1 File(s) copied
>A_
```

Neither of the batch file commands above explicitly states file names to be copied. Actual file names will be specified when the batch file is initiated. The next example does just that:

```
A>copycomp a:accounts.dat b:
```

The first part of the command line above initiates the batch file named COPYCOMP.BAT. The second and third parts specify actual characters to replace variables %1 and %2 in the batch file. When you press the ◄─┘ key, batch processing takes over and the following messages appear:

```
A>copy a:accounts.dat b:
      1 File(s) copied
A>comp a:accounts.dat b:
Insert diskette(s) with files to compare
and strike any key when ready

Files compare ok
Compare more files (Y/N)?
A>
A>__
```

In the batch process above, you only have to type the file names once. You do still have to press two more keys: one starts the file compare and one ends it.

Each batch file variable corresponds to a specific group of characters on the command line. The first group of characters is always the batch file name (including the drive designation prefix if there is one), and it only replaces variable %0. The second group of characters only replaces variable %1 in the batch file, the third group only replaces variable %2, and so on.

On the one hand, characters that have no matching variable are simply not used. For example, a batch file without variable %0 does not use the batch file name as replacement characters, period. The previous example illustrates this.

On the other hand, variables that have no matching characters are ignored during batch file execution, and the results are unpredictable. Errors may occur, or you may have to supply the missing characters during batch file execution. Compare the following example with the previous example:

```
A>copycomp b:backup.bat
A>copy b:backup.bat
      1 Files(s) copied
A>comp b:backup.bat
Enter 2nd file name or drive id
__
```

There are no characters to replace variable %2, the target file name above. The COPY command uses the default drive, drive A, as the target drive, and uses the same file name as the source file; that may or may not be what you wanted. But the COMP command must have both drives explicitly designated, so it interrupts batch processing to ask for the missing target drive from the keyboard.

If you want to use an actual file name that contains a percent symbol inside a batch file, you must type the character % twice. For example, type TAX%%.DAT inside a batch file to specify a file named TAX%.DAT.

Displaying Remarks

The PC DOS command REM is designed especially for displaying remarks during batch processing. When the first three characters on a command line are REM (small letters or capitals), the entire line is displayed but no other action takes place. For example, adding comments to batch file COPYAB.BAT (Fig. 5-7) can turn it into a general backup procedure. This could be done with a new batch file that displays comments with a bunch

```
A>copy con backup.bat
rem ********************************
rem *    Use your write-protected   *
rem *active diskette as the "source."*
rem *    Use its backup diskette as  *
rem *the "target."                   *
rem *    Use the "N" key to respond  *
rem *to all questions and prompts.   *
rem ********************************
copyab
^Z
            1 File(s) copied

A>_
```

Fig. 5-8. REM commands in a batch file.

of REM commands and then, on its last line, initiates existing batch file COPYAB.BAT (Fig. 5-8).

At least one blank space must follow the command word REM. The message that follows it can be blank, or it can have up to 123 characters.

Batch Processing Pauses

Many of the PC DOS commands use messages like "Strike any key when ready" and then pause, waiting for you to press the space bar, ← key, or some other key. The PAUSE command lets you add your own pauses to a batch file. Batch file COPYAB.BAT (Fig. 5-7) uses the DISKCOPY and DISKCOMP transient commands. But if command files DISKCOPY.COM and DISKCOMP.COM are not on the default drive, PC DOS cannot execute the commands. You can use PAUSE commands to display instructions for disk switching to obviate the error messages that occur when command files are absent (Fig. 5-9).

The AUTOEXEC Batch File

When you load PC DOS by turning on the system unit or pressing the **Ctrl|Alt|Del** keys, the system looks on drive A for the batch file AUTOEXEC.BAT. If that file is present, PC DOS takes its first commands from it, not from the keyboard. In that case, the system does not ask for the date and time unless file AUTOEXEC.BAT includes the DATE and TIME commands. Like any other batch file, AUTOEXEC.BAT can contain any number of valid PC DOS commands, resident or transient. Transient commands do require the presence of the appropriate file, of course. The following example creates an AUTOEXEC.BAT file that will ask for the date and

```
A>copy con a:copyab.bat
pause <<Put DOS disk in default drive>>
diskcopy a: b:
pause >>Put DOS disk in default drive<<
diskcomp a: b:
^Z
                1 File(s) copied

A>_
```

Fig. 5-9. PAUSE commands in a batch file.

time and then shift the display 2 characters to the right whenever PC DOS is loaded:

```
A>copy con: autoexec.bat
date
time
mode ,r
mode ,r
∧Z
       1 File(s) copied
A>__
```

Upon loading PC DOS, the following messages appear on the display screen:

```
A>date
Current date is Tue 1-01-1980
Enter new date: 2/12/84
A>time
Current time is 0:00:13.29
Enter new time: 16:15

A>mode ,r
A>mode ,r
A>
A>__
```

Each MODE command in the batch file clears the screen and shifts it one character to the right, assuming the display is attached to a color/graphics monitor.

PART 2

PROGRAMMING IN BASIC

CHAPTER 6

THE FUNDAMENTALS

This chapter and the nine that follow teach you how to program the PC in BASIC. In this chapter, you will learn how BASIC relates to other programming languages. You will learn some simple commands that produce displays on the screen, and you will also learn how to input things from the keyboard. The new editing techniques presented here, added to the ones already covered in Chapter 4, will simplify the job of typing programs into the computer and correcting mistakes. This chapter also describes how to store and retrieve programs on disk.

PROGRAMMING LANGUAGES

A computer needs to be given specific, unambiguous instructions to perform any task. That is what programming is all about, designing a sequence of instructions that the computer can follow to perform a task. But computers cannot yet understand instructions given in natural languages like English, Spanish, German, or French. Instead, their instructions must be expressed in any one of several computer languages. Computer languages differ from natural languages chiefly in the rigor of their grammar and the dearth of their vocabulary.

The basal computer language is the language of the computing machine itself, the microprocessor. Machine language instructions are made up of patterns of zeros and ones, which actually represent patterns of electrical pulses. No one uses machine language directly; working exclusively with patterns of zeros and ones is just too taxing. Instead, people use other computer languages that approximate natural languages (usually English) to some degree, and have those languages translated into machine language.

The computer language closest to machine language is *assembly language*. It lets you use mnemonic words and letters instead of numbers alone, but instructions are still oriented towards internal events rather than the task at hand. Therefore you must know how the computer works internally in order to write an assembly language program.

The easiest languages to write programs in are oriented towards problems or procedures rather than the inner workings of the computer, and include BASIC, COBOL, Pascal, and FORTRAN. Each individual instruction in these *high-level* languages corresponds to a sequence of machine language instructions, so programs can be shorter and less complex.

Syntax and Logic

All programming languages have strict rules about spelling, punctuation, and the order of words and symbols in an instruction. Taken together, the rules are called *syntax*. Some syntax rules are natural but others require rote memorization. For example, a plus sign (+) represents addition, but an asterisk (*) represents multiplication, and a slash (/) represents division. The keyboard does not have the customary symbols × or • for multiplication nor the ÷ symbol for division, so other symbols were chosen.

Learning a host of syntax rules will not make you a programmer. You must also learn how to analyze a problem, break it down into logical steps, and select the proper instructions that tell the computer how to perform each step. The technique is best acquired through practice and will come to some people easier than it does to others.

About BASIC

BASIC is the most popular high-level language used on small computers. It is powerful yet simple and easy to learn. It is a general language that can handle applications in business, industrial, professional, and home life equally well.

The core of BASIC emerged in 1964 from Dartmouth College as a language for the limited programming requirements of those who shared a single large computer system. BASIC originally used teletypes for communication, not keyboards and display screens, and it had little provision for using disk drives. Over the years dozens of computer manufacturers expanded and improved the language so it could display graphics, use disk drives, and handle other specialized peripheral equipment. Unfortunately, no standard ever developed for those extensions; each manufacturer changed BASIC differently. The result is that BASIC, like most natural languages, has many somewhat incompatible dialects. That is why a program written in BASIC for an Apple or Radio Shack computer may not work on the PC. However, once you learn even one version of BASIC, it will be easy to learn new facets of another version.

Versions of PC BASIC

The PC itself has three dialects of BASIC, though all are related: Advanced BASIC is expanded from Disk BASIC, which is expanded from Cassette BASIC. The interpreter for Cassette BASIC resides in PC read-only memory, so it is always present and ready to translate BASIC program instructions into machine language when you turn the machine on. The interpreters for Disk BASIC and Advanced BASIC are extensions of the Cassette BASIC interpreter that must be loaded into dynamic memory before the PC can understand Disk BASIC or Advanced BASIC instructions. Most programmers use Disk BASIC or Advanced BASIC because Cassette BASIC cannot use a disk drive.

This book distinguishes between the versions of PC BASIC only when there is a difference. Otherwise you can assume the term "PC BASIC" refers to all three versions.

STARTING AND ENDING PC BASIC

Starting BASIC involves handing over control of the PC to one of the three interpreters. The procedure for doing that is somewhat different for each of the interpreters. You may have already deduced it from your experience with purchased software.

Cassette BASIC

Since the Cassette BASIC interpreter resides in read-only memory it is always present when the system unit power is on. To start Cassette BASIC when the power is already on, open the door of drive A and then reset the computer with the **Ctrl|Alt|Del** multiple keystroke. The display screen clears and the cursor flashes in the home position. Within five seconds drive A comes to life briefly, but quiets down when the PC discovers the drive A door is open. About 10 seconds later the Cassette BASIC identification message appears (Fig. 6-1A).

Turning on the system unit power with no diskette drives or with the drive doors open also starts Cassette BASIC. Due to the automatic system test that occurs when the power comes on, it takes longer for the identification message to appear, between 30 seconds and two minutes, depending on the amount of dynamic memory in your PC system.

If drive A is a Winchester partition, the Winchester drive must be switched off before you can start Cassette BASIC. If that is impossible, you must use Disk BASIC or Advanced BASIC instead of Cassette BASIC.

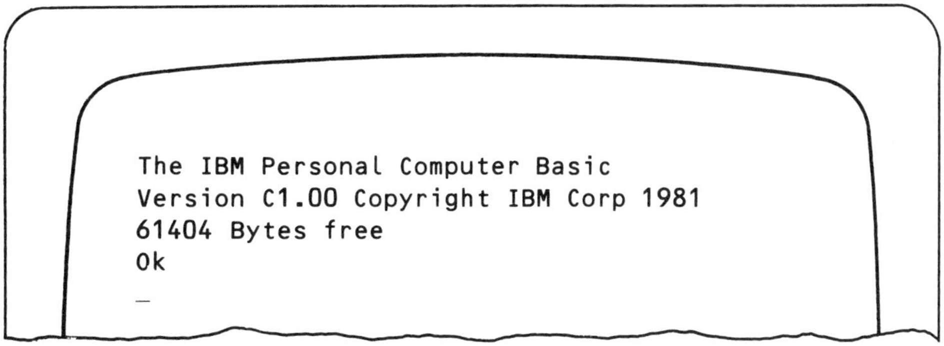

```
The IBM Personal Computer Basic
Version C1.00 Copyright IBM Corp 1981
61404 Bytes free
Ok
_
```

(A)   Cassette BASIC.

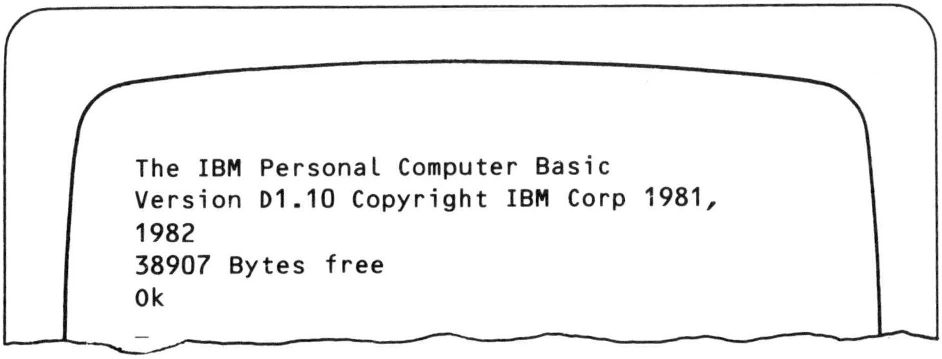

```
The IBM Personal Computer Basic
Version D1.10 Copyright IBM Corp 1981,
1982
38907 Bytes free
Ok
_
```

(B)   Disk BASIC.

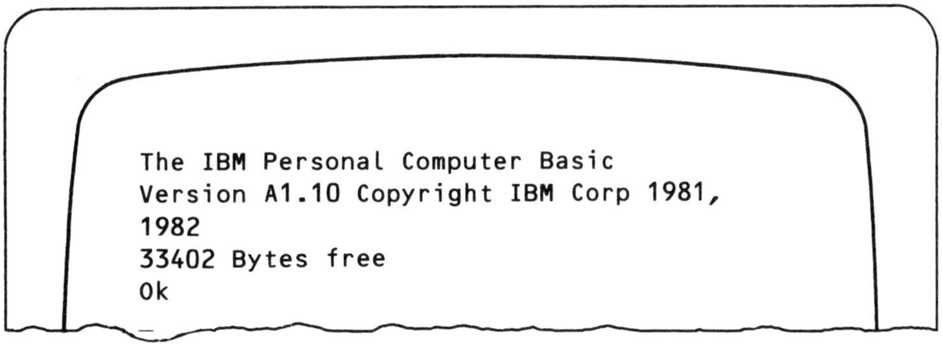

```
The IBM Personal Computer Basic
Version A1.10 Copyright IBM Corp 1981,
1982
33402 Bytes free
Ok
_
```

(C)   Advanced BASIC.

Fig. 6-1.   PC BASIC identification messages.

Disk BASIC and Advanced BASIC

Both Disk BASIC and Advanced BASIC need PC DOS, so you must load it as explained in Chapter 3. The program file named BASIC.COM contains the Disk BASIC interpreter and the program file named BASICA.COM contains the Advanced BASIC interpreter. To start either interpreter, type its file name without the COM extension and press the ← key. You may prefix the file name with a drive designation if the file is not on the default drive. For example, the following command to PC DOS will start Advanced BASIC from drive A, even though the default drive is B:

```
B>a:basica
```

In less than five seconds the display screen clears and an identification message appears (Figs. 6-1B and 6-1C).

Ending BASIC

Turning off the system unit will end any of the three BASIC interpreters. Be careful not to turn the power off while the computer is in the middle of a command or program, though.

Both Disk BASIC and Advanced BASIC recognize the SYSTEM command, which transfers control of the PC to PC DOS. Here is an example:

```
Ok
system
A>_
```

The command prompt A> tells you that PC DOS has regained control of the computer. Any BASIC program you had been using or working on prior to the SYSTEM command is erased from dynamic memory. It will be gone if you subsequently restart one of the BASIC interpreters.

IMMEDIATE MODE

The message "Ok" that you see on the display screen below the identification message means the interpreter is ready for a BASIC command. This is called *immediate mode* or *direct mode*, because the PC responds immediately to each command you type. Here is an example:

```
Ok
print  "When in doubt tell the truth."
```

When you type in the command above and press the ← key, the computer responds with this:

```
When in doubt tell the truth.
Ok
__
```

The message that was enclosed in quotation marks is displayed. The prompt "Ok" appears above the flashing cursor, telling you the computer is ready for another command.

The example above demonstrates how the PRINT statement displays a message. The message can be short, or it can be long like this:

```
Ok
print  "When  angry,  count  four;  when  very
angry,  swear"
When  angry,  count  four;  when  very  angry,
swear.
Ok
—
```

The example above was typed on a display screen with 40-character lines. Notice how the PRINT command occupies two display lines. If a command will not fit on one display line, it automatically wraps around to the next display line; you do not press the ◄┘ until the end of the command. PC BASIC allows 255 characters in a single command; it ignores any characters after the 255th.

The PRINT command also does arithmetic calculations and displays the answers. Consider these examples:

```
Ok
print  169/13+87
100
Ok
print  82*14-91
1057
Ok
—
```

Neither of the examples above uses quotation marks, because a PRINT command displays verbatim whatever it finds enclosed in quotation marks. Compare the next example with the last one above:

```
Ok
print  "82*14-91"
82*14-91
Ok
—
```

Error Messages

The PC will not tolerate typographical errors or sloppy syntax. If you make a mistake typing a command, the computer will probably balk and squawk like this:

```
Ok
prnt  430*22
Syntax  error
Ok
—
```

The message "Syntax error" is a catch-all that means the interpreter could not understand what you just typed. Sometimes it can identify the nature of the error, as is the case when you put characters in an arithmetic problem, like this:

```
Ok
Print  "one" /2
Type mismatch
Ok
—
```

Occasionally the erroneous command is still a valid command. Suppose you want to multiply 555 by 33, but you type this instead:

```
Ok
Print 555+33
588
Ok
—
```

Even though the command above does not give the answer you want, it is still a valid command. The PC cannot second-guess what you want.

If an error occurs, with or without an error message, review the typed command carefully. When you spot the mistake, retype the command, but more carefully this time.

PROGRAMMED MODE

Instead of typing commands for direct execution in immediate mode, you can type them into a program for deferred execution. This is called *deferred mode*, *programmed mode*, or *indirect mode*, and it is the key to unlocking the computer's full power. In deferred mode, commands are usually called *statements*, but the two terms are used somewhat interchangeably. This is because most immediate mode commands work as deferred mode statements and the reverse is also true. However there are some commands that only work in immediate mode and some statements that work only in deferred mode. Appendix A summarizes all BASIC commands and statements.

Line Numbers

The distinguishing feature of a programmed mode statement is its *line number*. It is a one- to five-digit number with a value between 0 and 65529 with which you preface the statement, like this:

```
Ok
10 print  "Always do right."
—
```

Program Execution

When you enter a line with a line number, the PC does not execute the line; it just puts the line in dynamic memory. Because it has not executed a direct command, it does not redisplay the "Ok" message, but it is ready for another command or program line anyway.

A program is made up of many lines like the one above, each with its own unique line number. When you press the ← key to terminate each line, the new line is added to program lines already stored in dynamic memory. Then when you give the RUN command, the program lines are executed. The line numbers determine the order in which the lines will be executed. The following example adds two lines to the one in the last example, then executes all three:

```
Ok
20 print  "This will gratify some
people,"
30 print  "and astonish the rest."
run
Always do right.
This will gratify some people,
and astonish the rest.
Ok
—
```

A plain RUN command like the one above starts the program at its lowest line number. A variation of the RUN command allows you to specify a line number at which to start execution. With the three-line program still in memory from the last example, the following example only executes the last two lines:

```
Ok
run 20
This will gratify some people,
and astonish the rest.
Ok
—
```

The PC returns to immediate mode when it runs out of program lines. You can formally end a program with a STOP statement. When the PC encounters one, it halts program execution, displays a message stating where it stopped, and returns to immediate mode. The following example adds a STOP statement to the middle of the previous program, then executes the new program:

```
Ok
25 stop
run
Always do right.
This will gratify some people,
Break in 25
Ok
—
```

The message "Break in 25" means the program stopped at line 25. You can continue execution from there with the CONT command, like this:

```
Ok
cont
and astonish the rest.
Ok
—
```

The END statement also halts program execution, but unlike the STOP statement, it does not display a message announcing the last-executed line number. Sometimes the CONT command can restart a program halted by an END statement, but not always.

You can interrupt program execution by pressing the **Ctrl** and **Scroll Lock** keys in unison. The same "Break . . ." message appears as after executing a STOP statement, and the CONT command will resume execution.

TYPING BASIC STATEMENTS

The PC will only execute statements correctly if you type them correctly. A few statements consist of a single command word, but most have several components. Study the rules for each statement carefully and make sure you include all the necessary components, in the right order, and separated by punctuation marks and blank spaces as required.

Some programmers wonder about extra blank spaces in BASIC programs. The PC ignores all blank spaces between the line number and the beginning of the command. It ignores most, but not all other blanks too. Sometimes the existence or absence of a blank changes the effect of a command. Use examples from this book and other sources as models, and use caution when experimenting with original combinations, because errors may show up not when you type a statement, but later when you run the program it is part of.

You can use any mixture of small letters and capitals for the command words themselves; the PC converts them all to capitals as you type them in. That does not hold true for all components of every statement, though. For example, sample commands earlier in this chapter have shown that the characters inside quotation marks in a PRINT statement are displayed as is.

Controlling Display Screen Width

Any display screen can be set to either 40 or 80 characters per display line with the commands WIDTH 40 and WIDTH 80, respectively. WIDTH 80 may produce unsatisfactory results on a home television or a color video monitor—characters may be too fuzzy to read.

Long Commands and Program Lines

It is possible to combine several immediate mode commands or deferred mode statements on a single line. Each command or statement is separated from the next by a colon, like this:

```
Ok
10 print  "one" :print "two" :print "three"
—
```

The example above shows three PRINT statements on a single display line, but it is possible to type even longer compound statement lines. The maximum number of characters in immediate and programmed modes is the same, 255. Long lines may occupy as many as seven 40-character display screen lines or four 80-character display screen lines, but the PC considers each to be a single, unbroken program line. It folds the program line in order to accommodate the display screen. When typing a long line, you press the ◄┘ key just once, at the end of the last statement or command.

The line folding you will see in the rest of the examples printed in this book may not match the line folding you will see on the display screen if you type those same examples into the PC. The PC obstinately folds lines at the 40th (or 80th) character even if that happens to come in the middle of a word, while this book does not.

Typing Shortcuts

PC BASIC presets the function keys to provide a shortcut method of typing ten commonly used BASIC commands. For example, pressing **F2** has the same effect as typing the RUN command and pressing the ◄┘ key. The bottom line of the display screen shows the function key uses, and Table 6-1 elaborates. The preset function keys meanings are not permanent; Chapter 11 explains how to change or disable them under program control.

Immediate mode has a permanent shorthand for entering some commands. Pressing the **Alt** key in unison with one of the 26 letter keys enters a predetermined command word that starts with the same letter as the letter key used. For example, the combination keystroke **Alt|P** generates the command word ''PRINT.'' Table 6-2 lists the command words available through this shorthand.

Table 6-1. Preset Function Key Uses in BASIC

Key	Definition	Key	Definition
F1	LIST	F6	,"LPT1:"*
F2	RUN*	F7	TRON*
F3	LOAD"	F8	TROFF*
F4	SAVE"	F9	KEY
F5	CONT*	F10	SCREEN 0,0,0*

*Includes the equivalent of the ← key.

Table 6-2. Command Words Generated With the Alt Key

Key	Command	Key	Command	Key	Command
A	AUTO	J	J	R	RUN
B	BSAVE	K	KEY	S	SCREEN
C	COLOR	L	LOCATE	T	THEN
D	DELETE	M	MOTOR	U	USING
E	ELSE	N	NEXT	V	VAL
F	FOR	O	OPEN	W	WIDTH
G	GOTO	P	PRINT	X	XOR
H	HEX$	Q	Q	Y	Y
I	INPUT			Z	Z

Most BASIC dialects, PC BASIC included, let you abbreviate the command word PRINT with a question mark. When the PC sees a question mark in the context of a command word, it expands it to the full unabbreviated word PRINT.

Activating a Printer

Pressing the ⌂ and **PrtSc** keys in unison dumps whatever is on the display screen onto the printer, just as in PC DOS. However, **Ctrl‖Prt Sc**, which also activates the printer in PC DOS, does not affect the printer at all in BASIC. Normally PC BASIC uses a parallel printer, but you can change that default with the MODE command in PC DOS, as Chapter 3 explains.

Program Comments

Sometimes you can easily tell what a BASIC statement does just by looking at it, but not always. It is especially difficult to determine a particular statement's role in a complex program that you have not seen for some time. Rather than constantly rediscover how a program works, most programmers use REM statements to include remarks or comments that describe the action.

The REM statement has no effect on program execution. Its sole purpose is for program clarification. Everything on a program line that follows the command word REM is treated as an explanatory remark. Therefore, a comment that is part of a multiple-statement line must be the last statement on the line.

The PC recognizes an apostrophe as shorthand for the command word REM. There is no need to precede the apostrophe with a colon when it introduces a remark at the end of a multiple-statement line. Here are some sample program comments:

```
Ok
10 rem display boiling point of water
20 '    in several temperature scales
30 print 212 'Fahrenheit
40 print 100 'Celsius
50 print 80:rem Reaumur
—
```

EDITING BASIC STATEMENTS

PC BASIC includes editing features that let you correct or change any immediate mode command line or deferred mode program line, as long as it is visible on the display screen. Chapter 4 describes the editing features in detail, including the EDIT command and the use of cursor movement and editing keys (review Figs. 4-3, 4-4, and 4-5, and Table 4-1).

Listing Program Lines

Once an immediate mode command disappears off the top of the display screen, there is no way to edit it, but that is not the case with programmed mode statements. The LIST command redisplays all or part of the program currently in memory. The following example illustrates, assuming the last sample program is still in memory:

```
list
10 REM display boiling point of water
20 '    in several temperature scales
30 PRINT 212 'Fahrenheit
40 PRINT 100 'Celsius
50 PRINT 80:REM Reaumur
Ok
—
```

Notice that when PC BASIC redisplays the program, it uses capital letters in command words like REM and PRINT.

When the program in memory occupies more than 22 display lines, it will not all fit on the display screen at one time. Use a simple LIST command, and the first part of the program flows off the top of the display screen. You can use the **Ctrl|Num Lock** multiple keystroke to freeze the display screen, the **Ctrl|Scroll Lock** multiple keystroke to interrupt the listing, or you can specify a range of lines to be listed, like this:

```
list 10-20
10 REM display boiling point of water
20 '    in several temperature scales
Ok
list 40-
40 PRINT 100 'Celsius
50 PRINT 80:REM Reaumur
Ok
list -30
10 REM display boiling point of water
20 '   in several temperature scales
30 PRINT 212 'Fahrenheit
list 10
10 REM display boiling point of water
Ok
```
—

Above you see four variations of the LIST command. The first lists a range of lines bounded by explicit line numbers, the second lists from an explicit line number to the end of the program, the third lists from the beginning of the program to an explicit line number, and the fourth lists a single explicit line number.

Anywhere you type an explicit line number you can type a period instead, and the number of the last-displayed line will be used. Here are two examples:

```
list 40
40 PRINT 100 'Celsius
Ok
list .-
40 PRINT 100 'Celsius
50 PRINT 80:REM Reaumur
Ok
list .
50 PRINT 80:REM Reaumur
Ok
```
—

Program lines can be listed to the printer as well as to the display screen. For the printer, there is a special command, LLIST. The variations for specifying lines to be listed work with LLIST the same as with LIST.

Replacing Program Lines

It is extremely easy to replace an existing program line with a new one. Simply type the new line with the same line number as the old line. When you press the ← key to make the new line permanent, it will replace any existing line with the same number.

Inserting Program Lines

To insert a program line between two existing lines in a BASIC program, merely give it a line number that falls in between the line numbers of the existing lines. When you press the ← key to place it in memory, the PC automatically inserts it in the correct spot.

The only difficulty arises when line numbers are so close together that there are too few unused ones between the existing ones. Avoid that by assigning line numbers in multiples of ten when you first write a program. If necessary you may renumber the program as described later in this chapter.

Deleting Program Lines

You can delete a single program line by typing its line number and pressing the ← key. In addition, the DELETE command will eliminate one line or several. Its format is similar to that of the LIST command, as shown in the examples below:

```
list 20
20 '   in several temperature scales
Ok
delete .
Ok
list 10-30
10 REM display boiling point of water
30 PRINT 212 'Fahrenheit
Ok
delete 30-50
Ok
list
10 REM display boiling point of water
Ok
```

The DELETE command does differ somewhat in format from the LIST command. When specifying a range of lines to be deleted, both beginning and ending line numbers must be explicitly stated. You cannot delete all lines from the beginning of the program simply by omitting the first line number, nor can you delete all the lines to the end of the program by omitting the second line number in a DELETE command. Furthermore, the line numbers you specify in the DELETE command must exist in the program or the message "Illegal function call" appears and no deletion occurs.

Clearing Program Memory

To clear all program lines from memory at once, use the NEW command. You must use it before typing in a new program, or the new program lines will merge with the old ones.

Renumbering Program Lines

The RENUM command assists in renumbering program lines. It assigns new, equally spaced line numbers to the block of program lines starting at an existing line number you choose and ending with the last line in memory. You also choose the first new line number and the increment between new line numbers. Here is an example:

```
list
10 REM display boiling point of water
20 '   in several temperature scales
30 PRINT 212 'Fahrenheit
40 PRINT 100 'Celsius
50 PRINT 80:REM Reaumur
Ok
renum 35,30,5
Ok
list
10 REM display boiling point of water
20 '   in several temperature scales
35 PRINT 212 'Fahrenheit
40 PRINT 100 'Celsius
45 PRINT 80:REM Reaumur
Ok
—
```

The RENUM command in the example above starts renumbering with line 30 by changing its number to 35 and giving each successive line a number 5 higher than the previous line.

You may omit any of the numbers in a RENUM command. When the first number is absent, 10 is used as the first new line number. When the second number is absent, the first line of the program will be the first one renumbered. An increment of 10 is used if no other increment is specified.

The line numbers you specify in the RENUM command must exist in the program or the message "Illegal function call" appears and no renumbering occurs. The same message appears if you try to change statement sequence with the RENUM command.

The statements GOTO, GOSUB, IF-THEN, ON-GOTO, and ON-GOSUB, which are covered in later chapters, all contain references to other line numbers. RENUM changes those line number references too, unless it encounters a reference to a nonexistent line. In that case it displays a message that reports the missing line number and the number of the line where the reference occurred, and then it continues with the renumbering.

Automatic Line Numbering

You can save some typing effort by having PC BASIC supply line numbers. The AUTO command specifies the first line number to be used and the increment between line numbers. Here is an example:

```
auto 70,10
70 print 459.67+212 'Rankine
80 print 273.15+100 'Kelvin
90 _
```

To terminate automatic line numbering, you must press the **Ctrl** and **Scroll Lock** keys in unison. Pressing the **Esc** key will erase the current line from the display screen, but that does not cancel automatic line numbering. The invisible line number is assigned to whatever you type on the vacated line.

An asterisk will appear alongside an automatically generated line number that already belongs to a program line in memory, warning you that a new line entered after the asterisk will replace the existing line. (A blank space will replace the warning asterisk in such a new line.) To retain the existing line, type nothing but ←. You can use the ← key that way to skip past any automatically created line number, not just those with asterisks.

You may omit the numbers in the AUTO command. There are six variations altogether, as Table 6-3 shows.

Table 6-3. AUTO Command Variations

Variation	First line number	Increment
AUTO	10	10
AUTO 10	As specified	10
AUTO 10,	As specified	Same as last*
AUTO ,10	0	As specified
AUTO ,	0	Same as last*
AUTO 10,10	As specified	As specified

*If none previously specified, defaults to 10.

BASIC PROGRAMS ON DISK

Since the PC can conveniently keep just one BASIC program at a time in dynamic memory, there must be some way to store a program outside memory and retrieve it on demand. The five commands LIST, SAVE, LOAD, MERGE, and RUN transfer programs between dynamic memory and a disk file. (Cassette BASIC cannot access a disk drive, but it can transfer programs to and from cassette tape files using the SAVE and LOAD commands.) When you wish to store or retrieve a program on disk, you must provide a file name that follows the rules presented in Chapter 3 (review Fig. 3-6). As usual, the file name may be prefixed with a drive designation, but if it is not, the default drive established by PC DOS will be used. If you omit the file name extension, PC BASIC will use the extension BAS.

Storing Programs

The LIST and SAVE commands transfer the BASIC program in memory to a disk file. If the destination is a disk file that already exists on the specified drive, the old file is erased before the new file is stored. Both of the following commands store a program on disk file BOILPT.BAS, in drive B:

```
save "b:boilpt"
Ok
list ,"b:boilpt"
Ok
```

The LIST command transfers every character of a program to any output device in exactly the same way as it displays it on the display screen. The SAVE command is different. It normally compresses the program by abbreviating command words with one-character tokens. To inhibit the compression and force the SAVE command to spell out every command word, add a comma and the letter A to the end of the command line, like this:

```
save "boilpt" ,a
Ok
```

The LIST command will store a program on disk in a format similar to that of the SAVE command, but the two are not identical. The MERGE command, described later in this chapter, works only with programs stored by a SAVE command suffixed with the letter A.

Another SAVE command option encrypts the program it stores to protect it against future viewing. When the program is brought back into memory, the LIST and EDIT commands will not work with it. Use this option with caution, because there is no way to unprotect a program. To effect encryption, place a comma and the letter P after the closing quotation mark for the file name in the SAVE command, like this:

```
save "boilpt" ,p
Ok
```

The SAVE command always stores an entire program, and normally the LIST command does too. To store just part of a program, use the LIST command and specify an appropriate range of line numbers, like this:

```
list 10-50, "boilpt"
Ok
```

Retrieving Programs

The LOAD statement retrieves programs saved by a LIST or SAVE statement. It clears program memory just like a NEW statement, so the new program replaces any existing one. Here is an example:

```
load   "boilpt"
Ok
```

The LOAD command will not only retrieve a program but will run it too, if you include a comma and the letter R at the end of the command line, like this:

```
Ok
load   "program" ,r
```

An alternate form of the RUN command will do the same thing. Just add a file name to a RUN command to make the LOAD command an implicit part of it. Here is an example:

```
Ok
run  "program"
```

An error message appears if the LOAD or RUN commands cannot find the file specified. In that case, any existing program in memory is unaffected.

Disk File Utility Commands

For convenience, Disk BASIC and Advanced BASIC have BASIC commands that mimic three PC DOS commands. One lists disk directories, another deletes files, and the third renames a file.

A simple FILES command lists the entire directory of the default drive, or you can specify the drive and even the files to list. The latter options require a drive designation, file name, or both, all enclosed in quotation marks. The file name can be specific or generic. The examples below only show the commands, not the directories that would result:

```
files
files  "b:"
files  "*.bas"
```

The FILES command most closely matches PC DOS command DIR /W (described in Chapter 3), but the two are not identical. Both allow the characters * and ? to specify generic file names, but their interpretations differ somewhat. The FILES command requires you to explicitly state any file name extension. For example, the command FILES "*" lists all files that have two or more characters in their names and have no extensions whatever. To list all file names, you must use a command like FILES "*.*". In PC DOS, the commands DIR "*" and DIR "*.*" are equivalent. Another disparity occurs when an * character follows an explicit character, as in "P*.*". In that case, the * character in a FILES command matches one or more characters, but in a DIR command it will also match no characters. For example, the command FILES "P*.*" will not list a file named P.BAS, whereas the command DIR "P*.*" will.

The KILL command removes a specified file name from a disk directory. It interprets wild card characters literally, so generic file names are not allowed. The file name must be inside quotation marks, like this:

```
kill  "temp.bas"
Ok
```
—

The NAME-AS command changes the name of a disk file. You specify the old and new file names, both enclosed in quotation marks. If the file is not on the default drive, you must prefix the old file name with a drive designation. Any drive designation prefixing the new file name is ignored. Generic file names are not allowed. The following example changes the name of file TEST.BAS to PERM.BAS:

```
name "test.bas" as "perm.bas"
Ok
```

CHAPTER 7

CONSTANTS, VARIABLES, AND ARRAYS

Every program you write will use data in some way. This chapter introduces the types of data available in PC BASIC and shows some of the ways you can use them in a program.

STRINGS

A *string* is any series of characters in uninterrupted succession. String values are usually written with enclosing quotation marks, like those in the following PRINT statement:

```
PRINT "25 Rue Madeleine"
```

Strings can include capital and small letters, numerals, and punctuation; in fact they can contain any of the 256 characters listed in Appendix D. The only restriction is on the number of characters, with 255 being the maximum. The shortest string has no characters and is called an *empty string* or *null string*.

The computer only works with numbers, so it cannot store characters directly. It converts them according to numbers using a code known as *ASCII* (American Standard Code for Information Interchange). For example, the ASCII code number for the capital letter A is 65 and for the small letter b it is 98. Appendix D relates each PC BASIC character to its ASCII code number.

You can type many characters just by pressing the appropriate key, but others require a special typing technique using the **Alt** key in conjunction with the ten numbered keys of the dual-mode keypad. Here's how it works. First you determine the code number of the character you want to type. Then you press and hold the **Alt** key while you type the code on the keypad. The corresponding character will appear when you release the **Alt** key. For example, if you press and hold the **Alt** key while you press the **1**, **7**, and **2** keys in succession, the symbol ¼ will appear on the display screen when you release the **Alt** key.

However, you cannot generate the character with code number 127 or those with codes 0 through 31 directly from the keyboard in immediate mode. Chapter 8 explains how a program can display them, and Chapter 11 describes a way they can be entered from the keyboard under program control.

NUMBERS

PC BASIC features five kinds of numbers (Fig. 7-1), and each exists for a specific reason. Three offer increasing degrees of numeric precision at the expense of memory requirements and arithmetic calculation speed. Two others are provided as a convenience for more advanced programming.

Integers are numbers without decimal points and may range in value between −32768 and 32767. Each integer value occupies two memory cells, and most arithmetic that involves only integers proceeds at top speed. PC BASIC treats any number without a decimal point as an integer as long as its value is within range.

Integer	Octal	Hexadecimal
32767	&77777	&H7FFF
100	&144	&H64
23	&27	&H17
2	&2	&H2
0	&0	&H0
−1	−&1	−&H1
−187	−&273	−&HBB
−32767	&77777	−&H7FFF

Single precision	Double precision
1234567	1234567890123456
9999.99	99999999999999.99
123.123	12345678.123456789
.1234567	.12345678904123456
0	0
−.1234567	−.12345678904123456
−123.123	−12345678.123456789
−9999.99	−99999999999999.99
−1234567	1234567890123456

Fig. 7-1.   **Examples of the different kinds of numbers in PC BASIC.**

Floating point numbers can include a decimal point and a decimal fraction component. They may be written in the usual way or in scientific notation (Fig. 7-2). The largest possible number is equal to 1701412 times 10^{32}, and the closest a number can get to zero is equal to .5877471 divided by 10^{38}. There are two kinds of floating point numbers, and they vary only in the degree of accuracy they are capable of, six digits or 16.

Single Precision

Single-precision numbers, which use four memory cells each, are floating point numbers with seven or fewer digits. However, because of the way PC BASIC does arithmetic, the seventh digit is unreliable, so only the first six digits are accurate. For example, a single-precision number with four digits ahead of the decimal point would be accurate to the nearest hundredth

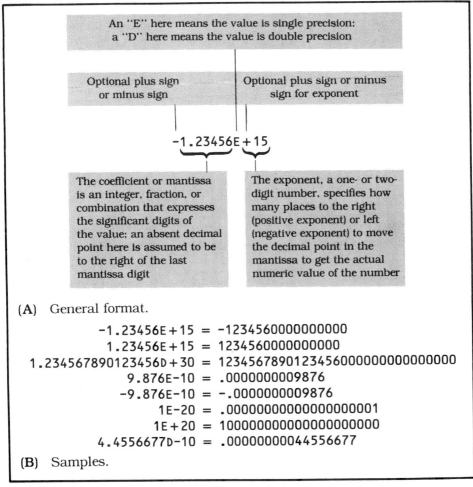

An "E" here means the value is single precision; a "D" here means the value is double precision

Optional plus sign or minus sign

Optional plus sign or minus sign for exponent

$$-1.23456E+15$$

The coefficient or mantissa is an integer, fraction, or combination that expresses the significant digits of the value; an absent decimal point here is assumed to be to the right of the last mantissa digit

The exponent, a one- or two-digit number, specifies how many places to the right (positive exponent) or left (negative exponent) to move the decimal point in the mantissa to get the actual numeric value of the number

(A) General format.

```
            -1.23456E+15 = -1234560000000000
             1.23456E+15 = 1234560000000000
 1.234567890123456D+30 = 1234567890123456000000000000000
                9.876E-10 = .0000000009876
               -9.876E-10 = -.0000000009876
                    1E-20 = .00000000000000000001
                    1E+20 = 100000000000000000000
          4.4556677D-10 = .00000000044556677
```

(B) Samples.

Fig. 7-2. Scientific notation.

and a single-precision number with one digit ahead of the decimal point would be accurate to five decimal places. PC BASIC treats any number suffixed with an exclamation point as a single-precision number by rounding it off internally to seven digits. The following PRINT statement illustrates:

```
Ok
print 1234.56789!
1234.568
```

Double Precision

Double-precision numbers, which use eight memory cells each, are accurate up to 16 digits. PC BASIC maintains 17 digits internally for each double-precision number but only shows the first 16, thus ensuring their complete accuracy. You would need a double-precision number to maintain all the digits in a dollar-and-cents amount greater than $9999.99.

PC BASIC automatically treats any number with more than seven digits as a double-precision value, unless it is suffixed with an ! character. You can force it to treat any number as a double-precision value by suffixing it with a # symbol. If the value has fewer than seven digits, PC BASIC internally adds zeros after the last decimal digit.

Hexadecimal and Octal

Most BASIC programmers write numbers using the familiar base 10 number system, with digits 0 through 9, called *decimal* numbers. But inside the computer, all numbers are stored using the base 2 number system, as patterns of zeros and ones, called *binary numbers*. The BASIC interpreter automatically converts from base 10 to base 2, so BASIC programmers can simply use the base 10 numbers they are used to. Because the conversion requires some arithmetic, you cannot tell just by looking at a base 10 number what its equivalent is in base 2.

Some programmers (especially those accustomed to assembly language) occasionally find it more convenient to write numbers using a number system that is easier to convert to base 2. Base 8, called *octal*, and base 16, called *hexadecimal*, are the most popular. For example, ASCII character codes are sometimes expressed as hexadecimal numbers. Each octal or hexadecimal digit translates directly to a binary number, as Table 7-1 shows for low-value numbers. Larger values are easy to convert one octal or hexadecimal digit at a time (Fig 7-3). The conversion between octal or hexadecimal numbers and decimal numbers does require arithmetic, the use of a conversion table, a special pocket calculator, or a computer program.

Table 7-1. Number Base Conversion (Hexadecimal–Octal–Binary)

Hexadecimal	Octal	Binary	Hexadecimal	Octal	Binary
0	0	0000	8	10	1000
1	1	0001	9	11	1001
2	2	0010	A	12	1010
3	3	0011	B	13	1011
4	4	0100	C	14	1100
5	5	0101	D	15	1101
6	6	0110	E	16	1110
7	7	0111	F	17	1111

```
10101001   Binary              10101001   Binary
 A   9    Hexadecimal          2  5  1    Octal
```

(A) For hexadecimal–binary, group binary digits into fours and use Table 7-1.

(B) For octal–binary, group binary digits into threes (assume leading 0's as needed) and use Table 7-1.

Fig. 7-3. Converting between hexadecimal or octal numbers and binary numbers.

To type an octal integer in PC BASIC, prefix the number with an ampersand (&), like this:

```
print &40
32
Ok
```

Hexadecimal numbers use the letters A, B, C, D, E, and F as digits along with the numerals 0 through 9. To type a hexadecimal integer, prefix the number with an ampersand and the letter H, like this:

```
print &hda0
3488
Ok
```

PC BASIC does not allow hexadecimal and octal fractions, only integers. The range is −&77777 to &77777 (octal) or −&H7FFF to &H7FFF (hexadecimal). For more information on the binary, octal, and hexadecimal numbering systems, see the book *Microcomputer Primer* by Mitchell Waite and Michael Pardee (Howard W. Sams & Co., Inc.), pages 320 to 332 and 341 to 346.

VARIABLES

The computer would be a pretty limited machine if it could only use constant data values (called *constants*) like those described so far. Fortunately it can use part of its memory to keep track of variable values. Each value is identified by a unique name, and the whole package, value and name, is called a *variable*. You make up the names according to certain rules (Fig. 7-4). A variable name can be any length as long as it fits on the program line, but PC BASIC ignores characters past the 40th. The only names you cannot use are those listed in Table 7-2; they are reserved for command words and the like. However, you may use the reserved words as part of a longer variable name. For example, DATAVAL is a valid name even though DATA and VAL are reserved words and cannot be used separately as variable names.

Variable Types

Each type of data—string, integer, single precision, and double precision—has a corresponding variable type. The last character of the variable name declares the value type of the value; Table 7-3 lists the possibilities. Variable names that are identical except for the type suffix are nonetheless unrelated. Thus A$, A!, A#, and A% all name different variables.

Each time PC BASIC encounters a new variable name in a program, it earmarks an area of memory to keep track of the associated value. Table 7-3 tabulates the amount of memory each variable type uses.

Usually, a name without one of the type-identifying suffixes (%, #, $, !) denotes a single-precision numeric variable by default. Four variations of the DEF statement override the standard rule and specify single letters that determine variable types when they occur at the beginning of variable

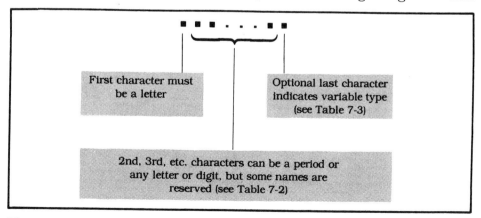

First character must be a letter

Optional last character indicates variable type (see Table 7-3)

2nd, 3rd, etc. characters can be a period or any letter or digit, but some names are reserved (see Table 7-2)

Fig. 7-4. PC BASIC variable name rules.

Table 7-2. Reserved Words (Cannot Be Used as Variable Names*)

ABS	CVS	FRE	LOG	POINT	SQR
AND	DATA	GET	LPOS	POKE	STEP
ASC	DATE$	GOSUB	LPRINT	POS	STICK
ATN	DEF	GOTO	LSET	PRESET	STOP
AUTO	DEFDBL	HEX$	MERGE	PRINT	STR$
BEEP	DEFINT	IF	MID$	PRINT#	STRIG
BLOAD	DEFSNG	IMP	MKD$	PSET	STRING$
BSAVE	DEFSTR	INKEY$	MKI$	PUT	SWAP
CALL	DELETE	INP	MKS$	RANDOMIZE	SYSTEM
CDBL	DIM	INPUT	MOD	READ	TAB(
CHAIN	DRAW	INPUT#	MOTOR	REM	TAN
CHR$	EDIT	INPUT$	NAME	RENUM	THEN
CINT	ELSE	INSTR	NEW	RESET	TIME$
CIRCLE	END	INT	NEXT	RESTORE	TO
CLEAR	EOF	KEY	NOT	RESUME	TROFF
CLOSE	EQV	KILL	OCT$	RETURN	TRON
CLS	ERASE	LEFT$	OFF	RIGHT$	USING
COLOR	ERL	LEN	ON	RND	USR
COM	ERR	LET	OPEN	RSET	VAL
COMMON	ERROR	LINE	OPTION	RUN	VARPTR
CONT	EXP	LIST	OR	SAVE	WAIT
COS	FIELD	LLIST	OUT	SCREEN	WEND
CSNG	FILES	LOAD	PAINT	SGN	WHILE
CSRLIN	FIX	LOC	PEEK	SIN	WIDTH
CVD	FN†	LOCATE	PEN	SOUND	WRITE
CVI	FOR	LOF	PLAY	SPACE$	WRITE#
				SPC(	XOR

*Suffixes ($, %, !, #) do not affect reserved status, but reserved words can be imbedded in long variable names.

†FN can be used freely anywhere except the first two characters of a variable name, where it invokes a user-defined function (see Chapter 8).

Table 7-3. Variable Types

Type	Name suffix*	Length bytes	Value range
Integer	%	2	-32768 to 32767
Double-precision number	#	8	-1.701411733192644D+38 to 1.701411733192644D+38
Single-precision number	!	4	-1.701412E38 to 1.701412E+38
String	$	2+†	0 to 255 characters

*A variable name without one of the listed suffixes usually has a single precision value, but a DEF statement can change that (see Chapter 8).

†String length is 2 bytes plus the number of characters.

names that have no type identifying suffixes. Here is an example that defines integer variables:

```
10 DEFINT A,J-M
```

The statement above makes every variable whose name starts with the letter A, J, K, L, or M an integer variable, with no percent sign (%) suffix required. Thus names AARD, J1, K, LOOP, MARK would all denote integer variables. In a similar fashion, the statement DEFSTR defines string variable prefixes, DEFSNG defines single-precision prefixes, and DEFDBL defines double-precision prefixes. However, the standard type-identifying suffixes (%, #, $, !) override the effects of any DEF statement to explicitly determine a variable's type.

DEF statement execution should precede any use of affected variables. The DEF statement initializes the values of any existing variables that start with listed letters. Numeric values are set to zero and strings are set to null length. Variables that have specific type-identifying suffixes, however, are not initialized or affected in any way by a DEF statement.

Assigning Values

Variables are no good without values. PC BASIC automatically assigns every new variable it encounters a value of 0 (if numeric) or null (if string) and it includes several statements that let you assign other values to variables. One of them, the LET statement, is one of the most common statements in any program. Its full form looks like this:

```
500 LET TAX.RATE=6.5
510 LET TAX.AUTH$= "Board of Eq."
```

The command word LET is optional, so most programmers omit it to simplify the statement, like this:

```
500 TAX.RATE=6.5
510 TAX.AUTH$= "Board of Eq."
```

The LET statement assigns the variable named on the left-hand side of the equals sign (=) the value written on the right-hand side. The value and the variable must be compatible data types. If one is string and the other numeric, the error message "Type mismatch" appears.

Numeric Type Conversions

A double-precision value like 1.2345678 that is assigned to a single-precision or integer variable like A! or B% is rounded to match the variable. Similarly, a single-precision value like 1.2 assigned to an integer variable like N% is rounded to the nearest whole number. The following example illustrates:

```
a! = 1034500.89
Ok
print a!
1034501
Ok
```

Going the other way, an integer value like 253 is converted to single- or double-precision variable like CD# or CD! by adding an imaginary decimal point and zeros after it. Conversion of a single-precision value to a double-precision variable is similar, but a single-precision value assigned to a double-precision variable still has at most six digits of accuracy.

ARRAYS

BASIC has a way to systematically name an entire array of variables. Instead of giving each individual variable a unique name, the array of variables gets a single name and each element in the array is indexed by number. For example, suppose you are writing a program to analyze the sales of several items. You could use a separate variable name for the sales of each item (Fig. 7-5), and each variable name could describe the value it represents. But every time you have a new item to track sales for, you have to add another variable name to the program, and that generally involves rewriting the program. Instead, you could keep the sales figures in an array and use its indexes to choose individual sales items (Fig. 7-6). For reasons that will become clear in later chapters, it is usually easier to use arrays.

To specify an array element, enclose the index in parentheses and write it after the array name. The index can be a constant or a variable, and that is the real power of arrays, because it lets one program line act on any element in the whole array. Consider the following example:

```
10  A = 12.3
20  B(J) = 12.3
```

Line 10 above always assigns the variable A the same value, namely 12.3. But line 20 could assign any element of array B the value 12.3; the value of variable J determines which element gets the value.

Naming procedures for PC BASIC arrays are the same as for individual variables (Fig. 7-4 and Table 7-2). Arrays and independent variables with the same names are completely unrelated, however. An array can only contain one type of data values: string, integer, single-precision numbers, or double-precision numbers. The single-letter prefixes in DEF statements affect array types like they do simple variables, as described earlier in this

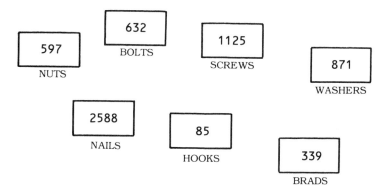

Fig. 7-5. Storing values in separate variable names.

597	632	1125	871	2588	85	339
ITEM(1)	ITEM(2)	ITEM(3)	ITEM(4)	ITEM(5)	ITEM(6)	ITEM(7)

Fig. 7-6. Storing values in an array.

chapter. Similarly, the standard type-identifying suffixes (%, #, $, !) override the effects of DEF statements to explicitly determine an array's type.

Array Dimensions

A PC BASIC array can have more than one index. You could think of an array with one index as a one-dimensional row or column of values (Fig. 7-6). A second index adds a second dimension (Fig. 7-7). For example, suppose you wanted to analyze sales figures for several items during each

ITEM(1,1)	ITEM(1,2)	ITEM(1,3)	ITEM(1,4)	ITEM(1,5)	ITEM(1,6)	ITEM(1,7)
597	632	1125	871	2588	85	339
691	705	1004	759	3412	60	352

0	0	0	0	0	0	0
0	0	0	0	0	0	0
ITEM(52,1)	ITEM(52,2)	ITEM(52,3)	ITEM(52,4)	ITEM(52,5)	ITEM(52,6)	ITEM(52,7)

Fig. 7-7. Storing values in a two-dimensional array.

week of the year. You could use 52 individual variables for each item you plan to track, but what a chore! A better solution would be to use 52 one-dimensional arrays, but the best solution is to use one two-dimensional array. The first index chooses the sales item, and the second index chooses the week.

Three, four, five, and more indexes are allowed in a single array. You can think of a three-dimensional array as a cube, but four-dimensional and higher arrays are harder to visualize. The maximum number of dimensions in one array is 255.

Dimensioning Arrays

Before a program can use a one-dimensional array with an index higher than 10, or any multidimensional array, it must define the array dimensions and maximum indexes. To dimension an array, list it in a DIM statement, stating the largest index the program will use for each dimension. The following example dimensions a four-dimensional string array with maximum indexes of 4, 8, 2, and 50:

```
110 DIM S$(4,8,2,50)
```

A single DIM statement can dimension many arrays. List the arrays following the command word DIM, and separate the arrays with commas. Here is an example:

```
10 DIM ITEM$(35), COST#(2,35), UNIT%(2,35)
```

If a DEF statement affects any of the array names listed in a DIM statement, the DEF statement should precede the DIM statement. Then executing a DIM statement allocates sufficient dynamic memory to hold the arrays listed, initializes numeric array values to zero, and sets string array values to a null length. If memory runs out in the process, the message "Out of memory ..." appears. In that case, arrays near the front of the DIM statement list will probably be dimensioned, but arrays starting with the one that exhausted memory will not be dimensioned.

DIM works in immediate mode too. However, arrays dimensioned there cannot be used in programmed mode after a RUN command, which undimensions all arrays.

Changing Array Dimensions

Once set, an array's dimensions cannot be changed simply by executing another DIM statement. First, an ERASE statement must eliminate the array from memory. The statement consists of the command word ERASE followed by a list of one or more array names. The names are separated by commas, but do not include any parentheses or index values. The following example illustrates:

```
10 DIM ITEM$(40),COST(40),PRICE(40)
20 REM there might be some other
90 REM statements here
100 ERASE PRICE,COST
110 DIM COST(2,40)
120 REM and some more statements here
```

Of course, subsequently redimensioning the array with another DIM statement will initialize all its elements; any previous values will be gone.

Lowest Array Index

Unless otherwise stated in advance, the lowest index of every array is 0. However, many programmers never use the 0 element of arrays because they are accustomed to counting from one, not zero. To avoid the memory waste that results from that practice, use a statement like the following:

```
100 OPTION BASE 1
```

The OPTION BASE command tells PC BASIC what the lowest array index is, 0 or 1. It must be executed before any array name is used in *any* other way, including in DEF or DIM statements, or else the message "Duplicate Definition" will appear. The command works in immediate or programmed mode, but the RUN command resets the lowest index to 0 before it starts executing a program. Therefore an OPTION BASE 1 command in immediate mode has no effect on arrays in programmed mode. Every program requires its own OPTION BASE statement if it is to deviate from the default.

CHAPTER 8

WORKING WITH STRINGS AND NUMBERS

There are many ways to control, manipulate, and combine constants, variables, and arrays. This chapter explains some new ways to assign values to variables. It also tells you how to use expressions and functions to combine data values and convert them from one type to another, how to assign values to variables and array elements, and how to display values on the display screen.

ASSIGNING VALUES

The LET statement, introduced in Chapter 7, is the most common way to assign values to variables one at a time. It is not well suited to assigning values to large numbers of variables nor in assigning values entered from the keyboard during program execution. PC BASIC has other statements that do those kinds of assignments better.

DATA and READ Statements

The DATA and READ statements provide a clear-cut and efficient means of assigning constant values to large numbers of variables and array elements. DATA statements establish a list of constant values and READ statements assign the values to variables and array elements. Here is a simple example:

```
list
99 'Account number table
100 DATA 100, Fern Herzberg, 150, Augie Bogdis,
     200, Xavier Decoto
```

```
1139 'Assign account no. and name
1140 READ acct(1),cust$(1),acct(2), cust$(2),
     acct(3), cust$(3)
Ok
```

DATA statements can include any valid numeric constant (review Fig. 7-1) or string constant. A string constant only requires enclosing quotation marks when it has important leading or trailing blank spaces, or when one of its characters is a comma or a colon. However, a string enclosed in quotation marks cannot itself contain quotation marks.

If there is more than one DATA statement, they all contribute to the same list of values. The list is built sequentially, starting with the values from the first DATA statement listed in the program and ending with the last (Fig. 8-1). None of the DATA statements need ever be executed.

The first READ statement executed assigns the first value from the DATA statements' list to the first variable. Its second variable gets the second value, the third value goes to the third variable, and so on until all variables have been assigned values. If another READ statement is subsequently executed, it takes values from the DATA statements' list starting where the previous READ statement quit (Fig. 8-2).

Unused values on the DATA statements' list are ignored, but if the list runs dry before it can satisfy a READ statement, the error message "Out of DATA . . ." appears. Also, READ statement variables and array elements

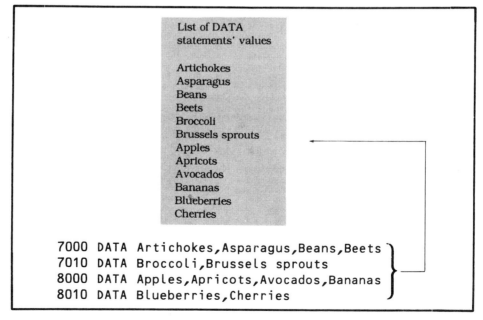

Fig. 8-1. All DATA statements build a single list of values.

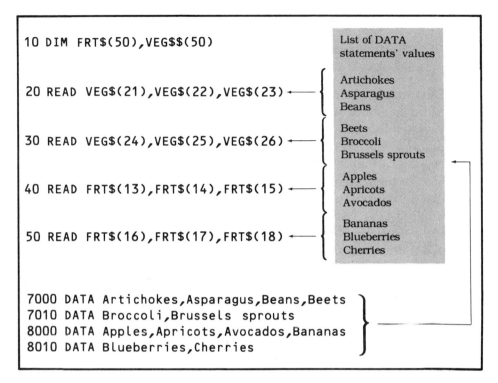

```
10 DIM FRT$(50),VEG$$(50)                List of DATA
                                         statements' values

                                         Artichokes
20 READ VEG$(21),VEG$(22),VEG$(23)       Asparagus
                                         Beans

                                         Beets
30 READ VEG$(24),VEG$(25),VEG$(26)       Broccoli
                                         Brussels sprouts

                                         Apples
40 READ FRT$(13),FRT$(14),FRT$(15)       Apricots
                                         Avocados

                                         Bananas
50 READ FRT$(16),FRT$(17),FRT$(18)       Blueberries
                                         Cherries


7000 DATA Artichokes,Asparagus,Beans,Beets
7010 DATA Broccoli,Brussels sprouts
8000 DATA Apples,Apricots,Avocados,Bananas
8010 DATA Blueberries,Cherries
```

Fig. 8-2.   READ statements assign values from the DATA statements' list.

must be compatible with the values they receive. One cannot be string and the other numeric or the message "Syntax error ..." will appear along with the READ statement where the type mismatch occurred. The READ statement handles disparity in precision between numeric values and variables the same way as the LET statement, as described in Chapter 7.

The DATA statement causes no error in immediate mode, but its values on it are inaccessible either from immediate mode or programmed mode. An immediate mode READ statement takes the next available values from the list established by any programmed mode DATA statements in memory at the time.

The RESTORE Statement

PC BASIC keeps track of its position on the DATA statements' list of values with a pointer, and it moves the pointer ahead each time a READ statement gets a value from the list. The RESTORE statement manipulates the pointer directly. In its simplest form, it moves the pointer back to the beginning of the DATA statements' list. The next READ statement after a RESTORE statement will reuse the values on the DATA statements' list.

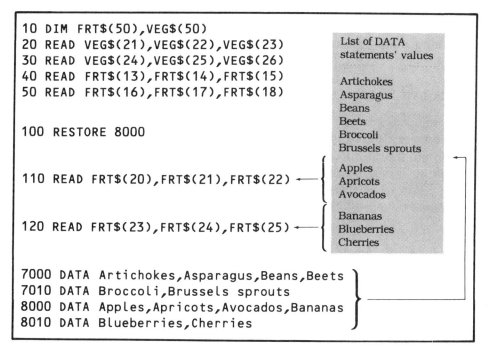

```
10 DIM FRT$(50),VEG$(50)
20 READ VEG$(21),VEG$(22),VEG$(23)
30 READ VEG$(24),VEG$(25),VEG$(26)
40 READ FRT$(13),FRT$(14),FRT$(15)
50 READ FRT$(16),FRT$(17),FRT$(18)


100 RESTORE 8000



110 READ FRT$(20),FRT$(21),FRT$(22)



120 READ FRT$(23),FRT$(24),FRT$(25)



7000 DATA Artichokes,Asparagus,Beans,Beets
7010 DATA Broccoli,Brussels sprouts
8000 DATA Apples,Apricots,Avocados,Bananas
8010 DATA Blueberries,Cherries
```

List of DATA
statements' values

Artichokes
Asparagus
Beans
Beets
Broccoli
Brussels sprouts
Apples
Apricots
Avocados
Bananas
Blueberries
Cherries

Fig. 8-3. RESTORE statements move the pointer in the DATA statements' list of values (in this case, to line 8000).

The RESTORE statement can also move the pointer to an intermediate DATA statement by specifying a line number (Fig. 8-3). If there is no DATA statement on the specified line, the next DATA statement in the program will be used.

Entering Values From the Keyboard

Programmers frequently need to have program users specify string or numeric values. The INPUT statement accepts keyboard entries and assigns them to variables or array elements. Here is an example of a simple INPUT statement:

```
350 INPUT A
```

When PC BASIC encounters a statement like the one above, it displays a question mark. That cues the program user to type something on the keyboard. The ← key acts like a backspace key during entry, moving the cursor left one character at a time. The **Esc** key will erase the whole line, question mark and all, permitting a fresh start on the entry. Both keys work until the ← key is pressed to terminate the entry.

When responding to an INPUT statement, string values need only be enclosed in quotation marks if they include commas or important leading or trailing blank spaces. However, a string enclosed in quotation marks cannot itself contain quotation marks.

Keyboard Entry Cues

Few programs can get by with keyboard entry cues as terse as a single question mark. Fortunately the INPUT statement will display a message in addition to the question mark, or instead of it. In the INPUT statement, the prompting message takes the form of a string constant placed after the command word, enclosed in quotation marks, and separated from the variable name by a semicolon. Here is an example in immediate mode:

```
input "Life of loan in years "; life
Life of loan in years? 10
Ok
```

To suppress the question mark that appears after the prompting message, use a comma instead of a semicolon in the INPUT statement. The program user's input will immediately follow the last character of the prompting message. Here is an example:

```
input "Life of loan in years = ", life
Life of loan in years = 10
Ok
```

Keyboard Entry of Several Values

A single INPUT statement can accept values for more than one variable or array element. Just list the additional variables or array elements at the end of the INPUT statement and separate them from each other with commas. PC BASIC still only cues the program user with a single question mark or prompting message, if one is included in the INPUT statement. The program user must respond with a value for every variable listed in the INPUT statement, separating the values with commas. Here is an example:

```
list
10 INPUT "Name and Soc Sec No" ;N$,SS#
Ok
run
Name and Soc Sec No? Alvin Fox, 123-45-678
Ok
```

Keyboard Entry Error Checking

When the program user presses the ◄┘ key to terminate his entry, PC BASIC checks the entry. Numeric values are converted to match the precision of their destination variables the same way as in a LET or READ statement. If there are too many or too few values for the number of variables and array elements in the INPUT statement, or if the user entered a string value where a numeric is required, the message "?Redo from start" appears. Then the program user must re-enter all the values from the beginning of the line.

Exchanging Variable Values

The SWAP statement exchanges the values of two variables. For example

```
COST1 = 5
Ok
COST2 = 21
Ok
SWAP COST1,COST2
Ok
PRINT COST1
21
Ok
PRINT COST2
5
Ok
```

The variables must have exactly the same data types, or the message "Type mismatch" appears. Either one or both variable names can be a simple variable or an array element.

Clearing Variable and Array Values

The CLEAR statement will clear all variables and arrays from memory at once, without affecting the program lines. Numeric variables will have a value of zero and string variables will have a null value. The CLEAR statement also negates the effect of previously executed DIM and DEF statements.

DISPLAYING VALUES

The PRINT statement can be used in immediate or programmed mode to display the values of variables and arrays. The next example shows how it works with numeric and string variables:

```
list
100 INPUT  "Item name" ; ITEM$
110 INPUT  "Value"; VALUE
200 PRINT
210 PRINT ITEM$;"    value is $";VALUE
```

```
Ok
run
Item name? Brass lamp
Value? 83.50

Brass lamp value is $ 83.5
Ok
```

The example above illustrates several new features of the PRINT statement. Notice on line 200 that a simple PRINT statement generates a blank line on the display screen. Then notice on line 210 that a single PRINT statement can display several values, in this case a string variable, a string constant, and a numeric variable.

Spacing

The amount of blank space displayed between values depends on the value types and the punctuation used between them in the PRINT statement. Any two values separated by a semicolon will be displayed right next to each other. String values are displayed verbatim, so successive strings separated by semicolons seem to run together. Concatenating strings in this manner can be useful, but abutted numbers seldom make sense. Therefore a single blank space always follows every numeric value. The previous example illustrates how semicolons work with numeric and string values.

Commas that replace semicolons between values in PRINT statements cause values to align in uniform columns. To this end, the PRINT statement divides the display screen into zones. All zones are 14 spaces wide except the last one, which is 12 spaces wide on a 40-character display screen and 10 spaces wide on an 80-character display screen. Each comma that precedes a value in a PRINT statement moves the cursor to the start of the next zone before that value is displayed. Here is an example:

```
list
50 PRINT   "-----Item----- ","-Cost-"
100 READ  ITEM$,COST
110 PRINT  ITEM$,,COST
120 READ  ITEM$,COST
130 PRINT  ITEM$,,COST
140 PRINT
1000 DATA  Desk,875,Chair,260
Ok
run
```

```
-----Item-----                      -Cost-
Desk                                  875
Chair                                 260
Ok
```

In the program above, the first string constant displayed encroaches on the second zone (line 50), so the second string appears in the third zone. In order to maintain column alignment, subsequent PRINT statements use two commas between values, thereby skipping the second zone (lines 110 and 130).

Carriage Returns

A PRINT statement that does not end with a semicolon or comma finishes by moving the cursor to the left edge of the screen, one line down. In language reminiscent of typewriters and teletypes, that action is called a *carriage return*.

Putting a comma or semicolon at the end of a PRINT statement suppresses the carriage return that otherwise would occur. A semicolon holds the cursor at the end of the last value displayed and a comma advances the cursor to the start of the next zone and holds it there. The following example demonstrates a way to put a variable in an entry prompt as it illustrates the terminal semicolon:

```
list
100 INPUT "What is your name"; N$
110 PRINT "How old are you,  ";N$;
120 INPUT AGE
Ok
run
What is your name? Iola
How old are you, Iola? 32
Ok
```

The program above inputs a string value (line 100), and on the next line it uses a PRINT statement to incorporate the user's response into a second prompting message (line 110). The semicolon at the end of that PRINT statement prevents a carriage return so that the user's response to the second INPUT statement (line 120) occurs on the same display line as its prompting message.

On long lines a carriage return occurs automatically when the cursor reaches the rightmost character position of the display screen. That automatic carriage return is a permanent feature of the display screen; semicolons and commas have no effect on it. There is an unexpected side effect of this feature: a PRINT statement that exactly fills a display line will generate *two* carriage returns unless it has a terminating semicolon. The extra carriage return produces a blank line, and if that happens on the last line of the display screen, the whole screen rolls up one line. Consider the following example, run on a 40-character display screen:

```
list
10 PRINT ,, "123456789012";
20 PRINT ,, "abcdefghijkl"
30 PRINT ,, "123456789012";
Ok
run
                            123456789012
                            abcdefghijkl

                            123456789012
Ok
```

All three PRINT statements above put a character in the last character position of the display screen. The first PRINT statement (line 10) ends with a semicolon, suppressing the carriage return that normally occurs at the end of every PRINT statement, but not the carriage return that occurs when the cursor reaches the last character position on the display screen. The second PRINT statement (line 20) has no terminating semicolon, so it yields two carriage returns and a concomitant blank line.

The PRINT statement has another interesting feature that affects the way it prints long lines: it tries to display an entire value on one line. If it sees that a value will go past the end of the line, it starts the value at the beginning of the next full line. This example illustrates:

```
print "A" ,, "1234567890123"
A
123456790123
Ok
```

The two commas in the PRINT statement above put the cursor at character position 30 just before the 13-character string value is displayed. Since the value is too long to fit in the 10 remaining character positions (on a 40-character screen), it is displayed starting at the beginning of the next line.

Numeric Values

How a numeric value will appear depends on several factors. If the value is negative, a minus sign (−) precedes the displayed value, and if the value is positive, a blank space precedes the displayed value, in lieu of a plus sign. In either case, the PRINT statement adds a blank space after the last digit. For example:

```
list
240 INPUT "Enter a number: ",N
```

```
250 PRINT
260 PRINT N;"plus ";-N;"is 0"
Ok
run
Enter a number: 3

3 plus -3 is 0
Ok
```

As long as the number does not have too many digits, it appears in regular decimal notation. But single-precision values with more than seven digits and double-precision values with more than 16 digits appear in scientific notation (review Fig. 7-2). The following example illustrates:

```
list
1300 DEFSNG S:DEFDBL D
1400 INPUT "Single";SINGLE
1410 INPUT "Double";DOUBLE
1420 PRINT
1430 PRINT "Single: ";SINGLE
1440 PRINT "Double: ";DOUBLE
Ok
run
Single? 12345678900
Double? .001234567890123456789

Single: 1.234568E+10
Double: 1.234567890123457E-03
Ok
run
Single? 1234.56789
Double? 123456789.123456789

Single: 1234.568
Double: 123456789.1234568
Ok
```

Numeric constants are treated as double-precision values unless they are suffixed with an exclamation point (!) to indicate single-precision or a percent sign (%) to indicate integer. All numbers are displayed as decimal (base 10) values; octal or hexadecimal constants are converted before they are printed.

The PRINT statement never displays leading zeros in front of the decimal point nor trailing zeros behind it. This yields somewhat unsatisfactory results when displaying monetary amounts. For instance, the amount 83.50 will appear as 83.5, as an earlier example showed. Chapter 10 explains the PRINT USING statement, which will display properly formatted monetary amounts.

EXPRESSIONS

The values of variables, array elements, and constants can be combined or compared, and the result can be used in a number of ways. *Expressions* perform the combinations and comparisons.

Every expression has *operands*, which are the values that are combined or compared, and *operators*, which specify the nature of the combinations or comparisons. Most people understand how common arithmetic operators like addition, subtraction, multiplication, and division work, but there are more obscure numeric operators too. What's more, there are *relational operators*, which compare the values of two operands, *logical operators*, which combine operands according to logical rules, and even one string operator.

Expressions can be used just about anywhere a variable or constant is used to supply a value. For example, an expression can supply a value for a PRINT statement to display, it can provide the index for an array, and it can even specify an array dimension in a DIM statement.

Some restrictions do apply to expression use, but for the most part they are common sense. Expressions cannot be assigned a value by a LET, READ, or INPUT statement. Expressions listed as values in DATA statements are treated as literal string constants; they are not evaluated. And expressions must yield a type of value that is compatible with its context. For example, an expression with a string value will fail as an array index.

Operator Precedence

Programs frequently have complicated expressions involving many operators and operands. How does PC BASIC know which operation to perform first? Sometimes it makes no difference, as is the case with the expression $6-3+1-23$; no matter which occurs first, addition or subtraction, the result is the same: -19. More often the order of evaluation does matter. For example, the expression $100+10*5$ results in 150 if multiplication occurs first ($10*5=50$, and $100+50=150$), or 550 if addition occurs first ($100+10=110$, and $110*5=550$).

PC BASIC evaluates expressions according to the standard rules of operator precedence outlined in Table 8-1. It says, for example, that multiplication takes precedence over addition, so the result of the expression $100+10*5$ is 150. Some operators have equal precedence. When they appear in the same expression, the leftmost is evaluated first, the second leftmost next, and so on. For example, $200/5-4*10$ is 0, since $200/5=40$, $4*10=40$, and $40-40=0$.

Overruling Precedence

Parentheses in expressions can overrule standard operator precedence, because the operations they enclose are evaluated first. For example, 200/(5−4)*10 equals 2000, because (5−4)=1, 200/1=200, and 200*10= 2000. Standard operator precedence applies inside parentheses, unless an inner set of parentheses overrides it. You can nest parentheses inside each other almost indefinitely; the innermost set is always evaluated first. The rarely encountered theoretical limit to parentheses nesting varies with the complexity of the expression. When an expression does exceed it, the message "Out of memory . . ." appears.

Numeric Expressions

Numeric expressions may involve operations between integer, single-precision, double-precision, octal, and hexadecimal values. When a numeric expression has operands of several types, PC BASIC converts them all to the highest precision present in the expression, and it evaluates the expression in that precision. However, the conversion does not increase the precison of lower-precision operands. For example, an integer value converted to single- or double-precision value will not suddenly acquire fractional digits (other than zeros). By the same token, a single-precision value converted to double precision will still have at most six digits of accuracy; the extra double-precision digits are just set to zero.

The ultimate precision of the value of a numeric expression depends on its context. If the expression appears in a PRINT statement, the value is displayed in the precision it was calculated in. If the value is assigned to a lower-precision variable, it is *rounded* to the precision of that variable. If the value occurs in some other context, it is converted to the appropriate precision. For example, a single- or double-precision value appearing as an array index is rounded to an integer.

Table 8-1 lists all eight numeric operators. Four of them are more obscure than the familiar addition, subtraction, multiplication, and division. *Exponentiation* multiplies a value times itself a number of times. *Negation* yields the negative of a number. *Integer division* is the same as regular division, except its operands must be in the range −32768 to 32767, and any remainder or fraction in the quotient is discarded (the quotient is not rounded), leaving just an integer value. *Modulo* returns the remainder after one number is divided by another. The following example illustrates all four operands:

```
list
10 INPUT "1st number";N1
20 INPUT "2nd number";N2
30 PRINT "Exponentiation: ";
```

```
        N1; " ∧ " ;N2; " = " ;N1∧N2
40 PRINT  "Negation:  - " ;N1; " = " ;-N1
50 PRINT  "Integer division:  ";
        N1; " \ " ;N2; " = " ;N1\N2
60 PRINT  "Modulo:  ";
        N1; " MOD " ;N2; " = " ;N1 MOD N2
70 RUN  'Restart; press  <Break> to end
Ok
run
1st number? 10
2nd number? 3
Exponentiation:  10 ∧ 3 = 1000
Negation:  - 10  =-10
Integer division:  10 \ 3 = 3
Modulo:  10 MOD 3 = 1
1st number?
Break in 10
Ok
```

Notice the example above uses the RUN command to restart the program (line 70). To interrupt it and return to immediate mode, use the **Ctrl|Scroll Lock** combination keystroke (the **Break** key).

String Expressions

PC BASIC has one true string operator: concatenation. It joins string values together end to end, forming one long string value. The following program illustrates:

```
list
10 INPUT  "1st string";S1$
20 INPUT  "2nd string";S2$
30 S$=S1$+S2$
40 PRINT S1$;"  +  ";S2$;"  =  ";S$
Ok
run
1st string? over
2nd string? due
over + due = overdue
Ok
```

Relational Expressions

A relational expression compares two values to determine whether a proposed relationship between them is true or false. It will check for any one of six relationships: equal, unequal, less than, greater than, less than or equal, or greater than or equal. Table 8-1 lists the relational operators.

Table 8-1. Standard Operator Precedence

Operator	Precedence[a]	Operands	Operation
		Numeric[b]	
$\wedge$	12	2 numeric	Exponentiation
-	11	1 numeric	Negation (unary minus)
*	10	2 numeric	Multiplication
/	10	2 numeric	Division
\	9	2 numeric[c]	Integer division[c]
MOD	8	2 numeric	Modulo[d]
+	7	2 numeric	Addition
-	7	2 numeric	Subtraction
		String	
+	7	2 string	Concatenation
		Relational[e]	
=	6	2 alike	Equal
< >	6	2 alike	Not equal
> <	6	2 alike	Not equal
<	6	2 alike	Less than
>	6	2 alike	Greater than
< =	6	2 alike	Less than or equal to
= <	6	2 alike	Less than or equal to
> =	6	2 alike	Greater than or equal to
= >	6	2 alike	Greater than or equal to
		Logical[f]	
NOT	5	1 logical	Logical complement
AND	4	2 logical	Conjunction
OR	3	2 logical	Disjunction
XOR	2	2 logical	Exclusive conjunction
EQV	2	2 logical	Equivalence
IMP	1	2 logical	Implication

[a]Operators are listed from highest precedence to lowest; those with equal precedence are evaluated in sequence, from left to right. Parentheses overrule standard precedence; expressions within parentheses are evaluated first.

[b]When numeric operands have different precisons, all in an expression are converted to the highest precision present.

[c]The operands of integer division must be between −32768 and 32767, and any remainder is discarded from the quotient.

[d]The Modulo operation returns the remainder after the first operand is divided by the second.

[e]Relational operands must be compatible, either two numeric values or two string values.

[f]Table 8-2 has more on logical operators. Logical operands can be relational expressions or numeric values between −32768 and 32767.

A numeric value can be compared to another numeric value of any type. The values will be equal only if they are exactly the same, and that will be rare if they have different precisions. For example, the single-precison value 1.23456789! is less than—not equal to nor greater than—the double-precision value 1.23456789. This might seem puzzling, since 1.234568, which is the actual value of the single-precision constant, looks larger than the value of the first constant. But PC BASIC remembers that the seventh digit of a single-precision value is unreliable and ignores it during the comparison. Effectively, the numbers compared are 1.23456789 and 1.23456000.

The best way to compare two numeric values is to subtract one from the other and then see how close the difference is to zero. You can consider the values equal if the lower precision value is an integer and the difference is less than 1; when single precision is lower use .000001; for double precision use 1E-16. For example, instead of A# = B!, use ABS(A#-B!)<.000001.

A string value may only be compared to another string. Strings are compared character by character until a mismatch occurs, and then the code numbers of the mismatched characters are compared and the string whose character has the highest code number is considered greater. If one string runs out of characters before a mismatch occurs, the longer string is considered greater. If both strings have identical characters and equal length, they are considered equal. Two null strings are also considered equal.

Expressions with more than one relational operator are rare when the operands are numeric values and virtually illegal when the operands are string values. The reason hinges on the arcane fact that relational expressions evaluate to integer values: 0 for false, −1 for true. For example, the expression A=B=C will always be false unless A=B and C=−1, or A<>B and C=0. An expression like A$=B$=C$ induces the error message "Type mismatch," because the first part of the expression, A$=B$, evaluates to a numeric value and cannot be compared to C$, a string value.

Programmers most often use relational expressions in conditional statements to let a program make dynamic decisions about which statements to execute. Chapter 9 covers that topic.

Logical Expressions

Logical expressions deal with the logical values True and False. Since those values result from relational expressions, it should be no surprise that the most common operands in logical expressions are in fact relational expressions.

PC BASIC has six logical operators: NOT, AND, OR, XOR, IMP, and EQV. Each evaluates two operands (except NOT, which uses one) and deduces from them a single value, True or False, according to prescribed rules of logic. Table 8-2 enumerates the rules.

Most people find it easier to understand logical expressions when they involve real-life operands instead of abstract programming operands. For

Table 8-2. Logical Expression Evaluation

First value	Oper- and	Second value	Value of expression	First value	Oper- and	Second value	Value of expression
-	NOT	T	F	T	XOR	T	F
-	NOT	F	T	T	XOR	F	T
				F	XOR	T	T
				F	XOR	F	F
T	AND	T	T	T	EQV	T	T
T	AND	F	F	T	EQV	F	F
F	AND	T	F	F	EQV	T	F
F	AND	F	F	F	EQV	F	T
T	OR	T	T	T	IMP	T	T
T	OR	F	T	T	IMP	F	F
F	OR	T	T	F	IMP	T	T
F	OR	F	F	F	IMP	F	T

example, you could use logical expressions to decide your stance on issues in an election. You might make the official positions of the Republican and Democratic parties the operands. For each issue, the first logical operand is ''The Republicans favor this issue (True or False?)'' and the second operand is ''The Democrats favor this issue (True or False?).'' A logical expression will then decide, ''I favor this issue (True or False?).''

If you apply the NOT operator to the Republicans' position, your stance will be opposite theirs. The AND operator says that only if both Republicans and Democrats endorse an issue will you favor it. An OR expression says that if either one party or the other approves, so do you. The XOR operator decides that as long as one party or the other, but not both, endorse an issue, you will too. EQV is the opposite of XOR; it says if both parties endorse an issue, or if both oppose it, then you will approve. An IMP expression says unless the Republican platform (the first operand) endorses and the Democratic platform (the second operand) opposes, you will approve.

FUNCTIONS

Functions are like a cross between commands and expressions. Like commands, they have a command word, and like expressions they calculate a value from one or more operands. PC BASIC has 61 predefined functions and by far the greatest number of them return numeric values. They perform mathematical calculations, analyze strings, convert data types, allow direct control of the computer and its peripheral equipment, and analyze data files. Seventeen functions return string values and another seven, though they return numeric values, are string related. The more common functions are explained in detail in various places throughout the rest of this book, and Appendix A summarizes them all.

A function can replace an expression or it can be part of an expression. To use one, specify the command word that identifies it and then list its operands, enclosed in parentheses. Here is an example of a string function:

```
print string$(40,"*")
****************************************

Ok
```

As illustrated above, the STRING$ function builds a string value that consists of a repeated single character. It has two operands: the second operand specifies the character to repeat and the first operand specifies the number of times to repeat the character. The repetition factor must be between 0 and 255.

Not all functions have two operands. Many have one and a few have three. The latter category includes the INSTR function, which searches all or part of one string for the occurrence of another string. Its operands are the string to search, the string to look for, and the first character position to start with in the searched string. The function returns the integer equal to the position of the first matched character in the searched string. The following example demonstrates:

```
list
10 INPUT "String to search: ", S$
20 INPUT "String to find: ", F$
30 INPUT "Start search at: ", P%
40 PRINT "Found at: ";INSTR(P%,S$,F$)
Ok
run
String to search: Saint-seducing gold
String to find: ing
Start search at: 7
Found at: 12
Ok
```

The operand that specifies the starting position for the search is optional. If it is absent, the search starts with the first character.

Substring Functions

Three popular string functions extract pieces of a string value, called *substrings*: LEFT$ starts with the leftmost character, RIGHT$ starts with the rightmost character, and MID$ takes characters from anywhere in the string. In each case, you must specify a source string value and the number of characters to extract from it. For MID$, you must also specify a starting position in the source string; characters are extracted starting there and proceeding to the right, towards the end of the string. The follow-ing example illustrates:

```
list
10 INPUT "String: ", S$
20 INPUT "No. of characters: ",N%
30 INPUT "Starting pos. for MID$: ",SP%
40 PRINT "Right: ";RIGHT$(S$,N%)
50 PRINT " Left: ";LEFT$(S$,N%)
60 PRINT "  Mid: ";MID$(S$,SP%,N%)
Ok
run
String: They laugh that win
No. of characters: 4
Starting pos. for MID$: 12
Right: win
 Left: They
  Mid: that
Ok
```

No error occurs if you specify more characters than there are; LEFT$ and RIGHT$ simply return the whole source string and MID$ returns the entire right-hand part of the string, starting at the specified position. A null sub-string results when the number of characters requested is zero or when the starting position for MID$ is past the end of the source string.

The MID$ function can also specify a substring that receives a value, like this:

```
MID$(S$,5,3) = "cement"
```

In this case, the first operand specifies the destination string and the sec-ond operand specifies the first character position in that string that will receive a value. The third operand specifies how many characters from the source string will be assigned to the receiving string, starting with the first source string character. The third operand is optional; if missing, the entire source string is used.

User-Defined Functions

You can define functions to supplement the predefined ones. The following example defines a function that rounds numeric amounts to the nearest hundredth (useful in monetary calculations):

```
10 DEF FNCENT(X) = INT(X*100 + .5)/100
```

A function definition statement begins with the command word DEF. After that comes the function name, which must begin with the letters FN. The rest of the function name can be any valid variable name (review Fig.

7-4 and Table 7-2). Following the function name comes a list of *parameters*, enclosed in parentheses. They are dummy variable names that act as place holders for the actual values supplied each time the function is used. The remainder of the statement line is a model expression that defines what the function does.

The model expression usually includes the dummy variables from the parameter list, and it may use other variables, array elements, constants, and functions as well. It can be any valid expression as long as it will yield a value compatible with the function name; value and name must both be string or both be numeric.

The expression is not actually evaluated until the function is used. The following example shows how that happens:

```
list
10 DEF FNCENT(X)=INT(X*100+.5)/100
100 INPUT "Amount of sale: $",AMT#
110 INPUT "Sales tax rate: ",RATE
120 TAX=FNCENT(RATE/100*AMT#)
500 PRINT ,,AMT#
510 PRINT ,"Sales tax",TAX
520 PRINT ,"Total",FNCENT(TAX+AMT#)
Ok
run
Amount of sale: $9.97
Sales tax rate: 6.5
                              9.97
              Sales  tax      .65
              Total           10.62
Ok
```

To employ a user-defined function, state its name (starting with the letters FN) and then list (inside parentheses) a value to take the place of each dummy variable in the function definition's parameter list. Each value must be compatible with the type of the corresponding dummy variable, string or numeric. When such a function reference is executed, the specified values replace the dummy variables in the model expression, but they have no effect on other variables in the program with the same names as the dummies. The resulting expression is evaluated using the current values of any nondummy variables present in the model expression. The function name determines the type and precision of the final function value.

Numeric Conversion Functions

PC BASIC features many functions that convert data from one type to another. No less than three of them convert a single- or double-precision value to a whole number without any fractional part. The FIX function simply chops off any digits after the decimal point, the INT function calculates the largest integer that is less than or equal to its operand, and the CINT function rounds to the nearest integer. The following example illustrates the difference between the three functions:

```
list
10  INPUT  "Number";A
20  PRINT  "FIX(";A";") =  ";FIX(A)
30  PRINT  "INT(";A";") =  ";INT(A)
40  PRINT  "CINT( ";A ";") =  ";CINT(A)
50  PRINT
60  RUN 'Repeat; use <Break> to end
Ok
run
Number? 101.625
FIX( 101.625 ) = 101
INT( 101.625 ) = 101
CINT( 101.625 ) = 102

Number? 500.1
FIX( 500.1 ) = 500
INT( 500.1 ) = 500
CINT( 500.1 ) = 500

Number? -265.1
FIX(-265.1 ) = -265
INT(-265.1 ) = -266
CINT(-265.1 ) = -265

Number? -133.9
FIX(-133.9 ) = -133
INT(-133.9 ) = -134
CINT(-133.9 ) = -134

Number?
Break in 10
Ok
```

The FIX and INT functions actually return single-precision values with zero fractional parts. However, the CINT function returns a true integer value within the range -32768 to 32767; its operand must be within that range or an error occurs.

The CSNG function rounds a double-precision value to seven significant digits or less, like this:

```
print csng(97.5436750000001)
97.54368
Ok
```

The CDBL function converts integer and single-precision values to double-precison values, but does not extend their accuracy. Here are some examples:

```
print cdbl(10%/3%)
3.333333253860474
Ok
print cdbl(1.1!/1.5!)
.7333333492279053
Ok
```

In both cases above, the correct double-precision numbers would end in a sequence of 3's. The numbers displayed are clearly incorrect after the seventh digit.

Numeric Strings

In addition to the three numeric formats, numbers can be represented in strings. For example, "1234.56" is a numeric string. There are times when it is easier to deal with numeric values than with numeric strings. Relational expressions, for example, can yield incorrect results with numeric strings. The expression "10"="10.0" is false, even though 10=10.0 is true.

The VAL function converts a numeric string to a numeric value. It starts converting with the leftmost character and continues until it runs out of characters or a nonnumeric character occurs. Numeric characters consist of any number of leading blank spaces, a single optional plus or minus sign, any number of digits, and an optional decimal point followed by any number of digits; scientific notation is also acceptable. If the string has no numeric characters (before the first nonnumeric), VAL returns zero. Here are some examples:

```
print val("1234.56789");val("-1234.56789!")
 1234.56789 -1234.568
Ok
print val("9.29558d7 miles"),val("ZIP 94596")
 92955800           0
val("47.5%")
Syntax error
Ok
```

The "precision" of the numeric string—that is, the number of digits and the magnitude of the value—determines the precision of the VAL conversion. If the first nonnumeric character is an exclamation point (!), VAL returns a single-precision value. The pound sign (#) and percent sign (%) do not affect precision in this context as they do in standard numeric constants. In fact, if the percent sign (%) is the first nonnumeric character, an error occurs.

The STR$ function is the opposite of the VAL function; it converts a numeric value to a numeric string. A numeric value has the same format in a string as it has when displayed by a PRINT statement, except there is no extra blank space after the last digit in the string. The following examples illustrate:

```
print 6620;" mph ",str$(6620);" mph "
 6620  mph         6620mph
Ok
print str$(&h3f)
 63
Ok
print str$(.0000000299792458);" meters/sec "
.0000000299792458 meters/sec
Ok
```

Five other functions convert numbers to numeric strings in different ways. The OCT$ and HEX$ functions convert decimal numeric values to octal and hexadecimal integer strings, respectively, rounding if necessary. The value to be converted must be between -32768 and 65535. Here are some examples:

```
list
10 INPUT "Number: ",N%
20 PRINT N%;"is ";HEX$(N%);" Hex, ";
   OCT$(N%);" Octal"
30 RUN 'Restart; use <Break> to end
Ok
run
Number: 100
 100 is 64 Hex, 144 Octal
Number: 129,8
 129 IS 82 Hex, 202 Octal
Number:
Break in 10
Ok
```

The MKI$, MKS$, and MKD$ functions convert numbers to integer, single-precison, and double-precison values, respectively, for disk data files; Chapter 12 describes them.

ASCII Conversion Functions

The ASC function returns the ASCII code number of a character (Appendix D relates codes to characters). Its reciprocal, CHR$, interprets a numeric value as a code number and generates the corresponding character. The following immediate mode commands illustrate:

```
print asc( "A" )
 65
Ok
print chr$(64+33)
a
Ok
```

CHAPTER 9

PROGRAM ORGANIZATION

Few programs have long uninterrupted stretches of sequential program statements. This chapter explores the ways you can control the order of statement execution, including unconditional branching, conditional statement execution, and statement iteration. It also looks at ways to structure programs for best efficiency and clarity by using program modules and chaining programs together.

BRANCHING

Unfettered program execution proceeds sequentially from one statement to the next and from one program line to the next. PC BASIC has several statements that change the order in which program lines execute.

The GOTO Statement

The GOTO statement changes program execution by branching to a different program line. You specify the destination program line by stating its line number, as line 20 in the following example illustrates:

```
list
10 INPUT "Item name: ",ITEM$
20 GOTO 100
30 ITEM$="Item name is "+ITEM$
100 PRINT ITEM$
Ok
run
Item name: Monthly
Monthly
Ok
```

Use a constant to specify the destination line number. If you happen to include a decimal point and decimal digits, PC BASIC ignores them, but an error occurs if you use scientific notation, a variable, or an expression to specify the line number. Also, a program line with the specified number must exist or the message "Undefined line number . . ." appears.

Any program line is a valid target for a GOTO statement, including lines with nothing besides comments, but because a REM statement is not executed, you may as well branch to the line after it. That way if you later delete the REM statement, the program will still work. The following example shows what could happen:

```
list
100 REM Initialize arrays
110 READ COST(N)
120 READ PRICE(N)
130 N=N+1:GOTO 100
9000 DATA 375,44.50,90
Ok
delete 100
Ok
run
Undefined line number in 130
Ok
```

The error above would not occur if the GOTO statement on line 130 was GOTO 110.

A GOTO statement in immediate mode is like a RUN command, except it simply restarts the program at the first statement on the indicated line number, without initializing any variables or changing any statuses. This feature is useful during program testing and development, but you should avoid it otherwise. It is too easy to specify the wrong line number or to inadvertently change a variable in such a way that you actually change the program, opening the door to unsuspected errors.

The ON-GOTO Statement

The ON-GOTO statement gives a program some decision-making power. Instead of always branching invariably to the same line number, a program can choose from a list of line numbers to branch to. The ON-GOTO statement includes an expression and a list of line numbers. The value of the expression is an index into the list of line numbers: a value of 1 means program execution branches to the first line number on the list, a value of 2 means it goes to the second line number, and so on. Here is an example:

```
list
1000 INPUT "Enter element number (1 to
     3): ",N%
1010 ON N GOTO 1100,1200,1300
1020 PRINT "Unknown":GOTO 1000
```

```
1100 PRINT  "Hydrogen":GOTO 1000
1200 PRINT  "Helium":GOTO 1000
1300 PRINT  "Lithium":GOTO 1000
Ok
run
Enter element number (1 to 3): 2
Hydrogen
Enter element number (1 to 3): __
```

Fractional expression values are rounded to the nearest whole number. If the expression evaluates to 0 or a number greater than the number of line numbers on the list, no branch occurs and program executions falls through to the next consecutive statement. Negative expression values cause the message "Illegal function call ..." to appear.

CONDITIONALS

With some manipulations, the ON-GOTO statement will take care of most decision making in a BASIC program, but at times it will be awkward at best. Fortunately, PC BASIC has a statement, IF-THEN, that is easy to apply to general decision-making situations.

IF-THEN Statements

The IF-THEN statement says that *if* a condition is true, *then* it will perform some action. A relational or logical expression specifies the condition, and a regular BASIC statement specifies the action. If the expression is true, PC BASIC executes the statement. If the expression is false, the statement is skipped. The following program has four simple examples:

```
list
100 INPUT "Enter two numbers: ",A,B
110 IF A>B THEN PRINT "1st no. is larger"
120 IF B>A THEN PRINT "2nd no. is larger"
130 IF B=A THEN PRINT "Nos. are equal"
139 ' Restart unless both numbers are 0
140 IF A<>0 AND B<>0 THEN GOTO 100
150 END
Ok
run
Enter two numbers: -3,5
2nd no. is larger
Enter two numbers: 1e4,1000
Nos. are equal
Enter two numbers: 0,0
Nos. are equal
Ok
```

When the statement to be conditionally executed is a GOTO statement, as it is in line 140 in the example above, you may omit either of the command words THEN or GOTO, but not both. Thus the statement on line 140 above could be written:

```
140 IF A<>0 AND B<>0 THEN 100
```

or

```
140 IF A<>0 AND B<>0 GOTO 100
```

You can list several statements for conditional execution, separating one from another with a colon, like lines 1100, 1200, and 1300 below:

```
list
90 GOTO 1000
900 PRINT "Atomic wt. of ";ELMT$;"is";AW
1000 INPUT "Enter an element number: ",N%
1010 IF N%=0 THEN END
1100 IF N%=18 THEN ELMT$="Argon"
     :AW=39.948:GOTO 900
1200 IF N%=26 THEN ELMT$="Iron"
     :AW=55.847:GOTO 900
1300 IF N%=82 THEN ELMT$="Lead"
     :AW=207.2:GOTO 900
1400 PRINT "Atomic weight of element";
     N%; "unknown"
1410 GOTO 1000
Ok
run
Enter an element number: 26
Atomic wt. of Iron is 55.847
Enter an element number: __
```

Any statement is allowed as part of the conditionally executed sequence, but if a GOTO statement is included, it will naturally be the last one executed. Also, be sure to put a REM statement, if any, at the very end of the line, because PC BASIC ignores everything after the command word REM.

The ELSE Clause

A typical IF-THEN statement scenario has two divergent execution paths that converge again in short order. Program execution follows one path if the relational or logical expression is true and another path if it is false. Both paths generally come together again later in the program. The following example illustrates:

```
list 940-960
940 IF TERMS$= "S " THEN DSCNT=40:GOTO 960
950 DSCNT=30
960 PRINT STR$(DSCNT);"% NET PRICE $";
    FNCENT(TOTAL*(1-DSCNT/100))
```

The statements that are executed when the IF-THEN expression is false can be put on a separate program line, as they are above, or they can be incorporated in the IF-THEN statement itself. The command word ELSE joins them to the end of an IF-THEN statement. Compare the following to the previous example:

```
list 940-960
940 IF TERMS$= "S " THEN DSCNT=40 ELSE
    DSCNT=30
960 PRINT STR$(DSCNT);"% NET PRICE $";
    FNCENT(TOTAL*(1-DSCNT/100))
```

Note that there is no colon before the command word ELSE.

LOOPS

Many occasions arise when the same program steps are repeated over and over. Rather than duplicate the same program lines several times, you can have the program loop back and re-execute the statements. This happened in a few earlier examples in this chapter and in the end of Chapter 8, where a GOTO or RUN statement kept a program going indefinitely. But suppose you want to re-execute just part of a program just a few times. In that case, the program must decide while it is running when it should stop repeating. It can count iterations using an integer variable and can decide when to stop with an IF-THEN statement. Here is an example:

```
list
30 CTR%=1
40 IF CTR%>8 THEN 70 'Initialize loop counter
50 PRINT 2^CTR%;
60 CTR%=CTR%+1:GOTO 40
70 REM Sequential execution resumes
80 END
Ok
run
2  4  8  16  32  64  128  256
Ok
```

This program repeats lines 50 and 60 as long as the value of variable CTR% is less than or equal to 8, but each time it repeats line 60, it increments the value of CTR% by 1. Therefore the program stops looping back to line 50 after eight iterations.

The FOR and NEXT Statements

The FOR and NEXT statements take over some of the routine and make it easier to write program loops. They replace the statement that sets the initial loop counter value, the IF-THEN statement that decides when to terminate the loop, and the statement that increments the loop counter. Compare the following example to the previous one:

```
list
40 FOR CTR%=1 TO 8
50 PRINT 2∧CTR%;
60 NEXT CTR%
70 REM Sequential execution resumes
80 END
Ok
run
 2  4  8  16  32  64  128  256
Ok
```

The FOR statement identifies the start of a program loop, names a numeric variable that will count loop iterations, assigns a starting value to the iteration counter, and states the iteration counter's maximum value. The iteration counter must be a simple variable; it cannot be an array element. The FOR statement checks to see if the current value of the counter exceeds the maximum. If not, the program executes the statements between the FOR and the NEXT statements. When the program executes the NEXT statement, it loops back to the statement that follows the FOR statement.

FOR and NEXT statements must occur in matched pairs. If a NEXT statement is executed before a FOR statement with the same iteration counter variable, the error message "NEXT without FOR . . ." appears. A similar message appears if there are too few NEXT statements to match all the FOR statements in a program.

When the FOR statement determines that the value of the counter variable exceeds the stated maximum, program execution branches to the first statement after the NEXT statement. Thus if the counter's initial value exceeds the maximum, the loop statements are not executed. The following example illustrates:

```
list
10 FOR K=10 TO 9
20 PRINT "Loop executed"
30 NEXT K
40 PRINT "Final value = ";K
Ok
run
Final value = 10
Ok
```

The FOR / NEXT Step Value

Normally, the iteration counter is incremented by 1 at the end of each loop iteration. To specify a different increment, append the word STEP, followed by the value of the increment, to the FOR statement. Any value is allowed, including negative and fractional values. The following example illustrates a negative fractional "increment" (actually a decrement):

```
list
40 FOR L=3.5 TO 1 STEP -.5
50 PRINT L;
60 NEXT L
70 REM Sequential execution resumes
80 END
Ok
run
3.5  3  2.5  2  1.5  1
Ok
```

When the step size is negative, the program loops until the iteration counter is *less* than its final value, as defined by the FOR statement. In that case, the counter's starting value must be higher than its ending value.

Using the FOR / NEXT Counter Variable

The iteration counter variable can be used anywhere inside the loop as any other numeric variable might be used; you can even change its value, but this practice is not recommended. Doing so will affect the number of loop iterations because a NEXT statement always increments the most recent value of the iteration counter variable.

Branching out of a FOR/NEXT loop leaves the iteration counter variable at the last value it had in the loop. Terminating a loop normally, through a NEXT statement, leaves the iteration counter variable at the last value it had plus the step value. In the last example, variable CTR% will equal .5 on line 70.

Specifying FOR / NEXT Loop Extents

The FOR statement can use constants, variables, or expressions to specify the initial, final, and increment values for the iteration counter. But once the FOR statement has been executed, those values are set for the duration of the loop. Changing variable values inside the loop will have no effect on the initial, final, or increment values established when the loop began.

Nesting FOR / NEXT Loops

FOR/NEXT loops can be nested one inside another (Fig. 9-1). You can omit the variable name from the NEXT statement and the statement will match the most recently executed FOR statement. Do not use this technique with nested FOR/NEXT loops if there is any chance of branching out of an inner loop—it will not work. Consider the following program segment:

```
list
10 DIM N$(2,10)
20 FOR J%=1 TO 2
30 FOR K%=1 TO 10
40 INPUT "Name: ",N$(J%,K%)
50 IF N$(J%,K%)=" " THEN GOTO 70
60 NEXT
70 NEXT
Ok
run
Name: Milton
Name: Chaucer
Name:
NEXT without FOR in 70
Ok
```

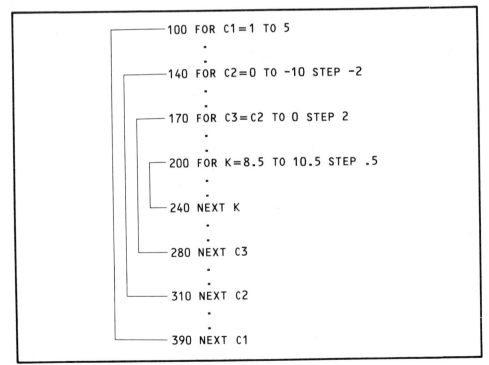

```
100 FOR C1=1 TO 5
       .
       .
140 FOR C2=0 TO -10 STEP -2
       .
       .
170 FOR C3=C2 TO 0 STEP 2
       .
       .
200 FOR K=8.5 TO 10.5 STEP .5
       .
       .
240 NEXT K
       .
       .
280 NEXT C3
       .
       .
310 NEXT C2
       .
       .
390 NEXT C1
```

Fig. 9-1.   Nested FOR/NEXT loops.

In the preceding program, the NEXT statement on line 60 is the nominal terminus of the inner loop, which begins on line 30. However, if line 50 branches to line 70, the NEXT statement there will terminate the inner loop instead. Unfortunately, that NEXT statement was supposed to terminate the outer loop, which began on line 20. The program halts with an error message when it discovers the outer loop no longer has a terminal NEXT statement.

The WHILE and WEND Statements

FOR/NEXT loops work well when you want to repeat something a fixed number of times. But vary the number of iterations during loop execution or subject the loop to interruption by an unscheduled event, and you must corrupt the FOR/NEXT loop with an IF-THEN statement that tests for a special condition and ends the loop abnormally by branching out of it. The WHILE and WEND statements are designed to handle irregular, uneven, and unpredictable loop situations without lumpy IF-THEN statements.

The WHILE statement, which starts a WHILE/WEND program loop, consists of the command word and a relational or logical expression. If the expression is true, the statements that follow the WHILE statement are executed until a WEND statement occurs. Then program execution loops back to the WHILE statement. There the expression is re-evaluated, and if it is still true, the loop is executed again. If the expression in the WHILE statement is ever false, program execution skips ahead to the statement that follows the WEND statement and continues sequentially from there. Here is an example:

```
list
1000 INPUT "String to compress: ",S$
1010 RMV$= " "  'Remove these from input
2000 WHILE INSTR(1,S$,RMV$)<>0
2009 '--Remove one character at a time----
2010 S$=LEFT$(S$,INSTR(1,S$,RMV$)-1)+
     RIGHT$(S$,LEN(S$)-INSTR(1,S$,RMV$))
2020 WEND
3000 PRINT S$
Ok
run
String to compress: a b c d e f
abcdef
Ok
```

The program above compresses a string by removing all blank spaces. It uses the INSTR function to search the string for blanks. As long as there are blanks present, the relational expression in the WHILE statement (line

2000) will evaluate true, and the WHILE / WEND loop (lines 2000 to 2020) will be executed. Each iteration of the loop removes one blank space (line 2010). When all blanks are gone, the program skips around the loop and displays the compressed string (line 3000). The character compressed out can be changed by changing the value of variable RMV$ (line 1010).

A numeric expression will work in the WHILE statement too. As long as its value is nonzero, the statements in the WHILE / WEND loop are executed. For example, the WHILE statement in the program above could be rewritten as follows:

```
2000 WHILE INSTR(1,S$,RMV$)
```

You can nest WHILE / WEND loops, but each WHILE statement must have a corresponding WEND statement or an error occurs.

PROGRAM STRUCTURE

As programs get longer and more complex, the need for organization and planning becomes more and more imperative. The thought of writing a large program can be overwhelming, like the idea of eating a whole salami at once, but slice it up and it becomes palatable. The simplest way to subdivide a program is by function: dimensioning and defining, initializing, inputting, processing, and outputting are typical divisions. To demarcate the sections, use separate and distinct ranges of line numbers for each one. Establish a standard scheme for numbering the sections of any program and you will always know where to look for the DIM statements, the DEF statements, the DATA statements, and so on.

Some of the program sections can themselves be subdivided into modules, and the modules can be divided again. The goal is to make each final module small enough to be easily planned, written, and tested. As a side benefit, many modules can be used like superinstructions in any program you write. The remainder of this chapter explores the PC BASIC commands that make modularization possible.

SUBROUTINES

It often happens that the same procedure occurs in several places in the same program. For example, a program that needs to compress strings in several different places could duplicate the recent WHILE / WEND loop example in each place. That seems somewhat wasteful. Instead, you could isolate the procedure from the main program and branch to it as needed. Then it is called a *subroutine*, and branching to it is termed *calling* the subroutine. When the subroutine finishes, it returns to the point in the program from which it was called.

The GOSUB and RETURN Statements

The GOSUB statement calls a subroutine. Like the GOTO statement, it branches to a specified line number, but it also remembers where to branch back to when the subroutine ends. Executing a RETURN statement marks the end of a subroutine. The program branches back to the statement following the GOSUB that called the subroutine. Here is a simple example:

```
list
1000 INPUT "String to compress:  ",FS$
1009 'Remove blanks from FS$
1010 S$=FS$:RMV$="  ":GOSUB 2000
1030 PRINT S$
1040 END
1997 '==Subroutine compresses strings=====
1998 '  RMV$ has character to extract
1999 '  S$ has original string & result
2000 WHILE INSTR(1,S$,RMV$)<>0
2010 S$=LEFT$(S$,INSTR(1,S$,RMV$)-1)+
     RIGHT$(S$,LEN(S$)-INSTR(1,S$,RMV$))
2020 WEND
2030 RETURN
Ok
```

The program above uses a subroutine to remove all blank spaces from a string value. The subroutine (lines 2000 through 2020) removes every occurrence of whatever character is in variable RMV$ from variable S$, so before calling it, the main program must assign values to both variables (line 1010). The GOSUB statement (line 1010) starts the subroutine. When the subroutine finishes, the RETURN statement (line 2030) branches back to the statement after the GOSUB, which in this case is a PRINT statement (line 1030). The END statement (line 1040) separates the main program from the subroutine.

A program may call the same subroutine from two or more places. For example, the following line added to the last example would call the subroutine again to remove hyphens from variable S$:

```
1020 RMV$="-":GOSUB 2000 'Remove hyphens
```

Subroutines and the Run-Time Stack

Repeatedly exiting subroutines with GOTO, ON-GOTO, or IF-THEN statements (instead of RETURN statements) results in the "Out of memory . . ." error, so avoid the practice. The reason for that particular error is a bit esoteric: PC BASIC dedicates a relatively small amount of dynamic memory to keeping a list of return locations for subroutines. It is called the *stack* or *run-time stack*. Each time a subroutine is called, its return location is added to the stack. When a RETURN statement is executed, the most recently added return location is removed from the stack and program execution branches there. Statements like GOTO and IF-THEN exit a subroutine all right, but they never touch the stack. If that happens often enough, the stack runs out of memory and the program halts with the error message. Chapter 15 explains a way to increase the size of the stack.

There are occasions when you will want to leave a subroutine unexpectedly and branch to a specific program line. In Advanced BASIC you can do that by using a RETURN statement with a line number. Instead of returning to the statement following the most recent GOSUB, it clears the most recent entry from the stack and branches to the specified line number. Use this feature with caution, though. If the subroutine was in the midst of FOR/NEXT or WHILE/WEND loops, they will still be active.

The ON-GOSUB Statement

The ON-GOSUB statement calls a subroutine just like a simple GOSUB statement does, but it chooses the line number to branch to from a list, according to the value of an expression. In that respect it is like the ON-GOTO statement described earlier in this chapter. Here is an example:

```
890 ON ASC(R$)-48 GOSUB 910, 930, 950, 970
```

The value of the expression is an index into the list of line numbers: a value of 1 means program execution branches to the first line number on the list, a value of 2 means it goes to the second line number, and so on. Fractional expression values are rounded to the nearest whole number. If the expression evaluates to 0 or a number greater than the number of line numbers on the list, no branch occurs and program execution falls through to the next consecutive statement. Negative expression values cause the message "Illegal function call . . ." to appear.

Subroutine Nesting

Subroutine calls can be nested. This is a bit different from nesting loops or parentheses, however. The subroutines themselves are not nested one inside another; the GOSUB statements that call them are nested. Thus one subroutine can call another, which can in turn call a third, and so on. Here is a simple example:

```
List
1100 GOSUB 8000 'Display framed quotation
2000 END
7999 '==Subroutine prints quote==========
```

```
8000  GOSUB 9000 '1st print some asterisks
8010  PRINT " If  you  pick  up  a  starving
         dog  and  make  him  prosperous,  he  will
         not  bite  you."
8020  PRINT  "This  is  the  principal
         difference  between  a  dog  and  a  man."
8030  GOSUB 9000 'Finish with more asterisks
8040  RETURN
8999  '==Subroutine  prints  asterisks=======
9000  FOR XCOUNT%=1  TO 20
9010  PRINT  "*  ";
9020  NEXT XCOUNT%
9030  RETURN
Ok
```

The main program above consists of a single subroutine call (line 1100) and an END statement (line 2000). The first subroutine (lines 8000 through 8040) prints a quotation framed by asterisks. It calls a second subroutine (lines 9000 through 9030) to print the asterisks. The final result looks like this:

```
run
* * * * * * * * * * * * * * * * * * * *
   If  you  pick  up  a  starving  dog  and  make
him  prosperous,  he  will  not  bite  you.
   This  is  the  principal  difference  between
a  dog  and  a  man.
* * * * * * * * * * * * * * * * * * * *
Ok
```

Subroutine nesting is a powerful concept. It means that not only can you break a program into modules and write a subroutine to perform each module, but you can break a subroutine into modules too. The smaller you can make each program module, the easier it is to create and test it, and the better chance there is of re-using it.

Recursion

A subroutine may call itself. That kind of nesting is called *recursion*, and the concept includes a subroutine that calls another subroutine that in turn calls the first. The following program illustrates recursion:

```
list
1000  INPUT "String to compress:  ",FS$
1009  '--Remove blanks from FS$
```

```
1010  S$=FS$:RMV$=" ":GOSUB 2000
1030  PRINT S$
1040  END
1997  '==Recursive subroutine compresses strings=
1998  ' RMV$ has characters to extract
1999  ' S$ has original string & result
2000  IF INSTR(1,S$,RMV$)<>0
      THEN S$=LEFT$(S$,INSTR(1,S$,RMV$)-1)+
      RIGHT$(S$,LEN(S$)-INSTR(1,S$,RMV$)):
      GOSUB 20000
2010  RETURN
Ok
```

The program above compresses blank spaces out of a string value, just like the earlier subroutine example did. As long as this subroutine (lines 2000 and 2010) finds blank spaces in variable S$, it keeps calling itself. Each time it is called, it removes one blank space. When all the blanks are gone, it returns repeatedly until finally it returns from the first call, which occurred in the main program (line 1010).

The number of times a subroutine can call itself (directly or indirectly) is limited. The exact limit depends on several factors, including which version of BASIC you are using, how much concurrent nesting of other subroutines is going on, and the size of the run-time stack. Tests show that the maximum is 44 times with a standard run-time stack in either Cassette BASIC or Disk BASIC, and 33 times in Advanced BASIC. Chapter 15 explains how you can raise the limit by increasing the size of the run-time stack.

PROGRAM OVERLAYS

Programs vary in size from a few lines to hundreds of lines and they may use a handful of simple variables or many large arrays. At some point the program size will exceed the capacity of dynamic memory. Programs that are too large to fit in available dynamic memory must be split up into segments. Each segment is saved on the disk as if it were a full-fledged program, but each segment only does part of the overall task. When a segment finishes, it loads the program segment that does the next step and transfers control to it. Program segments are also called *overlays*, because an incoming segment overlays the existing segment.

The CHAIN statement is best for linking one segment to the next. It looks like this:

```
200 CHAIN "prog2"
```

The string value is the name of any BASIC program. If you omit the file name extension as the example above does, PC BASIC assumes the extension BAS.

To see how program chaining works, consider a program that translates numbers into different languages. The program will start out translating into one language and will switch to another language when the program user requests translation of any number greater than it can handle. The following statements and commands create a program that does that for numbers between zero and nine in Spanish:

```
list
10 DIM W$(9)
20 FOR XC%=0 TO 9:READ W$(XC%):NEXT 'Get
   translations
30 READ LANG$, CUE$ 'Get name of language
   & cue
50 PRINT CUE$;LANG$; ":"
100 PRINT CUE$;:INPUT N% 'Request number
   to translate
110 IF N%>9 THEN 200 'Switch languages if
   entry>9
120 PRINT N%;LANG$; "  ";W$(N%) 'Translate
130 GOTO 100
200 CHAIN "prog2" 'Load next language
6990 '--Table of translations, digits 0-9-----
7000 DATA zero,uno,dos,tres,cuatro,cinco,
   seis,siete,ocho,nueve
7010 DATA en Español es, Número
Ok
save "prog1"
Ok
```

When the program user enters a value greater than nine, the program above uses a simple CHAIN statement (line 200) to load and run another program segment. Assuming the first segment is still in memory, the following commands will create a second segment, for German translations:

```
200 chain "prog1"
7000 data nullpunkt,eins,zwei,drei,vier,
   funf,sechs,sieben,acht,neun
7010 data auf Deutsch ist, Nummer
save "prog2"
Ok
```

To run the program, you start with the first segment. Enter a number greater than nine, and the program will switch languages by chaining to the next segment. Here is a sample of program execution:

```
run "prog1"
Número en Español es:
Número? 4
4 en Español es cuatro
Número? 99
Nummer auf Deutsch:
Nummer? 7
7 auf Deutsch ist sieben
Nummer? 99
Número en Español es:
Número? __
```

Imagine how much could be done with several chained programs, each using all of memory.

Common Variables

A simple CHAIN command like the one above erases all program lines and variables from dynamic memory before it loads in the next segment. Suppose the second program needs variables from the first program. The COMMON statement is one answer to this problem. It lists the variables that must be held over from the current program segment to the next. Simple variables and whole arrays can be retained, but not selected array elements. Here is a sample:

```
COMMON ITEM$(),TOTAL,OMIT$,COST()
```

As you see above, variable names are separated by commas. Array names are suffixed with parentheses that have nothing enclosed.

Though the COMMON statements can occur anywhere in a program, it is a good plan to put them at the beginning with the DIM and DEF statements. Do not list the same variable in more than one COMMON statement in the same program segment.

A simple CHAIN command will not maintain special variable types defined by DEFINT, DEFSNG, DEFDBL, and DEFSTR statements, nor will it maintain the values of common variables affected by those type declaration statements. For continuity, you must repeat the type definitions in the chained program. The following example creates two linked program segments:

```
10 defstr u:defint d
20 common units,dist
30 input "Distance";dist
40 input "Miles or Kilometers";units
100 chain "ovly1"
save "mainpgm"
Ok
```

```
new
Ok
10 defstr u
20 print dist;units
save "ovly1"
Ok
run "mainpgm"
Distance? 1342
Miles or Kilometers? Mi.
0 Mi.
Ok
```

The values assigned to variables DIST and UNITS during the first program above (lines 30 and 40) are declared common (line 20), so their values should be maintained during the loading of the overlay (line 100). But the second program neglects to redefine the special integer variables (compare line 10 in each program segment). Therefore variable DIST is considered single precision in the overlay and its value is lost in spite of the COMMON statement.

The CHAIN statement has an option that lets you preserve the values of all variables from one program to the next, without any COMMON statement. It looks like this:

```
CHAIN "pgmnam",,ALL
```

There are two commas ahead of the word "ALL" because of another CHAIN statement option, omitted here for simplicity, that will be described shortly. This method of sharing variables suffers from the same type redefinition problem as the COMMON statement described above.

Neither COMMON statements nor the ALL option in the CHAIN statement pertain to functions defined by DEF FN statements. All such user-defined functions must be redefined in each chained program segment if they are used there. Furthermore, if the function name is affected by a type declaration statement like DEFSTR or DEFINT, that type declaration must be repeated too.

Merging Overlays

Another CHAIN statement option lets you merge incoming lines with the existing program in memory. The existing program lines are not cleared with this form of the CHAIN statement. Instead, incoming lines are interwoven with the existing lines. If an incoming line and existing line have the same line number, the incoming line replaces the existing line. The following example shows part of a program that will merge one of several overlays; one of the overlays is shown:

```
list 1600-1800
1600 '--Calculate shipping charges
1610 IF SHIP$="T" THEN CHAIN MERGE
     "truck",,ALL
1620 IF SHIP$="M" THEN CHAIN MERGE
     "mail",,ALL
1630 IF SHIP$="A" THEN CHAIN MERGE
     "air",,ALL
1700 TOTAL=TOTAL+SHIP
1800 GOSUB 3000 'Print invoice
Ok
load "mail"
list
0 GOTO 1640 'Branch to start overlay
1640 READ RATE(1),RATE(2) 'get rates
1650 ' compute charges based on weight
1660 SHIP=RATE(1)+CINT((LBS-1/16)/16)
     *RATE(2)
7000 DATA .30,.25
Ok
```

The main program above loads one of three overlays to calculate shipping costs (lines 1610 to 1630). In each case, the ALL option preserves variable values. The overlay fits into a gap left in the main program line numbers (between lines 1630 and 1700). In order to avoid re-executing main program statements, each overlay has a GOTO statement (line 0) that branches to its first line (line 1640). Execution continues normally from there, eventually falling through to the main program (line 1700).

Program overlays loaded by a CHAIN MERGE statement must have been saved by a SAVE command with the ",A" option, which is described in Chapter 6.

You can incorporate a DELETE command into the CHAIN MERGE statement in order to remove a range of program lines before loading an overlay. Only one range of contiguous lines can be deleted. The CHAIN statement with the DELETE option looks like this:

```
1600 CHAIN MERGE "prgname",,DELETE 100-900
```

The extra comma ahead of the DELETE option accommodates another option (unused here) that will be described in the next section.

Both starting and ending line numbers must exist in the program or an error occurs. If no ending line number is specified, just the one line listed is deleted. If you renumber a program that contains a CHAIN statement with the DELETE option, the line number range in it will be renumbered too.

When the ALL option is present also, the CHAIN statement looks like this:

```
1700 CHAIN MERGE "ovly2",,ALL,DELETE 1000
```

Specifying the Starting Line

The long-awaited CHAIN statement option alluded to earlier in this chapter lets you specify the line number where execution will begin in the next overlay. The line number comes right after the file name, like this:

```
1610 IF SHIP$= "T" THEN CHAIN MERGE
     "truck",1640,ALL
```

The ALL and DELETE options can be appended in the usual way. The specified starting line number need not be present in the source program, but must exist in the loaded program or the "Undefined line number" message appears when the CHAIN statement is executed. The RENUM command has no effect on this optional starting line number.

TRACING EXECUTION

As your programs get longer and more complex, you will have to spend more and more time testing them to make sure they work correctly under varying circumstances.

Thorough testing is a major part of careful program development. Errors that arise can be hard to track down, especially in long and complex programs. The TRON statement activates a program execution tracer that displays the number of each program line as it is executed, resulting in a map of the program execution path. The following short program illustrates:

```
list
10 TRON 'Trace mode on
20 GOSUB 100
30 END
90 '==Recursive subroutine=======
100 IF K>5 THEN K=K+1:GOSUB 100
110 RETURN
Ok
run
[10][20][100][100][100][100][100][100][1
10][110][110][110][110][110][30]
Ok
```

The program trace above shows that execution proceeds from line 10 to line 20, where the program calls the recursive subroutine at line 100. The subroutine calls itself five more times at line 100. At that point, variable K is 6, so execution falls through to line 110. The first five times the subroutine returns, it is returning from its own recursive calls, which means execution continues on line 110. The sixth return goes back to the main program, at line 30, where the program ends.

To cancel the trace mode, execute a TROFF statement. A plain RUN command does not cancel trace mode, so an immediate mode TRON command will cause tracing of subsequent programs until a TROFF statement occurs. Any command that clears the current program from memory, like NEW or LOAD, also cancels trace mode.

CHAPTER 10

DISPLAY SCREEN AND PRINTER OUTPUT

Earlier chapters used the PRINT statement to display values on the screen. This chapter describes new features of the PRINT statement as well as other statements that afford greater control of screen output. It also explains how to program paper output on a printer.

CONTROLLING THE DISPLAY SCREEN

PC BASIC has several functions that work with the PRINT statement, and several independent statements too, that clear the display screen, align numeric output, and control the cursor.

Clearing the Display Screen

There are three ways to clear the display screen. All three also move the cursor to its home position. In immediate mode, the **Ctrl|Home** multiple keystroke does the job. The CLS command does the same thing, but it works in programmed mode too. Or, you can clear the screen by displaying the character that has ASCII code number 12. CHR$(12) generates the character, so a statement like PRINT CHR$(12) will clear the display screen.

Display Screen Width

Most video monitors can display either 40 or 80 characters per line, but the smaller characters used on 80-character lines are barely legible on home televisions and some monitors. Programs that might use any kind of display screen should plan on only 40 characters per line. PC BASIC lets a program explicitly set the maximum line width of the screen display to 40 or 80 characters per line. Two consecutive statements are required, SCREEN and WIDTH. Here is an example:

```
1010 SCREEN 0:WIDTH 40
```

The SCREEN 0 statement tells PC BASIC to ignore the line width it started with and use the line length specified by WIDTH statements instead. Only the first WIDTH statement executed after starting BASIC need be preceded by a SCREEN 0 statement.

Column Formatting

Most people find it easier to assimilate large amounts of information when it is aligned in columns. Chapter 8 demonstrated how using commas to separate the values listed in PRINT statements aligns those values in columns at the start of predefined zones. Unfortunately, zone width is fixed and you only get three zones on a 40-character screen (six on an 80-character screen). Often the values you want to display are wider or much narrower than the predefined zones. In those cases you need to be able to define your own zones somehow.

You can use the TAB function with PRINT statements to establish your own zones. TAB advances the cursor to a specific position on the display line. Horizontal positions, called *columns*, are numbered from 1 on the left to either 40 or 80 on the right, depending on the display screen width. The following example shows how the TAB function works:

```
list
4000 CLS:SCREEN 0:WIDTH 40
4010 PRINT  "Description ";TAB(20);
      "Acquired" ;TAB(30); "Cost "
4030 READ  NR%,DSCR$,SN$,AQ$,COST# ,VALUE#
4040 PRINT  DSCR$;TAB(20);AQ$;TAB(30); "$" ;
      COST#
10001 DATA  1,Desk,n/a,9/11/78,875,1500
Ok
run
Description           Acquired  Cost
Desk                  9/11/78   $ 875
Ok
```

As the example above shows, the TAB function specifies the column number where the next character will appear. Not so obvious is the fact that it advances the cursor by printing blank spaces, erasing anything it passes over in the process.

If the cursor is already past the column specified, the TAB function moves it to that spot on the next lower line. This example demonstrates:

```
list
4010 PRINT  "Description" ;TAB(20);
      "Acquired" ;TAB(30); "Cost"
4030 READ NR%,DSCR$,SN$,AQ$,COST# ,VALUE#
```

```
4040 PRINT DSCR$;TAB(20);AQ$;TAB(30); "$" ;
     COST#
10012 DATA 12,Overstuffed leather sofa,
n/a, 12/2/79,1377,1377
Ok
run
Description        Acquired  Cost
Overstuffed leather sofa
                   12/2/79  $ 1377
Ok
```

The value that specifies the column number must be between -32768 and 32767. Values less than one specify column 1. If the value exceeds the screen width, the modulo operation is applied: the value is divided by the screen width, the quotient is discarded, and the remainder specifies the column number to use. For example, PRINT TAB(241) on a 40-column screen is the same as PRINT TAB(1), because 240 MOD 40 = 1.

The TAB function only works with the PRINT statement and with the LPRINT and PRINT# statements, which are described later in the book. If you need a function that simply generates a number of blank spaces as a string value, try the SPACE$ function.

Cursor Control

You may already have figured out one way to position the cursor anywhere on the display screen: use the CLS command to home the cursor, then simple PRINT statements for vertical movement, and finally a TAB function for horizontal movement. But that method is awkard and it erases the screen every time too.

PC BASIC provides the LOCATE statement to directly move the cursor to any location on the display screen, without affecting anything already displayed. For this purpose, the screen is divided into rows and columns (Fig. 10-1). Where a row and column intersect, a character can be displayed. The most straightforward version of the LOCATE statement specifies the row and column number to move to, like this:

```
LOCATE 13,29
```

The first number specifies the row and the second number specifies the column. Row and column numbers can be specified by any numeric expression. Normally, there are 24 rows, numbered 1 through 24 from top to bottom, and 40 or 80 columns (depending on the width of the display screen), numbered 1 through 40 or 80 from left to right. Values must be within those ranges or the error message "Illegal function call ..." appears.

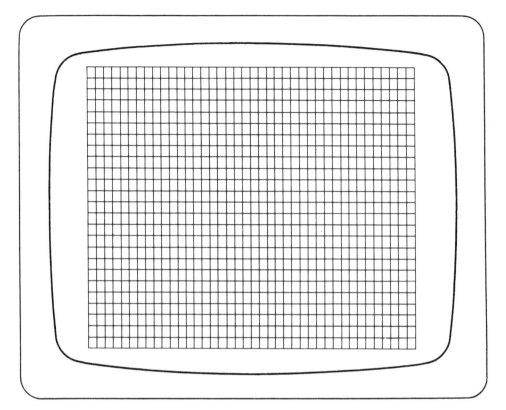

Fig. 10-1.   Rows and columns on the display screen.

As usual, displaying anything in the rightmost column causes an automatic carriage return. When that happens on line 24, the entire display screen shifts up one line, and the top line rolls off the top of the screen. There is no way to prevent this, so it is best to avoid the last column on line 24. Remember also from Chapter 8 that if a value is too long for the space remaining at the end of a line, PC BASIC displays the whole value at the beginning of the next line.

The following example uses one LOCATE statement to position a keyboard input, and a second LOCATE statement to position PRINT statement output:

```
list
10 CLS
100 LOCATE 1,20:INPUT "Row, column" R,C
110 LOCATE R,C:PRINT "*" ;
120 GOTO 100
Ok
run

                    Row, column? 2,20
                    *
```

Using Display Line 25

The 25th line is usually occupied by text that explains the function key definitions. The KEY OFF command makes the 25th display line available to the BASIC program for limited use. The only way to get to line 25 is with a LOCATE statement. A carriage return from line 24 rolls the screen up one line; it does not drop the cursor down to line 25. If a carriage return occurs for any reason on line 25, the rest of the display acts like a carriage return just occurred on line 24. Lines 1 through 24 roll up one line, and the cursor moves to the beginning of the now-blank line 24.

Determining Cursor Position

The POS function determines which column the cursor is currently in. It returns a value between 1 and 40 (40-column display screen) or 1 and 80 (80 column display screen). Here is an example:

```
PRINT POS(0)
```

The POS function does not use the dummy value in parentheses (0 in the example above) but it must be there. Any value will do.

Function CSRLIN determines the row that the cursor is currently in. It returns a value between 1 and 25. Here is an example:

```
PRINT CSRLIN
```

CSRLIN is an unusual function because it does not use parentheses. Even though it looks like a variable, you cannot assign it a value.

FORMATTED OUTPUT

The LOCATE statement, TAB function, and commas in PRINT statements all give you control over where a value will appear on the display screen, but they have little effect on how it will look. The PRINT statement always prints string values in their entirety and it has its own rules about the format of numeric values. Circumventing the PRINT statement's formatting conventions would require lots of tricky maneuvering with functions like STR$, RIGHT$, LEFT$, and MID$. Fortunately none of that is necessary.

The PRINT USING statement formats output according to your specifications. Like the PRINT statement, it has a list of values to be displayed. You must separate the values by semicolons; commas are not allowed. A semicolon at the end of the list inhibits the carriage return that otherwise occurs.

The first value in a PRINT USING statement must be a string. It specifies how the rest of the values will look when they are displayed. In most cases,

Table 10-1. PRINT USING Template Characters

Character(s)	Meaning
	Numeric formats*
+	Print an explicit + or − sign
**	Fill unused spaces on the left with asterisks
$$	Prefix values with a dollar sign
**$	Fill with asterisks and prefix with a dollar sign
#	Provide space for one digit
,	Punctuate with a comma between every third digit
.	Designate the decimal point position for output
-	Print a blank space (positive value) or − sign
∧∧∧∧	Force value to appear in scientific notation
	String formats
!	One character
\\	Two or more characters; enclose blank spaces to specify more characters
&	Variable length (entire string value appears)
	Literal characters
Any	Any character that is not part of a numeric or string zone definition is printed verbatim, except the __ character
__	The next character is printed verbatim even if it is normally a zone definition character

*Here is a guide to the general placement of numeric template characters:

$$+\left\{\begin{matrix} ** \\ **\$ \\ \$\$ \end{matrix}\right\} \#,\#\cdots\#.\#\cdots\# \left\{^+_-\right\} \wedge\wedge\wedge\wedge$$

the characters in the format string do not appear verbatim. Instead they are interpreted as a template that establishes string or numeric zones on the output line. The template fixes the length of each zone along with other characteristics. The actual values to be printed are modified as necessary so that they conform to the template. Table 10-1 identifies how different template characters affect output format. The following paragraphs discuss the options in some detail. PRINT USING is one of the most complex statements in PC BASIC, and it usually takes quite a bit of experimentation to understand all of its capabilities.

Formatting String Values

The PRINT USING statement will print string values as is or it will display a fixed number of characters from the left-hand part of the string. The following example illustrates several possibilities:

```
list
10 A$=''Tempus fugit''
20 PRINT USING "!" ;A$        '1 character
30 PRINT USING "\\" ;A$       '2 characters
40 PRINT USING "\ \" ;A$      '3 characters
50 PRINT USING "\  \" ;A$ '4 characters
60 PRINT USING "&" ;A$        'all chars.
Ok
run
T
Te
Tem
Temp
Tempus fugit
Ok
```

As you see above, a ! character in the template specifies a one-character string zone, while a & character specifies a zone of variable length to accommodate an entire string value, whatever its length may be.

A pair of backslash characters (|), possibly separated by some number of blank spaces, specifies a fixed-length string zone. The total number of characters, counting both backslashes and all of the blank spaces they enclose, determines the length of the zone. A string value starts printing at the left edge of the zone. If the string is too long for the template field, it has characters truncated on the right. If the value is shorter than the zone, blank spaces fill out the extra space on the right. For example, the following template specifies a seven-character zone, but there are only four characters to be printed:

```
print using " |      \" ;  "Desk" ;:print
      "$" ;875
Desk    $ 875
```

Formatting Numeric Values

Columns of numbers are easier to read if they are aligned at the decimal point. The PRINT USING statement makes that possible. It defines a fixed-length numeric zone, and the numeric value is modified to fit the zone. Knowing how much space a numeric value will occupy, you can design screen displays with more preciseness than the PRINT statement allows.

A numeric zone is defined by # characters, one for every digit to be printed. If the printed value is negative, a minus sign takes up one zone space. Numeric values always appear aligned at the right edge of the zone, like this:

```
print using  "####" ;12
   12
print using  "####" ;-123
-123
```

If the value has fewer digits than the zone allows, enough blank spaces are added to the left of the first printed digit to fill out the zone. If the value is too large to fit the template, it appears anyway, prefixed by a percent sign. Here is an example:

```
print using  "####" ;123456
%123456
```

Decimal Point

To get a decimal point and fractional digits in a numeric zone, put a decimal point after one of the # characters in the template. You decide where the decimal point will be, how many digits to allow before it, and how many digits to allow after it. On the one hand, a value that has more digits after the decimal point than the template allows will be rounded before it is printed. On the other hand, a value with fewer digits after the decimal point than the template allows has zeros appended to fill out the zone. The following example illustrates decimal points in templates:

```
list
10  INPUT "Enter a number: ",A
20  PRINT USING "####.##";A
30  GOTO 10
Ok
run
Enter a number: 1234.50
1234.50
Enter a number: 12.3456
  12.35
Enter a number: .123456
   0.12
Enter a number: __
```

Plus and Minus Signs in Templates

As earlier examples show, positive numbers normally appear without a sign, and negative numbers use one of the zone spaces for a minus sign. Incorporating an explicit sign in the template stipulates special treatment of signed numbers. You can put a + character ahead of the first # character or you can put a + or − character after the last one. The following example illustrates:

```
list
10 A$= " +###.#" :B$="###.#-" :
   C$= " ###.#+"
20 PRINT A$,B$,C$
30 FOR N=-88.8 TO 88.8 STEP 177.6
40 PRINT USING A$;N;:PRINT ,
50 PRINT USING B$;N;:PRINT ,
60 PRINT USING C$;N
70 NEXT
run
+####.#           ###.#-          ###.#+
   -88.8            88.8-           88.8-
   +88.8            88.8            88.8+
Ok
```

A plus sign used as a template prefix or suffix means a sign always appears: + for positive values, − for negative values. A minus sign only works as a suffix. Then it causes a minus sign to appear after negative values or a blank space to appear after positive values.

Commas in Templates

People often write long numbers with commas every three digits, like this: 100,000,000,000. The PRINT USING statement will punctuate such numbers if there is a comma present after the first # character. For example:

```
print using  " #,##########.## " ;1e7
   10,000,000.00
Ok
```

The comma can actually appear anywhere in the template after the first # character and before the decimal point. It specifies another digit position. The number output, including as many commas as necessary, will not exceed the zone width defined by the template.

Scientific Notation Templates

To force numeric values to be printed in scientific notation, suffix a normal numeric template with four $\wedge$ characters, as follows:

```
print using  "###.##∧∧∧∧" ;-.97654
-97.65E-02
Ok
```

As many digits as possible will appear in the coefficient portion and the exponent will be adjusted accordingly. If the template allows more than one digit before the decimal point, the leftmost digit will always be a blank space or a minus sign, depending on the sign of the printed value.

Monetary Templates

If you want a dollar sign printed ahead of the first digit in a number, just replace the first # character in the template with *two* $ characters. That increases the zone length by one to accommodate the dollar sign. For example:

```
print using  "$$###.##";15.95
   $15.95
Ok
```

In situations where negative dollar amounts may occur, most programmers suffix the template with a + character, as described earlier. That way the sign of the value always appears after the value itself. If you wish to prefix a monetary template with a + character, put it before the $$ characters. A monetary template that lacks an explicit sign causes negative amounts to appear with a minus sign ahead of the dollar sign.

The PRINT USING statement can use asterisks instead of blank spaces to fill the unused space at the left of a numeric value. All you do is replace the first two # characters with * characters, like this:

```
print using  "**#####.##";249.95
****249.95
Ok
```

To combine asterisk fill with a dollar sign, make the first three characters of a numeric template **$.

Constants in Templates

Any character can be part of the string that defines the template in a PRINT USING statement. Characters that do not participate in defining numeric or string zones appear exactly as written, and that includes blank spaces, letters of the alphabet, digits, and most punctuation. Here is an example:

```
tot=989457.82
Ok
print using "Total  #,######.##";tot
Total   989,457.82
Ok
```

You can also make the special characters that normally define string and numeric zones appear as written. In a template, any character preceded by a __ character will appear as a literal character. That includes the special zone-defining characters !, \, &, #, __, $\wedge$, $, *, ., +, and −. Of course some of those ($\wedge$, $, *, ., +, and −) appear as written anyway, unless they occur in the right combination and sequence as part of a numeric zone definition. The following example shows how the __ character works:

```
print using  "Weight:####_#";180
Weight: 180#
Ok
```

Templates for Several Values

A single template can provide the format for more than one value. The template can contain a separate format specification for each value, like line 100 in the program below:

```
list
100  FMT10$ = "\          \  \         \ $$#####.##"
4010 PRINT  "Description"  TAB(14);"Acquired";
     TAB(27);"Cost"
4030 READ NR%,DSCR$,SN$,AQ$,COST#,VALUE#
4040 PRINT USING FMT10$;DSCR$;AQ$;COST#
10101 DATA 101,Phone answering machine,G395298,
     6/22/81,215,215
Ok


run
Description  Acquired     Cost
Phone answer 6/22/81    $215.00
Ok
```

The template above, which is defined on line 100 and used on line 4010, has three zones. The first two are string; the third is numeric.

If the PRINT USING statement has more values to display than its template defines zones for, the template is reused from the beginning. The following example displays six values with a template that defines only two zones:

```
print using  "##.##% &   ";
78.11;"N";20.95;"O"; .93;"A"
78.11% N  20.95% O  0.95% A
Ok
```

If a template specifies more zones than there are values, the extra zones are ignored. Numeric values must have numeric templates and string values must have string templates or an error occurs.

PRINTER OUTPUT

Printed output is easier to create than displayed output. The ⇧|**PrtSc** combination keystroke will duplicate whatever is on the display screen onto

Table 10-2.   Equivalent Printer and Display Screen Statements

Display screen	Printer
PRINT	LPRINT
PRINT USING	LPRINT USING
POS	LPOS
TAB	TAB
SPC	SPC
CSRLIN	None
LOCATE	None

the printer anytime, even while the PC is waiting for keyboard input. However, not all character codes produce the same characters on a printer as they do on the display screen. Letters, digits, and most punctuation symbols are the same, but printers cannot duplicate all the special graphics characters available on the PC display screen. The interpretation of character code numbers above 127 and below 32 varies widely from one printer to the next. The IBM 80CPS Matrix printer, for example, prints block graphic characters where another printer would print italic letters.

The **PrtSc** key is not the only way to produce printed output. All of the statements and functions that display values on the screen either work directly on the printer or have counterparts that do. Table 10-2 correlates display statements and functions with equivalent printer statements and functions.

There are some differences between printing and displaying. A program can use the LOCATE statement to flit from line to line on the display screen, but not on the printer. A printer must print one line at a time. Most printers have limited backspacing capabilities, but cannot match the agility of the display cursor.

A printer always prints one whole line at a time. It has a one-line memory that stores characters sent by LPRINT or LPRINT USING statements that end with semicolons. When the printer gets a carriage return character, it prints the accumulated characters at once. For example, the following statement produces nothing visible on the printer:

```
LPRINT "I will make you shorter by a head";
```

In fact you can add to it and still see nothing printed:

```
LPRINT " (Elizabeth I)";
```

Any LPRINT or LPRINT USING statement without a terminal semicolon will send a carriage return, causing the accumulated characters to print. For example, a plain LPRINT statement executed after the last two examples would precipitate this:

```
I will make you shorter by a head (Elizabeth I)
```

```
10 GOTO 1000
790 '==End-of-page subroutine===============================
800 LCTR%=LCTR%+1 'increment line counter
810 IF LCTR%<=56 THEN RETURN 'Exit if page not full
820 LPRINT STRING$(66-LCTR%,CHR$(10)) 'Advance to next page
830 LPRINT TAB((80-LEN(TITLE$))/2);TITLE$ 'center title
840 LPRINT TAB(70);"PAGE";PAGE%
850 LPRINT
860 LPRINT "Column headings here"
870 LCTR%=5 'Reset line counter; allow for heading & margins
880 PAGE%=PAGE%+1 'Increment page number
890 RETURN
990 '--Demonstration program------------------------------
1000 PAGE%=1
1010 TITLE$="title"
1020 GOSUB 830
1030 FOR K%=1 TO 100
1040 LPRINT K%
1050 GOSUB 800
1060 NEXT K%
```

Fig. 10-2.   An end-of-page subroutine for printed output.

If enough characters accumulate to fill the line, PC BASIC automatically sends a carriage return character to print the line. Subsequent characters start accumulating for the next line. Standard line width is 80 characters, so the overall effect of printing a long line on the printer is just like displaying a long line on an 80-column screen. It is possible to change the printer line width, as described later in this chapter.

When PC BASIC sends the printer a carriage return character, it also sends another character to advance the paper to the next line. Without the line advance character, all printed lines would overprint each other.

Paging

A program can recognize when it is near the bottom of a printed page and can advance to the top of the next page, leaving suitable margins. At the same time, it can print a title, page number, and column headings.

The easiest way to handle this is with a subroutine, as shown in Fig. 10-2. It uses variable LCTR% to count how many lines have been printed since the page began and variable PAGE% for the page number. The subroutine increments the line count and compares it to the maximum number of lines per page (lines 800 and 810). As long as the line count is the smaller of the two, the subroutine does nothing special. But when the

Table 10-3. Common Printer Control Characters

Feature	Advances paper	Prints pending line	Control character
Carriage return	Next line	Yes	CHR$(13)
Line advance	1 line	Yes	CHR$(10)
Backspace	No	Yes*	CHR$(8)
Page advance	Next page	Yes	CHR$(12)
Sound alarm	No	No	CHR$(7)

*CHR$(8) prints the pending line, then positions to the last character printed.

line count equals the page size, the subroutine does its end-of-page ritual (lines 820 through 890).

Before a program starts to print, it should set the starting page number (usually to 1). For the first page, it can call the subroutine at an intermediate line number, bypassing the paper advance portion but printing the title and headings.

Every time the program prints a line, it must also call the subroutine in order to increment and check the line count. Alternatively, the program can increment the line count itself and only call the subroutine occasionally, but the bottom margins of the pages may be uneven that way.

Control Characters

The IBM 80CPS Matrix printer, like most contemporary printers, has a number of special features that are controlled by sending it one or two special characters. The control characters themselves are invisible. They do not print, but they affect the way later printing appears.

The single-character control codes affect the location of subsequent printing on the paper. Table 10-3 lists several common ones. Most printers

Table 10-4. Type Font Selection Characters (IBM 80CPS Matrix Printer)

Font	Control character(s) Activate	Deactivate	Characters per line*
Wide	CHR$(14)	CHR$(148)†	40
Condensed	CHR$(15)	CHR$(146)‡	132
Condensed wide	CHR$(15)+CHR$(14)	CHR$(148)+CHR$(146)†‡	66
Emphasized	CHR$(27)+"E"‡	CHR$(27)+"F"	n/a
Double-strike	CHR$(27)+"G"	CHR$(27)+"H"	n/a

*The standard type font prints 80 characters per line.
†The wide and condensed wide character fonts are automatically deactivated when the line is printed. Thus the following control characters deactivate them: CHR$(13), CHR$(10), and CHR$(12).
‡Emphasized automatically cancels condensed.

```
10 CC1$=CHR$(27) 'Prefix control character
20 '--Assign control character strings--------------------
30 W.ON$=CHR$(14):W.OFF$=CHR$(20) 'Wide font
40 C.ON$=CHR$(15):C.OFF$=CHR$(18) 'Cond. font
50 D.ON$=CC1$+"G":D.OFF$=CC1$+"H" '2-Strike font
60 E.ON$=CC1$+"E":E.OFF$=CC1$+"F" 'Emph. font
90 '--Print samples----------------------------------------
100 S$="ABCDEFabcdef0123#?!()"
110 LPRINT C.ON$;S$+" COMPRESSED TYPE";C.OFF$
120 LPRINT S$+" NORMAL TYPE"
130 LPRINT C.ON$;W.ON$;S$+" DOUBLE WIDTH COMPRESSED TYPE";C.OFF$
140 LPRINT W.ON$;S$+" DOUBLE WIDTH TYPE"
150 LPRINT
160 LPRINT S$+" NORMAL TYPE"
170 LPRINT D.ON$;S$+" DOUBLE STRIKE TYPE";D.OFF$
180 LPRINT E.ON$;S$+" EMPHASIZED TYPE"
190 LPRINT D.ON$;S$+" DOUBLE STRIKE EMPHASIZED TYPE";D.OFF$;E.OFF$
```

(A)   Program to print 12 type font samples.

```
ABCDEFabcdef0123#?!() COMPRESSED TYPE
ABCDEFabcdef0123#?!() NORMAL TYPE
ABCDEFabcdef0123#?!() DOUBLE WIDTH COMPRESSED TYPE
ABCDEFabcdef0123#?!()   DOUBLE   WIDTH   TYPE

ABCDEFabcdef0123#?!() NORMAL TYPE
ABCDEFabcdef0123#?!() DOUBLE STRIKE TYPE
ABCDEFabcdef0123#?!() EMPHASIZED TYPE
ABCDEFabcdef0123#?!() DOUBLE STRIKE EMPHASIZED TYPE
```

(B)   Printed output.

Fig. 10-3.   Type fonts available on the IBM 80CPS Matrix printer.

observe the codes listed there. For example the following statement prints any line that may be pending and advances the paper four lines after that.

```
LPRINT STRING$(4,CHR$(10))
```

Most printers have advanced features that require two control character codes, one to turn a feature on and another to turn it off. Unfortunately, few printers interpret control characters for advanced features the same way. The IBM 80CPS Matrix printer, for example, uses the control characters listed in Table 10-4 to change type fonts. Fig. 10-3 illustrates them. On another printer, those same control characters may have no effect or they may do something entirely different.

Table 10-5. Device Availability in BASIC

Name	Device	Input/output	BASIC version
KYBD:	Keyboard	Input	All
SCRN:	Screen	Output	All
LPT1:	1st printer	Output	All
LPT2:	2nd printer	Output	Disk, Advanced
LPT3:	3rd printer	Output	Disk, Advanced
COM1:	1st serial device	Both	All
COM2:	2nd serial device	Both	Disk, Advanced
CAS1:	Tape recorder	Both	All
A:	1st disk drive	Both	Disk, Advanced
B:*	2nd disk drive	Both	Disk, Advanced

*Systems with more than two drives use names C:, D:, etc.

Switchable Output

With the PRINT and LPRINT statements you can easily mix screen display and printer output, but what if you want the same output to be available on either device, under program user control? It would be a pain to have to duplicate all the output statements, once with PRINT and another time with LPRINT. You can avoid that with the PRINT# statement, which lets the program control what the output device will be.

The PRINT# statement identifies devices by number. The device number must be between 1 and 4 in Cassette BASIC. The other versions of BASIC normally allow only devices 1, 2, and 3, but Chapter 12 describes a way to increase that limit. Device numbers are not permanently assigned. They must be correlated with actual physical devices by OPEN statements, like this:

```
1100 OPEN "LPT1:" FOR OUTPUT AS #1
```

In the statement above, LPT1: is the device name of the system printer. Table 10-5 lists all device names.

The following program segment lets its user choose whether output will appear on the display screen or the printer:

```
1100 OPEN "LPT1:" FOR OUTPUT AS #1
1110 OPEN "SCRN:" FOR OUTPUT AS #2
1120 INPUT "Printer or display screen?
     (P/S) ",D$
1130 IF D$<>"S" AND D$<>"P" THEN 1120
1140 IF D$="P" THEN D%=1 ELSE D%=2
1430 PRINT#D%, TAB(33);"List of items"
1440 PRINT#D%,
1450 GOSUB 5500 'Get next item's values
```

```
1460 TMPL3$ = "\ \ \ " + SPACE$(18) +
     "\ $$#####.##"
1470 PRINT#D%, USING, TMPL3$;ITM$;DESCR$;COST#
```

The program segment above assigns one device number to the printer and another to the screen (lines 1100 and 1110). Variable D% is set to the device number that corresponds to the user's choice (line 1140). All of the bidirectional output will be programmed with PRINT#D% or PRINT#D%, USING statements (like lines 1430, 1440, and 1470). Notice that simple PRINT# statements (those without values to print) must still include the comma that follows the device number (line 1440), but that comma does not suppress the carriage return nor advance to the next print zone.

Before a program can change a device number assignment with another OPEN statement, it must cancel the existing assignment with a CLOSE statement. Here is an example:

```
1100 OPEN "SCRN:" FOR OUTPUT AS #1
1700 CLOSE #1
1710 OPEN "LPT1:" FOR OUTPUT AS #1
```

Printer Line Width

PC BASIC normally assumes that the printer has a line width of 80 characters. If a program tries to print more than 80 characters on the same line, PC BASIC automatically generates a carriage return character, ending the line and causing it to print. But the IBM 80CPS Matrix printer can print 132 characters per line with its condensed type font, and printers with wide carriages can handle more than 80 standard-size characters per line too.

A variation of the WIDTH statement lets you change PC BASIC's concept of the printer line width to anything between one and 255. Here is an example:

```
1120 WIDTH #1, 132
```

The first number in this form of the WIDTH statement is a device number, and the second number is the new line width. In order to affect printed line width, the specified device number must have been assigned to a printer by a previous OPEN statement. In addition, only PRINT# and PRINT# USING statements that use the specified device number will recognize the new line width. LPRINT and LPRINT USING statements always use an 80-character line width.

Yet another form of the WIDTH statement lets you defer the width change until the next time the printer appears in an OPEN statement. It looks like this:

```
1000 WIDTH "LPT1:", 132
```

A subsequent OPEN statement like the following one not only assigns the printer to a device number, but redefines the line width for that device number too.

```
1010 OPEN "LPT1:" FOR OUTPUT AS #2
```

Because the LPRINT, LPRINT USING, LLIST, and LIST ,"LPT1:" statements all implicitly open the printer, a deferred width setting affects them too.

Underlining and Overprinting

In Disk BASIC and Advanced BASIC you can suppress the normal automatic line advance that occurs right after a carriage return. That allows you to print right over the top of the just-printed line for special effects like underlining. You must use a special version of the OPEN statement and use a WIDTH statement to set the printer line width to 255. The new form of the OPEN statement does not include a FOR OUTPUT clause. The following program shows how to use this feature to underline and overprint:

```
2309 '--Regular auto line adv.
2310 OPEN "LPT1:" FOR OUTPUT AS #1
2319 '--No auto line adv.
2320 OPEN "LPT1:" AS #3:WIDTH #3, 255
2330 PRINT #3,"The Invisible Man"
2340 PRINT #3,"                    "
2350 PRINT #1,
2360 PRINT #3, "Strikeout"
2370 PRINT #3, STRING$(9,"-")
2380 PRINT #1
```

Printed output from the program above looks like this:

```
The Invisible Man
Strikeout
```

The program above uses device #1 to print normal lines to the printer, with line advances (line 2310). It suppresses line advances with device #2 (line 2320).

CHAPTER 11

KEYBOARD INPUT

PC BASIC has statements and functions that give a program much greater control over keyboard input than the INPUT statement affords. They can control the cursor shape and visibility, function key interpretation, and the effect of many control keys.

CURSOR SHAPE AND VISIBILITY

The cursor is usually not visible while a program is running. The INPUT statement does turn it on, but there are other methods of keyboard input that do not. You can make it visible any time with a variation of the LOCATE statement that looks like this:

```
300 LOCATE ,,1
```

The value 1 turns the cursor on. The same statement with the value 0 would turn the cursor off. The two commas in the statement above accommodate a LOCATE statement feature discussed in Chapter 10, namely specifying the cursor position. With the row and column values absent as they are above, the LOCATE statement does not change the cursor position.

The LOCATE statement has one other option: it can change the shape of the cursor. The cursor shape can vary from a thin horizontal line to a tall rectangle; it all depends on how much of the available space is filled in. The available space is about the size of a capital letter, but it is a little taller because it extends below the letter (Fig. 11-1).

The space available for the cursor is divided into a number of thin horizontal bars. Display screens attached to a monochrome adapter card have 14 bars, numbered from 0 at the top to 13 at the bottom (Fig. 11-2A). Display screens attached to a color/graphics adapter card have eight bars, numbered from 0 to 7 (Fig. 11-2B). The LOCATE statement specifies the top and bottom bars to use, like this:

```
300 LOCATE ,,1,12,13
```

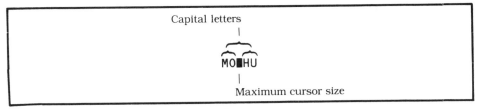

Fig. 11-1. Maximum cursor size.

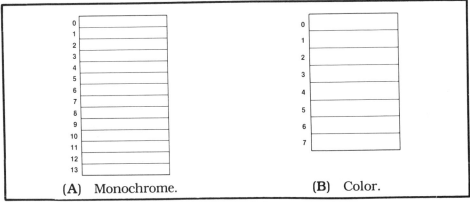

(A) Monochrome.   (B) Color.

Fig. 11-2. Thin horizontal bars form the cursor.

In the statement above, the first value determines the cursor visibility, the second value is the first cursor bar to use, and the third value is the last cursor bar to use. The first two commas hold the cursor at its current location. This statement defines a standard underscore cursor on a monochrome display screen.

Many cursor shapes are possible, including split cursors (Fig. 11-3). A split cursor results when the first cursor bar number is greater than the second. The second cursor bar number is optional. If it is absent, it is assumed to be the same as the first cursor bar number, resulting in a cursor that is one bar high.

FUNCTION KEYS

Press **F1** and the characters "LIST " appear, just as though you typed every one of them individually. The other nine function keys generate characters the same way. IBM calls these the *Soft Key* definitions, because they are not hard and fast like the other 76 keys on the keyboard. You can change a Soft Key definition so that it generates any string of up to 15 characters.

The 25th display line shows the first six characters of each Soft Key definition. The KEY OFF statement erases the Soft Key definition display from line 25, but it does not disable the Soft Key definitions. Press a function

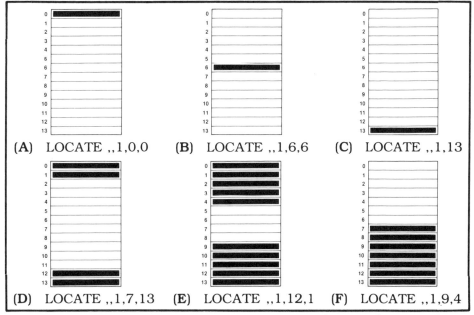

Fig. 11-3. Some different cursor shapes (monochrome shown; color is similar).

key and it still generates its defined string of characters. The KEY ON statement turns on the 25th line display of Soft Key definitions. To review all 15 characters of every Soft Key definition, use the KEY LIST command.

Another form of the KEY statement changes a Soft Key definition. The following example reassigns **F7** so that it generates the string "EDIT" when you press it:

```
KEY 7, "EDIT"
```

After executing the command above, pressing **F7** while in immediate mode will issue the command word EDIT. You can then type a line number and press the ← key to execute the EDIT command.

String constants, variables, and expressions are all acceptable in Soft Key definition statements. For example, you can use the CHR$ function to include a carriage return character, like this:

```
KEY 8, "FILES" +CHR$(13)
```

The carriage return character eliminates the need to press the ← key. Thus the statement above lets you execute a FILES command with a single keystroke.

Function keys work as Soft Keys whenever keyboard entry is accepted, for example, in immediate mode or in response to an INPUT statement.

However, assigning a function key a null Soft Key definition effectively disables it. If you press it subsequently, nothing happens.

Function Keys in Advanced BASIC

Advanced BASIC has a second way of interpreting function keys. Each one can be set up so that instead of entering a text string, it interrupts program execution and calls a subroutine. It takes two statements to set this up for each key.

A special version of the KEY statement activates a function key so it will trigger a subroutine call. The following example shows how this works for **F1**:

```
30 KEY (1) ON
```

The value in parentheses determines which function key will be activated. After executing the statement above, pressing **F1** no longer generates a string of characters.

Each activated function key requires a second statement to establish the line number of the subroutine that will be called after the key is pressed. The following example illustrates for **F1**:

```
35 ON KEY (1) GOSUB 20100
```

The value in parentheses determines which function key is involved. Until a statement like the one above is executed, a function key cannot trigger a subroutine call. Specifying a subroutine line number of 0 disables an activated function key.

Advanced BASIC checks at the beginning of each new program line to see if an activated function key has been pressed. If so, it then calls the specified subroutine.

To deactivate a function key for triggering subroutine calls and at the same time reactivate its original Soft Key definition, use a statement like this:

```
20170 KEY (1) OFF
```

As before, the value in parentheses indicates which key is affected.

The KEY-ON and KEY-OFF statements just described have no effect on line 25 of the display screen. Only plain KEY ON and KEY OFF statements turn on and off the display there of Soft Key definitions.

From time to time a program may need to temporarily shield itself from function key interruptions, but still remember if someone presses a function key. Later, it can trigger the appropriate subroutine call. The following statement does that for **F1**:

```
1430 KEY (1) STOP
```

If **F1** was pressed while deactivated by a statement like the one above, the appropriate subroutine will be called as soon as a KEY (1) ON statement is executed, reactivating **F1**. If several function keys are pressed while temporarily deactivated by KEY-STOP statements, corresponding subroutines will all be called in the order that the keys are reactivated.

The four cursor movement keys on the keypad can also be programmed to trigger subroutine calls. The procedure is exactly the same as just described for the ten function keys. For this purpose, the cursor control keys are identified by number, as follows: ↑ is 11, ← is 12, → is 13, and ↓ is 14. Use the number inside the parentheses of KEY-ON, KEY-OFF, KEY-STOP, or ON KEY-GOSUB statements. The following program uses the cursor control keys as function keys to call subroutines that move the cursor:

```
list
10 FOR K%=11 TO 14
20 KEY (K) ON 'Activate cursor keys
30 NEXT
40 ON KEY (11) GOSUB 1010 'up
50 ON KEY (12) GOSUB 1020 'left
60 ON KEY (13) GOSUB 1030 'right
70 ON KEY (14) GOSUB 1020 'down
80 CLS:LOCATE ,,1 'Cursor on
100 GOTO 100 'Wait for cursor key
1010 PRINT CHR$(30);:RETURN 'up
1020 PRINT CHR$(29);:RETURN 'left
1030 PRINT CHR$(28);:RETURN 'right
1040 PRINT CHR$(31);:RETURN 'down
Ok
```

CONTROLLING INPUT

The INPUT statement leaves the display screen vulnerable to attack. Its helpful editing keys come in a package with a bunch of troublesome ones. The ← key, **Esc** key, and the cursor control keys on the keypad are all capable of ruining the display, and the user will blame the program for that, not his own spirit of adventure. Fortunately PC BASIC has several features that give the program more control over the keyboard's effect on the display screen.

Disabling the INPUT Statement Carriage Return

In Disk BASIC and Advanced BASIC, you can put an extra semicolon in the INPUT statement, like this:

```
790 INPUT; "Serial no.";SN$
```

The extra semicolon suppresses the carriage return that otherwise occurs on the display screen when the user presses the ◄┘ key to end his entry. That is especially handy on line 24 or 25, where a carriage return makes the screen roll up one line, losing the contents of the top line.

The LINE INPUT Statement

The LINE INPUT statement assigns all characters input up to the first carriage return to a single string variable. Since it inputs only one value, it does not use commas to separate values, and that means commas can be freely used without having to enclose the whole entry in quotation marks. The LINE INPUT statement displays no question mark as an entry cue, but you may specify one as part of its optional prompting message. The following example will not generate a question mark:

```
790 LINE INPUT "Item description: " ;ITM$
```

The editing keys that work with the INPUT statement also work with the LINE INPUT statement. Its sole advantage for the program user is its attitude about commas in the input value.

The INPUT$ Function

For even more control over input, use the INPUT$ function. It inputs string values of a specified length. Here is an example:

```
310 K$ = INPUT$(1)
```

The value in parentheses specifies the number of characters to input. The PC waits until the program user enters as many characters as are called for. The ◄┘ key will not end entry early, but the **Ctrl│Scroll Lock** combination keystroke will still interrupt program execution.

INPUT$ does not turn the cursor on nor does it echo keystrokes on the display screen; it simply inputs the characters they generate. If you want the keyboard entry echoed on the screen, you can always display it with the PRINT statement. Before echoing it though, check for undesirable characters in the input string. The program can simply reject any characters that would adversely affect the display. The following short program shows one approach:

```
list
10 LOCATE ,,1 'Cursor on
20 K$ = INPUT$(1) 'Wait for 1 keystroke
40 IF ASC(K$)>31 THEN PRINT K$; 'Echo
50 GOTO 20 'Get another keystroke
Ok
```

The characters that cause trouble all have character code numbers less than 32. The simple program above avoids them by ignoring any keystroke that generates a code less than 32 (line 40).

You may have noticed that PC BASIC interprets some of character code numbers 0 through 32 and code 127 one way when it echoes keystrokes, and another way when it displays them with a PRINT or PRINT USING statement. In fact, only characters with codes 0, 8 through 13, or 28 through 31 cause trouble when displayed by PRINT or PRINT USING statements. Here is a modification of the previous example that ignores just the truly undesirable characters:

```
list
10 LOCATE ,,1 'Cursor on
20 K$ = INPUT$(1):K% = ASC(K$) 'Get 1 kystr
40 IF K%>31 OR (K%<28 AND K%>13) OR
   (K%<8 AND K%>0) THEN PRINT K$; ' Echo
50 GOTO 20 'Go get another character
Ok
```

The INKEY$ Function

The INKEY$ function reports which key was just pressed on the keyboard. It has a string value that may be null (length zero), one character, or two characters long. If the length is zero, the keyboard is inactive. A length of one means the string contains the character just typed. When the length is two, it means the last keystroke did not generate one of the 256 standard PC characters (more about that shortly).

The INKEY$ function does not wait for a key to be pressed, nor does it turn the cursor on, nor does it echo keystrokes on the screen. It merely reports if a keystroke occurred. Program execution continues immediately with the next statement. If you want the program to stop and wait for a keystroke, you must re-execute the INKEY$ function until that happens. Here is an example:

```
list
10 LOCATE ,,1 'Cursor on
20 K$ = INKEY$:IF LEN(K$)=0 THEN 20
   ELSE K% = ASC(K$) 'Wait for a keystroke
30 IF K%=13 THEN END <-' key ends
40 IF K%>31 OR (K%<28 AND K%>13) OR
   (K%<8 AND K%>0) THEN PRINT K$; ' Echo
50 GOTO 20 'Go get another character
Ok
```

The program above loops indefinitely until a key is pressed (line 20). If the ←key was pressed, the program ends (line 30). Otherwise it uses a

PRINT statement to echo acceptable keystrokes (line 40). Notice that the IF-THEN statement does not directly check the keyboard with an INKEY$ function. Instead, it assigns the current value of INKEY$ to a variable, thereby capturing the keyboard status at one instant. If the program used separate INKEY$ functions in the IF-THEN and PRINT statements, each would sample the keyboard at different instants, and the two instances of the INKEY$ function would almost certainly come up with different results.

Not all keystrokes generate a standard PC character. The INKEY$ function can identify 97 that do not. They include the cursor control keys on the keypad (**Home**, **←**, **End**, and so forth) and function keys that have a null (zero-length) Soft Key definition.

When one of the 97 keystrokes occurs, INKEY$ returns a two-character string value, which IBM calls an *extended code*. The first character always has a character code number of 0. The character code number of the second character determines which of the 97 keystrokes was typed. Appendix D lists all 97 extended codes and the keystrokes that generate them.

A program can use any of the 97 nonstandard characters to initiate a command or trigger some special action. If the length of the INKEY$ value is two, the program can test the second character to see what course of action to follow. The following example uses the cursor control keys to move the cursor left, right, up, and down:

```
List
10 LOCATE ,,1 'Cursor on
20 K$=INKEY$:IF LEN(K$)=0 THEN 20
   ELSE K%=ASC(K$) 'Wait for a keystroke
30 IF K%=13 THEN END ' <−' key ends
40 IF K%>31 OR (K%<28 AND K%>13) OR
   (K%<8 AND K%>0) THEN PRINT K$; ' Echo
50 IF LEN(K$)<2 THEN 20 ELSE K$=
   ASC(RIGHT$(K$,1)) ' Check for extended code
60 IF K%=72 THEN PRINT CHR$(30); 'up
61 IF K%=75 THEN PRINT CHR$(29); 'left
62 IF K%=77 THEN PRINT CHR$(28); 'right
63 IF K%=80 THEN PRINT CHR$(31); 'down
70 GOTO 10 ' Go get another keystroke
Ok
```

The program above is exactly the same as the previous example, except this one also checks for extended codes 72, 75, 77, and 80 (lines 50 through 63). Appendix D says they are the codes that INKEY$ returns when the cursor control keys are pressed. If the program detects one of those keys, it uses a PRINT statement with the CHR$ function to display the character that moves the cursor in the right direction (lines 60 through 63). Once again, Appendix D provides the code numbers for those characters.

DELINEATING ENTRIES

None of the statements or functions that do keyboard input tell the program user much about the number of characters allowed or whether the entry must be numeric or can include any character. That information would make the user's job much easier, and the program can supply it by displaying an entry template just before it requests keyboard entry. The entry template is no more than a string of asterisks or some such. The following example illustrates this.

```
list
10 CLS
190 '--Display template
200 LOCATE 12,20,1:PRINT STRING$(10,"*");
210 LOCATE 12,20,1 'Set cursor for entry
230 K$=INKEY$:IF LEN(K$)=0 THEN 230
    ELSE K%=ASC(K$) ' Wait for a keystroke
240 IF K%=13 THEN 1500 ' <─' key ends
265 'Echo keystroke and add to entry
270 IF K%>31 OR (K%<28 AND K%>13) OR
    (K%<8 AND K%>0) THEN PRINT K$;
    :NTRY$=NTRY$+K$
280 GOTO 230 ' Get another character
1500 PRINT:PRINT NTRY$:END
Ok
```

The example above is similar to previous examples but is more complex. It begins by clearing the screen and displaying the entry template at row 12, column 20 (lines 10 and 200). Then it repositions the cursor to the start of the entry area (line 210). After that, the program waits for a keystroke, and when one occurs, converts it to its character code number (line 230). It checks the character code number to see if the ◄─ was pressed (line 240) and ends by displaying the entered value if so. If not, the program echoes the keystroke and adds it to the entry value (line 270). However, it completely ignores any undesirable characters (line 270). Note that this example does not actually limit the number of characters a user may enter, but only suggests an appropriate size with the template.

A General Input Subroutine

The keyboard entry in the previous example still has some limitations. The user can still ruin the display by typing past the end of the entry zone, and he cannot use the ← key to correct mistakes. Also, the program only enters a string value. It could convert the entry to a numeric value and make sure the result is within prescribed limits. A few easy changes add those improvements, resulting in a general input subroutine (Fig. 11-4).

The subroutine uses several variables that it expects will have appropriate values when it is called. Variable INLEN% is the input length, INROW% and INCOL% specify the screen position where the input occurs, and INTMPL$ contains the entry template character. It returns the entered value in variable NTRY$, and variable NTRY# has the numeric equivalent.

The general input subroutine begins by displaying the template at the proper screen position (line 200) and repositioning the cursor to the start of the entry area (line 210). Then it clears anything left in variable NTRY$, which will return the keyboard entry (line 220). Next the subroutine waits for a keystroke, and when one occurs, converts it to its character code number (line 230). It checks to see if the ← was pressed (line 240). If so, it branches to check the numeric range of the entry. If not, it checks for the backspace key. If the ←key was not pressed, the subroutine checks for a full entry string (line 260), in which case it ignores all keystrokes except← and ←.

```
190 '==General input subroutine=============================
200 LOCATE INROW%,INCOL%,1:PRINT STRING$(INLEN%,INTMPL$); 'Display template
210 LOCATE INROW%,INCOL%,1 'Set cursor for entry
220 NTRY$="" ' Clear stale entry
230 K$=INKEY$:IF LEN(K$)=0 THEN 230 ELSE K%=ASC(K$) 'Wait for a keystroke
240 IF K%=13 THEN 300 ' <--' ends entry
250 IF K%=8 THEN 350 ' Backspace
260 IF LEN(NTRY$)=INLEN% THEN 230 'Entry full?
270 IF K%>31 OR (K%<28 AND K%>13) OR (K%<8 AND K%>0) THEN PRINT K$;
    :NTRY$=NTRY$+K$ 'Echo keystroke and add to entry
280 GOTO 230 ' Get another character
290 '--Done; check numeric range-------------
300 NTRY#=VAL(NTRY$) ' convert to numeric
310 IF NTRY#>INMAX# THEN 200 ' too big
320 IF NTRY#<INMIN# THEN 200 ' too small
330 RETURN
340 '--Backspace 1 character----------------
350 IF LEN(NTRY$)=0 THEN 230 ' Not if entry is empty
360 PRINT CHR$(29);LEFT$(INTMPL$,1);CHR$(29); 'Redisplay template
370 NTRY$=LEFT$(NTRY$,LEN(NTRY$)-1) ' Delete last character
380 GOTO 230 ' Get another character
```

Fig. 11-4.   The general input subroutine.

If the ◄─ was pressed, the subroutine branches to see if there is anything to backspace over (line 350). If not, it ignores the ◄─ key and goes back to wait for another keystroke.─Otherwise it moves the cursor one space left, replaces the character there with an cntry template character, and leaves the cursor at that position (line 360). Then it removes the backspaced character from the entry string (line 370) and goes to wait for the next keystroke (line 380).

The subroutine echoes any normal keystroke and adds it to the entry string (line 270). However, it ignores any undesirable characters (line 270).

The general input subroutine converts the entry to a numeric value after the user presses the ◄─┘ key (line 300). Then it checks the value to make sure it is within the range specified by the calling program (lines 310 and 320); variable INMAX# specifies the largest allowable entry and INMIN# specifies the smallest. If the entry is out of range, the subroutine rejects it by starting entry over again.

MULTIPLE ENTRIES

Programs that have many keyboard inputs are usually easier to write and use if their inputs are organized in some fashion. Rather than inputting values in a running stream, a program could display a form that identifies

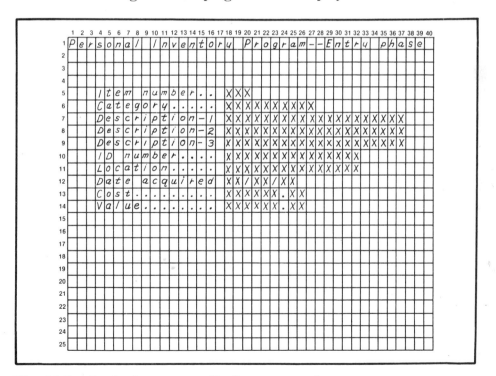

Fig. 11-5. Designing screen displays on graph paper.

several items to be entered and leaves a blank space for the user to fill in each value. That way the user can see what inputs are coming up and what he has entered so far. The general input subroutine (Fig. 11-4) affords enough control over keyboard entry to keep the form intact.

Graph paper is handy for designing entry forms for the screen (Fig. 11-5). Let each square on paper correspond to one character position on the screen. Write in the column numbers across the top of the paper and the row numbers down one side, for future reference. Write in the labels for each entry and mark off the space the entry itself will be allowed. Designing forms on paper first will save time in the long run; it's much faster to rearrange entry items or reword descriptive labels on paper than it is to constantly reprogram them.

Once you settle on a form design, you can easily write a program that displays it. The row and column numbers written on the paper design give you the row and column numbers to use with the LOCATE statements or TAB functions that position the cursor prior to displaying each label with a PRINT statement. After that, it's a simple matter to add more program statements that call the general input subroutine several times to enter all the items.

The program shown in Fig. 11-6 creates the form designed in Fig. 11-5 and enters values for it. It uses a CHAIN MERGE statement to incorporate the general input subroutine (line 10). The main program starts by setting up the display screen for keyboard input (line 1000) and displaying the entry form (lines 1300 through 1360). This program keeps the labels for the entry form in a DATA statement (line 7000), though many other schemes will work. After displaying the entry form, the program requests entry of every item (lines 1400 through 1420), using a subroutine (lines 4000 through 4800) to actually input each entry item. While this approach may seem excessively structured now, later examples will prove its worth. The program user must decide whether to fill in another form or end the program (lines 1900 through 1930). Notice how the program uses the TAB function to erase old messages and entries (lines 1900 and 1910) so that they do not confuse new messages or entries. When designing the display screen form, keep in mind there may be more than just inputs and their labels. You may have to display ancillary information or the result of some program calculation. It is usually a good idea to leave three or four lines vacant in case the program needs to input incidental information, display program status, or display a program title.

ENTRY ERRORS

Programs that do not anticipate user errors are simply being unrealistic. Errors will occur and your program must be ready to handle them.

```
200 CHAIN MERGE "11-4",1000 'Merge keyboard input subroutine
1000 CLS:KEY OFF:WIDTH 40
1290 '--Display entry form----------------------------------
1300 CLS
1310 PRINT "Personal Inventory Program--Entry phase"
1320 RESTORE 7000
1330 FOR ROW%=5 TO 14
1340 READ COL%,LABEL$
1350 LOCATE ROW%,COL%:PRINT LABEL$;STRING$(13-LEN(LABEL$),".")
1360 NEXT
1390 '--Enter all items in sequence----------------------
1400 FOR N%=1 TO 10
1410 GOSUB 4000
1420 NEXT
1800 REM Disk file output goes here (see Figure 16-2)
1890 '--Continue with entries?---------------------------
1900 LOCATE 2,1:PRINT "Enter another item? (Y/N)";TAB(40)
1910 LOCATE 3,1:PRINT TAB(40) 'Erase stale text
1920 INLEN%=1:INMAX#=0:INMIN#=0:INROW%=3:INCOL%=1:INTMPL$="*":GOSUB 200
1930 IF NTRY$=<>"N" AND NTRY$<>"n" THEN 1300
2090 '--End program---------------------------------------
2100 CLS
2110 PRINT "Personal Inventory Program--Ended";TAB(39);
2120 PRINT TAB(5);TIME$;TAB(15);DATE$
2130 END
3990 '==Input entry number N%============================
4000 LOCATE 2,1,0:PRINT "Type over the template.";TAB(40):PRINT
4010 PRINT "Press ";CHR$(17);CHR$(196);CHR$(217);" to end entry.";TAB(40)
4020 INMAX#=1D+20:INMIN#=-INMAX#:INROW%=N%+4:INCOL%=18:INTMPL$="*"
4050 ON N% GOTO 4100,4200,4300,4300,4300,4400,4500,4600,4700,4800
4090 '--Item number-----------------------------------
4100 INLEN%=3:GOSUB 200:ITMNR$=NTRY$
4110 '--Erase any unused template-------
4120 PRINT SPACE$(INLEN%-LEN(NTRY$));:RETURN
4190 '--Category---------------------------------------
4200 INLEN%=10:GOSUB 200:CTGRY$=NTRY$:GOTO 4120
4290 '--Description 1,2, & 3------------------------
4300 INLEN%=20:GOSUB 200:DSCR$(N%-2)=NTRY$:GOTO 4120
4390 '--ID number-----------------------------------
4400 INLEN%=15:GOSUB 200:IDNBR$=NTRY$:GOTO 4120
```

Fig. 11-6. Form entry program; uses the entry form designed in Fig. 11-5 and general input subroutine (Fig. 11-4).

```
4490 '--Location--------------------------------
4500 INLEN%=15:GOSUB 200:LCN$=NTRY$:GOTO 4120
4590 '--Date acquired------------------------------
4600 INLEN%=8:GOSUB 200:ACQRD$=NTRY$:GOTO 4120
4690 '--Cost-----------------------------------
4700 INMAX#=999999.99#:INMIN#=0:INLEN%=9:GOSUB 200:COST#=NTRY#
4710 '--Redisplay numeric entry---------
4720 LOCATE INROW%,INCOL%:PRINT USING "######.##";NTRY#;:RETURN
4790 '--Value----------------------------------
4800 INMAX#=999999.99#:INMIN#=0:INLEN%=9:GOSUB 200:VALU#=NTRY#:GOTO 4720
6980 '---locations and labels----------------------
6990 ' for entry form
7000 DATA 4,Item number,4,Category,4,Description-1,4,Description-2,4,
       Description-3,4,ID number,4,Location,4,Date acquired,4,Cost,4,Value
```

Fig. 11-6 —Cont.   Form entry program; uses the entry form designed in Fig. 11-5 and general input subroutine (Fig. 11-4).

There are two phases to error handling: recognition and notification. The general input subroutine (Fig. 11-4) illustrates how the INKEY$ function helps a program recognize entry errors, but it does little to advise the user an error has occurred. From the program user's perspective, its reaction to errors is confusing. For example, when the subroutine detects an unacceptable keystroke, it acts as though nothing at all happened. The user cannot tell whether the keystroke is not allowed or the keyboard is broken.

Announcing Entry Errors

One way to announce an error is with the PC's built-in speaker. The BEEP statement does that. All it takes to add it to the general input subroutine is an ELSE clause on line 270, like this:

```
270 IF K%>31 OR (K%<28 AND K%>13) OR
    (K%<8 AND K%>0) THEN PRINT K$;:
    NTRY$=NTRY$+K$ ELSE BEEP
```

Changed like this, the line still echoes a valid character and appends it to the entry string, but invalid entries make the speaker sound off as the keystroke is ignored.

A further refinement to the general input subroutine will tell the user if his entry is numerically too high or low. As it stands now, the subroutine gives no hint why it rejects an entry. The user just sees his entry vanish without a clue. Changing and adding a few lines will advise the user if his entry is too large or too small. Fig. 11-7 shows the new lines to use.

```
270 IF K%>31 OR (K%<28 AND K%>13) OR (K%<8 AND K%>0) THEN PRINT K$;
    :NTRY$=NTRY$+K$ ELSE BEEP 'If keystroke ok, echo it; otherwise ignore it
310 IF NTRY#>INMAX# THEN ERM$="smaller":GOTO 400 ' too big
320 IF NTRY#<INMIN# THEN ERM$="larger":GOTO 400 ' too small
390 '--Flash error message 3 times--------------
400 FOR X1%=1 TO 3
410 LOCATE INROW%,INCOL%,0:PRINT LEFT$(ERM$,INLEN%); 'Display message
420 BEEP
430 FOR X2%=1 TO 500:NEXT 'Pause
440 LOCATE INROW%,INCOL%,0:PRINT SPACE$(INLEN%); 'Erase message
450 FOR X2%=1 TO 500:NEXT 'Pause
460 NEXT X1%
470 GOTO 200 'Restart entry
```

Fig. 11-7. **Changes to the general input subroutine (Fig. 11-4) that announces entry errors.**

Here's how the changes in Fig. 11-7 work. If the entry is too large or too small, variable ERM$ is assigned the error message to be displayed (lines 310 and 320). Then a FOR/NEXT loop flashes the message three times over the top of the old entry (lines 400 through 460). First it displays as much of the message as will fit in the entry zone (line 410), then it sounds the speaker (line 420), and after that it uses a FOR/NEXT loop (line 430) to pause a couple of seconds before it erases the message (line 440) and pauses again briefly before repeating (line 450). After the third repetition, the general input subroutine is restarted from the beginning, forcing re-entry of the value (line 470).

Allowing Corrections After Entry

There are some errors the program cannot detect. These include misspellings, entering the wrong amounts, and other typographical errors that look like good entries to the program. Only the user can catch them, but the program can make it easy for him to do it.

It is a good idea to let the user review and correct his entries after he first finishes them all. If the program assigns every entry item a number, then the user can specify entry numbers he wants to change, one at a time. The program that enters data for the sample entry form does not do that (review Figs. 11-5 and 11-6).

Fig. 11-8 lists new lines to add to Fig. 11-6 in order to let the user change entries after his first pass through. The program must display entry num-

```
1590 '--Display item numbers------------------------------
1600 FOR X1%=1 TO 10
1610 LOCATE X1%+4,1:PRINT USING  "##)";X1%
1620 NEXT X1%
1630 '--Input number to change------------------------
1640 LOCATE 2,1:PRINT "Enter item no. to change (99 if none)";TAB(40)
1650 LOCATE 3,1:PRINT TAB(40)
1660 INLEN%=2:INMAX#=99:INMIN#=1:INROW%=3:INCOL%=1:INTMPL$="#":GOSUB 200
1670 IF NTRY#>10 THEN 1800
1680 N%=NTRY# :GOSUB 4000
1690 GOTO 1640
```

Fig. 11-8.   Additional lines for the form entry program (Fig. 11-7) to allow changing entry items by number.

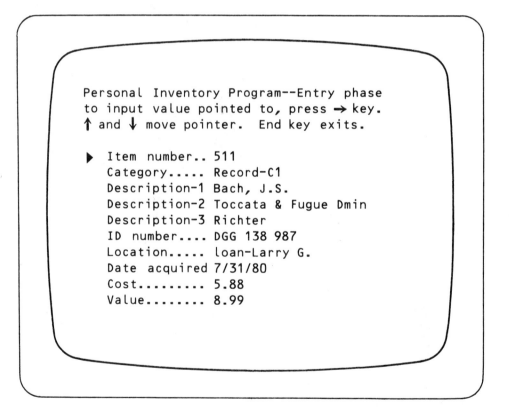

Fig. 11-9.   Using a pointer to indicate which entry item to change.

bers next to the form labels (lines 1600 through 1620) and input the entry number to be changed (lines 1640 through 1660). Then it can call the subroutine that inputs items (line 1680). The program stays in an endless loop

```
1590 '--Allow changes to entries--------------------------
1600 N%=1 'Start pointer at item 1
1610 LOCATE 2,1:PRINT "To input value pointed to, press ";CHR$(26);" key."
1620 PRINT CHR$(24);" and ";CHR$(25);" move pointer.  End key exits. "
1630 LOCATE N%+4,2,0:PRINT CHR$(16); 'Display pointer
1640 K$=INKEY$:IF LEN(K$)=0 THEN 1640 'Wait for keystroke
1650 PRINT CHR$(29);" "; 'Erase pointer
1660 '--Ignore meaningless keys
1670 IF LEN(K$)<>2 THEN BEEP:GOTO 1630 ELSE K%=ASC(RIGHT$(K$,1))
1680 IF K%=77 THEN GOSUB 4000:GOTO 1610 'right arrow
1690 IF K%=79 THEN 1800 'End key struck
1700 IF K%=72 AND N%>1 THEN N%=N%-1:GOTO 1630 'Up arrow
1710 IF K%=80 AND N%<10 THEN N%=N%+1:GOTO 1630  'Down arrow
1720 BEEP:GOTO 1630 'Meaningless key struck
```

Fig. 11-10. Additional lines for the form entry program (Fig. 11-6) to allow changing entry items with a pointer (use in lieu of Fig. 11-8).

pointer that the cursor movement keys can move from entry to entry (Fig. 11-9).

The programming that implements the moving pointer is shown in Fig. 11-10. It displays the pointer alongside the first entry (lines 1600 and 1630) and waits for a keystroke (line 1640). When any keystroke occurs, the program will erase the pointer (line 1650) and check for a significant key (lines 1670 through 1710). If the user pressed the → key, the program asks him to re-enter the item currently pointed to (line 1680). If he pressed the **End** key, the program stops allowing changes (line 1690). The ↑ or ↓ keys move the pointer up or down the list of entry items (lines 1700 and 1710). The program will ignore any other keystroke (lines 1670 and 1720). asking for changes until the user specifies an entry number of 99 to change (lines 1670 and 1690).

By making the user specify entry numbers, the program forces him to do work that it could do. Most people would find it easier to move from one entry to the next using the ↑ and ↓ keys. One approach uses a displayed

CHAPTER 12

DISK DATA FILES

When the amount of data a program handles gets large enough, it must be organized into files and stored outside the PC dynamic memory. Disks are the most efficient media for external data storage, and most PC systems have at least one disk drive. This chapter describes how a BASIC program can store and retrieve data on disk files and it assumes you understand the material presented in Chapter 3. The statements and functions described here apply only to Disk BASIC and Advanced BASIC.

DATA FILE STRUCTURE

Chapter 3 introduced the concept of disk files and likened them to the file drawers in a filing cabinet. Data file organization extends beyond that. Each file is further subdivided into one or more *records*, which are like the file folders in a file drawer. Each record usually contains several data values, just as file folders usually contain individual items. Each data value is called a *field*.

Typically, a file is organized so that every record has the same configuration. The number of fields, their sequence, and their lengths are all the same from one record to the next. The only things that vary are the values of the fields. Therefore two things define a file's layout: the configuration of its records and the number of records it has.

Thus a list of the fields in one record will adequately describe the structure of a file. Programmers often list the fields on a preprinted form and call the result a *file layout* (Fig. 12-1). The file layout usually shows the file name, states the number of records it has, and lists its fields in order. For

FILE LAYOUT

FILE NAME	RECORD SIZE	NO. OF RECORDS
ITEM, DAT	129	

DESCRIPTION *Personal inventory file — sequential*

VARIABLE	FIELD DESCRIPTION	MAX. SIZE	COMMENTS
ITMNR$	Item number	3	
CTGRY$	Category	10	
DSCR$(1)	Description—line 1	20	
DSCR$(2)	Description—line 2	20	
DSCR$(3)	Description—line 3	20	
IDNBR$	Identification number	15	
LCN$	Location	15	
ACQRD$	Date acquired	8	
COST#	Cost	9	
VALU#	Value	9	

Fig. 12-1.   File layout for a sample sequential-access personal inventory file.

each field, the layout shows the description, the length, and the variable name customarily used to hold its value in a BASIC program.

A single drive can only access a finite amount of data, so it's a good idea to calculate ahead of time whether enough space remains on a particular diskette for a new file you are planning. To calculate the disk space a file will require, add up the field lengths of one record and multiply the sum times the number of records in the file. Do that for every data file you plan to put on a disk and compare the total to the total disk capacity. (The PC DOS command CHKDSK, described in Chapter 3, reports disk capacity.) There must be enough room left over to accommodate the program files that you plan to put on the same disk.

Sometimes reducing the size of a field or two will make a too-large file fit. If not, you will have to divide it into several files and distribute the smaller files among several disks. You can split a file into several volumes, putting part of its records on one disk and part on another. Or you can split up each record, putting some of its fields into a file on one disk and other fields into a file on another disk.

Sequential and Random Access

PC BASIC offers two ways of locating a desired record. The simplest is called *sequential access*, because the program must always start at the beginning of a file and examine each record in turn, until it finds the one it wants. The alternative method lets the program access records by number, in any random order. It is called *random access*.

A file may be set up to use either sequential access or random access, but not both. Each method has its pros and cons. Sequential access is much simpler to program and tends to use less disk space, but it can be slow in finding a record near the end of a long file. Also, updating existing records is difficult with sequential-access files, and may be impossible. Random-access files require more programming and usually take more disk space, but they are very easy to update and all records can be found with equal speed.

Record length in a random-access file is constant, while in a sequential-access file it need not be. In a sequential-access file, the length of a record depends directly on the value of each field. Since field values are not the same in every record, record lengths will differ. Random-access record length is set when the file is created, and each field gets a fixed amount of space on the record. Values must fit in the space allocated. Long values are truncated and short values are padded with blank spaces. To minimize truncation, the size of each field is usually made large enough to accommodate its largest likely value.

Using Disk Data Files

To get at a particular field in a record, a program must first open the file, then locate the proper record, next transfer the record from disk to dynamic memory, and finally isolate the desired field as the value of a variable. Writing data to a file is similar, but this time the program transfers data values the other direction, from dynamic memory to the disk file.

To reduce the number of disk accesses, PC BASIC transfers data values to and from disk in blocks, not one value at a time. It sets aside part of dynamic memory for transfer areas, called *file buffers*. Each active file has its own file buffer.

Generally, PC BASIC manages the file buffers automatically, and you do not have to be concerned about them. But when a program finishes writing to a file, there will probably be some data left in the file buffer that PC BASIC has not written to the disk. Somehow the program must force PC BASIC to write out the final buffer contents. Closing a file will write out anything left over in the file buffer. At the same time, it updates the disk directory with changes to the file extents or other statistics kept there. Therefore, when a program finishes with a file, it must close the file or risk losing part of the file contents.

File Names and Numbers

Data files are identified on disk by a standard file name that conforms to the guidelines presented in Chapter 3 (review Fig. 3-6 and Table 3-1). Programs, though, refer to data files mainly by number. The OPEN statement correlates a file name with a file number. Here is an example:

```
1050 OPEN  "B:ITEM.DAT"  AS  #1
```

The file name can be specified by a string constant, variable, or expression. A drive designation prefix is required unless the file is on the default drive.

The file number can be specified by a numeric constant, variable, or expression. Normally, only file numbers 1, 2, and 3 are allowed. Each file number can identify just one file at a time, so a program can have at most three files open simultaneously. A way to raise that limit is described at the end of this chapter.

The file numbers described here and the device numbers described in Chapter 10 are one and the same. In fact, the term "file number" often means file or device number. A program can have fewer data files open while it uses PRINT# or PRINT# USING statements with the printer or display screen, because it must use one file/device number for each open device or file. If two devices are open (say the printer and display screen), the program can only have one data file open at the same time. However, the regular PRINT, PRINT USING, LPRINT, and LPRINT USING statements do not use file/device numbers, so a program can use those statements freely, even with all three file/device numbers assigned to data files.

The CLOSE statement frees a file/device number for re-use in a subsequent OPEN statement. Here is an example:

```
1100  OPEN  "LPT1:"  AS  #1
7510  CLOSE  #1
7520  OPEN  "A:TAXRATE.DAT"  AS  #1
```

A CLOSE statement that lists one number, like the one above (line 7510), closes just the specified file or device it is assigned to. To close more than one file with a single CLOSE statement, you can list several file numbers, separating them with commas, like this:

```
2140  CLOSE  #1,#3
```

A plain CLOSE statement that lists no file numbers will close all open files and devices. Several other BASIC statements do the same thing, including END, CHAIN (but not CHAIN MERGE), LOAD, NEW, RUN, and SYSTEM. However, most programmers prefer the positive, precise effect of a CLOSE statement with explicit file numbers listed.

SEQUENTIAL DISK FILES

A BASIC program can create a new sequential-access data file and store data values there, or it can add values to the end of an existing file. It can also retrieve values from an existing file. Data on a sequential-access file must be read or written in consecutive order. In order to retrieve a value from the middle of the file, a program must read past all the values that come before it. Values can only be written at the end of a sequential-access file. That means there is no way to read a value from a sequential-access file, change the value, and rewrite it in the same place on that file.

Sequential-access files use file buffers in a simple-minded way. Data sent to a sequential-access file accumulates in the file buffer. When the file buffer gets full, PC BASIC writes the whole thing at once onto the disk file, clearing the buffer for subsequent outgoing data. Going the other direction, program requests for data retrieval are filled from the file buffer, not directly from the disk surface. When the program has retrieved all the data in the buffer, PC BASIC replenishes it all at once from the disk file.

Opening and Closing Sequential-Access Files

In addition to assigning a file number to a named file, the OPEN statement determines the access mode that will be allowed with the file. For sequential-access files, a program may either write data starting at the beginning of a new file, write data starting at the end of an existing file, or read data. Table 12-1 lists the OPEN statement format that selects each access mode.

An OPEN statement with the FOR OUTPUT clause creates a new disk file with the specified file name. If a file already exists with that name, PC BASIC will automatically delete it and create a new file with the same name. An OPEN-FOR APPEND statement looks for an existing file to start at the end of, but if it finds none, it creates a new file with the specified name. An OPEN statement with the FOR INPUT clause must find the named data file or an error occurs.

It is possible to open a sequential-access file in append mode using one file number, and in input mode using another. But each file number uses a different file buffer, and there is no cross-communication between them. Therefore, in order to change access modes on a file, you need to close the file and reopen it. However, different files can be open simultaneously for unlike access modes.

Writing and Reading Sequential-Access Files

The PRINT# and PRINT# USING statements will write values to a disk file. INPUT# or INPUT# LINE statements will read the values back in and assign them to variables. Here is a simple example:

```
list
10 OPEN "SAMPLE.DAT" FOR OUTPUT AS #1
20 PRINT#1, 123 'Write value to disk file #1
30 CLOSE #1
40 OPEN "SAMPLE.DAT" FOR INPUT AS #1
50 INPUT#1, A 'Read value from disk file #1
60 PRINT "First value on file: ";A
70 CLOSE #1
Ok
run
First value on file: 123
Ok
```

Table 12-1. OPEN Statement Alternatives for Data Files

Access mode	Sample OPEN statement formats*
Write starting at the beginning of a new sequential-access file	1050 OPEN "B:ITEM.DAT" FOR OUTPUT AS #1
Write starting at the end of an existing sequential-access file	1835 OPEN "ADDRESS.DAT" FOR APPEND AS #3
Read starting at the beginning of an existing sequential-access file	2320 OPEN "A:ITEM.DAT" FOR INPUT AS #2
Write or read a random-access file	1040 OPEN "ITEM.DAT" AS #1 LEN=126

*The line numbers, file names, file numbers, and record length shown are all arbitrary and are for illustration only.

PRINT# statements format output in exactly the same manner no matter what the output device is. They always append an extra blank space to the end of each numeric value. Other than that, semicolons concatenate neighboring values and commas introduce extra blank spaces between them. The extra blank spaces needlessly use up disk space, so semicolons are preferable.

PRINT# USING statement template characters work the same with disk files as with the display screen or printer (review Table 10-1). Use caution with the monetary prefixes ($$, **, and **$), because they put numeric values into nonnumeric formats. Numeric values prefixed with $ or * characters on a disk file cannot be read back in as numeric values. The following example illustrates:

```
list
10 OPEN "SAMPLE.DAT" FOR OUTPUT AS #2
20 PRINT#2, USING "$$###.##";99.50
30 CLOSE #2
40 OPEN "SAMPLE.DAT" FOR INPUT AS #2
50 INPUT#2, A
60 PRINT "First value on file: ";A
70 CLOSE #2
Ok
run
First value on file: 0
Ok
```

In the program above, the PRINT# USING statement (line 20) sends the characters " $99.50" (the quotation marks are not sent) to file SAMPLE.DAT. The INPUT# statement tries to read them as a numeric value, but the $ character makes the value nonnumeric, so its numeric value is zero.

The absence of a terminal semicolon in a PRINT# or PRINT# USING statement yields a carriage return character after the last value. A terminal semicolon suppresses the carriage return character.

Separating Values on Sequential-Access Files

In order for the INPUT# statement to read values correctly from a disk file, the values must be separated from each other on the file. That means the PRINT# and PRINT# USING statements that write values to disk files must also write a character between each value to separate it from its neighbor. Without such a delimiting character, the INPUT# statement runs neighboring values together. The following example demonstrates what can happen:

```
list
10 OPEN "TEST.DAT" FOR OUTPUT AS #3
20 PRINT#3, "Silicon";14;28.0855
30 CLOSE #3
40 OPEN "TEST.DAT" FOR INPUT AS #3
50 FOR K%=1 TO 3:INPUT#3, A$
60 PRINT "Value no.";K%;":";A$
70 NEXT K%:CLOSE #3
Ok
run
Value no. 1 : Silicon 14 28.0855
Input past end in 50
Ok
```

The PRINT# statement (line 20) writes three values, but the semicolons that separate them cause them to be run together on the file. When the INPUT# statement tries to read them (line 50), they all come back combined into one value. There is no second or third value on the file, so an error occurs when the program tries to read past the last value on file.

For string values, the delimiting character can be a comma or a carriage return. Those same characters or blank spaces will delimit numeric values. There are any number of ways to make sure a delimiting character occurs between values. One of the simplest is to assign a comma to a string variable and write that variable between every value in a PRINT# statement, like this:

```
5  D$=","
20 PRINT#3, "Silicon";D$;14;D$;28.0855
```

The INPUT# statement interprets every comma it encounters as the end of a value. The only exception is a comma that is enclosed in quotation marks on the file itself. In other words, quotation marks must be written to the disk file around any string value that might contain a comma. The INPUT# statement will eliminate the quotation marks from the value. Here is an example:

```
list
10 OPEN "TEST.DAT" FOR OUTPUT AS #1
20 PRINT#1, CHR$(34);"Managua, Nicaragua";
   CHR$(34)
30 CLOSE #1
40 OPEN "TEST.DAT" FOR INPUT AS #1
50 INPUT#1, A$
60 PRINT "First value on file: ";A$
```

```
70 CLOSE #1
Ok
run
First value on file: Managua, Nicaragua
Ok
```

Ignoring Disk Field Delimiters

A related problem arises with a PRINT# USING statement that has a comma included in a numeric template. A single numeric value written with such a template ends up being several values on the disk file. Here is an example:

```
list
10 OPEN "SAMPLE.DAT" FOR OUTPUT AS #2
20 PRINT#2, USING "#,##########";
   123456789
30 CLOSE #2
40 OPEN "SAMPLE.DAT" FOR INPUT AS #2
50 INPUT#2, A
60 PRINT "First value on file: ";A
70 CLOSE #2
Ok
run
First value on file: 123
Ok
```

The LINE INPUT # statement, which reads a single string value, side-steps the comma problem by only recognizing carriage returns as value separators. Commas are just another string character. Here is an example:

```
list
10 OPEN "SAMPLE.DAT" FOR OUTPUT AS #3
20 PRINT#3, "Stine, Frank N."
30 CLOSE #3
40 OPEN "SAMPLE.DAT" FOR INPUT AS #1
50 LINE INPUT#1, A$
60 PRINT "First value on file: ";A$
70 CLOSE #1
Ok
run
First value on file: Stine, Frank N.
Ok
```

Recognizing the End of the File

An INPUT# or INPUT# LINE statement that tries to read past the end of a sequential-access file causes an error. To avoid that error, the program must somehow recognize when it has read the last value from the file and stop reading at that point. An EOF function in a WHILE or IF-THEN statement provides the easiest way to do that. Here is an example:

```
1850 IF NOT EOF(1) THEN 1700 ELSE CLOSE #2
```

The numeric value in parentheses specifies the file number. The EOF function returns a value of false (numeric 0) as long as there are more values left, but it returns a value of true (numeric -1) after the last value has been read.

USING SEQUENTIAL-ACCESS DATA FILES

Sequential access will work for most data files, though it is certainly less convenient than random access for files that must be updated periodically. But it is adequate for files with static contents, or for files which only have new records added to them from time to time. For example, a simple program that keeps track of major personal possessions is unlikely to change frequently. Fig. 12-1 presents a layout for such a file, and Fig. 12-2 lists a program that stores personal inventory records on a sequential-access disk file. Fig. 12-3 lists a program that reads back the records created by the program in Fig. 12-2 and displays them one at a time on the screen.

Personal Inventory File Creation Program Analysis

The personal inventory creation program (Fig. 12-2) begins by asking the user whether he wishes to add records to the existing file, or start a new file (lines 1030 and 1040). Depending on the user's response, the program opens file ITEM.DAT using the FOR OUTPUT or FOR APPEND access mode (line 1050). Variable D$ contains a comma for delimiting values written to the disk file (line 1060). The program uses two PRINT# statements to write each record on the sequential-access disk file (lines 1800 and 1810). After the user finishes entering items, he has a choice of reviewing the whole file or ending the program altogether (lines 2000-2040).

To keep the program simple, the keyboard entry phase is crude (lines 1400 through 1520), but the program listed in Fig. 11-6 can easily be adapted to do the job more elegantly. To combine Fig. 11-6 and Fig. 12-2, delete lines 1390 through 1520, 1900 through 1940, and 2090 through 2130 from Fig. 12-2 and merge the result with Fig. 11-6. The program will still contain two INPUT statements (lines 1040 and 2030). You may wish to replace them with calls to the general input subroutine, like line 1920 of Fig. 11-6.

```
 990 '--Open file----------------------------------------
1000 CLS:KEY OFF:WIDTH 40
1020 PRINT "Personal Inventory Program--Entry phase"
1030 PRINT "Erase existing file? (Y/N)"
1040 INPUT;"",NTRY$
1050 IF NTRY$="Y" OR NTRY$="y" THEN OPEN "ITEM.DAT" FOR OUTPUT
     AS #1 ELSE OPEN "ITEM.DAT" FOR APPEND AS #1
1060 D$="," 'Delimiting comma for file output
1390 '--Enter all items in sequence-----------------------
1400 CLS
1410 PRINT "Personal Inventory Program--Entry Phase"
1420 LOCATE 5,1
1430 INPUT "Item number";ITMNR$
1440 INPUT "Category";CTGRY$
1450 INPUT "Description-1";DSCR$(1)
1460 INPUT "Description-2";DSCR$(2)
1470 INPUT "Description-3";DSCR$(3)
1480 INPUT "ID number";IDNBR$
1490 INPUT "Location";LCN$
1500 INPUT "Date acquired";ACQRD$
1510 INPUT "Cost";COST#
1520 INPUT "Value";VALU#
1790 '--Output one record to data file--------------------
1800 PRINT#1,ITMNR$;D$;CTGRY$;D$;DSCR$(1);D$;DSCR$(2);D$;DSCR$(3);D$;
1810 PRINT#1,IDNBR$;D$;LCN$;D$;ACQRD$;D$;COST#;D$;VALU#
1890 '--Continue with entries?----------------------------
1900 LOCATE 2,1
1910 PRINT "Enter another item? (Y/N)"
1920 INPUT;"",NTRY$
1930 IF NTRY$<>"N" OR NTRY$<>"n" THEN 1400
1940 CLOSE #1 'no more entries this time
1990 '--Review file contents?----------------------------
2000 CLS
2010 PRINT "Personal Inventory Program-Review Phase"
2020 PRINT "Review file contents? (Y/N)"
2030 INPUT;"",NTRY$
2040 IF NTRY$="y" OR NTRY$="Y" THEN CHAIN"12-3",1000,DELETE 1000-7000
2090 '--End of program------------------------------------
2100 CLS
2110 PRINT "Personal Inventory Program--Ended";TAB(39);
2120 PRINT TAB(5);TIME$;TAB(15);DATE$
2130 END
7000 REM End of CHAIN-DELETE range (see line 2040)
```

Fig. 12-2. Personal inventory creation program—sequential-access output (can be combined with Fig. 11-6; see text for details).

```
1000 CLS:KEY OFF:WIDTH 40
1010 PRINT "Personal Inventory Program-Review phase"
1030 OPEN "ITEM.DAT" FOR INPUT AS #1
1190 '--Input next record from file---------------------
1200 WHILE NOT EOF(1)
1210 INPUT#1,ITMNR$,CTGRY$,DSCR$(1),DSCR$(2),DSCR$(3)
1220 INPUT#1,IDNBR$,LCN$,ACQRD$,COST#,VALU#
1290 '--Display review form-------------------------------
1300 CLS
1310 PRINT "Personal Inventory Program-Review phase"
1320 RESTORE 7000
1330 FOR ROW%=5 TO 14
1340 READ COL%,LABEL$
1350 LOCATE ROW%,COL%:PRINT LABEL$;STRING$(13-LEN(LABEL$),".")
1360 NEXT
1390 '--Display all values-------------------------------
1400 LOCATE 5,18:PRINT ITMNR$
1410 LOCATE 6,18:PRINT CTGRY$
1420 LOCATE 7,18:PRINT DSCR$(1)
1430 LOCATE 8,18:PRINT DSCR$(2)
1440 LOCATE 9,18:PRINT DSCR$(3)
1450 LOCATE 10,18:PRINT IDNBR$
1460 LOCATE 11,18:PRINT LCN$
1470 LOCATE 12,18:PRINT ACQRD$
1480 LOCATE 13,18:PRINT USING "######.##";COST#
1490 LOCATE 14,18:PRINT USING "######.##";VALU#
1890 '--Continue with entries or end program?------------
1900 LOCATE 2,1:PRINT "Review another item? (Y/N)";TAB(40)
1910 LOCATE 3,1:PRINT TAB(40) 'Erase stale text
1920 LOCATE 3,1:INPUT;"",NTRY$
1930 IF NTRY$="N" OR NTRY$="n" THEN 2100
1940 WEND
2090 '--End of program------------------------------------
2100 CLS
2110 PRINT "Personal Inventory Program--Ended"
2120 PRINT TAB(5);TIME$;TAB(15);DATE$
2130 CLOSE #1
2140 END
6980 '---locations and labels-----------------------------
6990 '   for entry form
7000 DATA 4,Item number,4,Category,4,Description-1,4,Description-2,4,
     Description-3,4, ID number,4,Location,4,Date acquired,4,Cost,4,Value
```

Fig. 12-3. Personal inventory review program—sequential-access input.

Personal Inventory File Review Program Analysis

The personal inventory file review program (Fig. 12-3) displays one record at a time on a display screen form like the one designed in Chapter 11 (review Fig. 11-5). The program starts by opening file ITEM.DAT for input (line 1030). Then until it finds the end of the file (line 1200), it reads the values in the next record (lines 1210 and 1220). It displays the screen form (lines 1300-1360) and the values it just read (lines 1400-1490). After that, the program asks whether it should continue with the next item (lines 1900-1930). If so, it continues reading records; if not, it ends.

RANDOM-ACCESS FILES

PC BASIC has a special set of statements designed to read and write random-access files. The only familiar statements are OPEN and CLOSE. There are new statements to use instead of PRINT# for output and INPUT# for input. Another new statement declares which variables will identify field values, and there are even special statements and functions for assigning those variables new values.

Random-access files use file buffers to minimize the number of disk accesses. A file buffer is always large enough to hold one record, sometimes more. When a program wants a certain record, PC BASIC first looks to see if that record is in the file buffer. If so, no disk access is necessary. If not, it transfers the contents of the buffer back to its proper spot on the disk and then transfers the desired record into the file buffer.

Opening Random-Access Files

Opening a file for random access assigns it a file number and establishes the length of each record on the file. All records in a single file must have the same length. Here is an example:

```
1010 OPEN "ITEM.DAT" AS #1 LEN=128
```

The absence of a clause between the file name and the AS specification in an OPEN statement means the file will be opened for random-access mode, which allows both reading and writing. Such an OPEN statement must include a LEN clause, which specifies the record length.

All records in a random-access file have the same fixed length. It is important to specify the record length correctly in order to avoid garbling the file contents. Normally, the maximum record length is 128 bytes, but there is a way to increase that, as explained at the end of this chapter.

To compute the length of a record, add up the lengths of the fields in it. Allow two characters for an integer field, four characters for a single-precision field, and eight characters for a double-precision field. For a string field, use the maximum number of characters you plan to allow its value to have. Write these numbers on the file layout you prepare (Fig. 12-4).

FILE LAYOUT

FILE NAME	RECORD SIZE	NO. OF RECORDS
ITEM. DAT	126	10

DESCRIPTION *Personal inventory file — random access*

VARIABLE	FIELD DESCRIPTION	MAX. SIZE	COMMENTS
ITMNR$	Item number	2	ITMNR%
CTGRY$	Category	10	
DSCR$(1)	Description-line 1	20	
DSCR$(2)	Description-line 2	20	
DSCR$(3)	Description-line 3	20	
IDNBR$	Identification number	15	
LCN$	Location	15	
AC2RD$	Date acquired	8	
COST$	Cost	8	COST#
VALU$	Value	8	VALU#

Fig. 12-4.   File layout for a sample random-access personal inventory file.

$A = 20$

Declaring Record Structure

After opening a random-access file, a program must declare the structure of the file's records. The FIELD statement does that. Here is an example:

```
1020 FIELD #2, 3 AS I$, 10 AS C$, 10 AS
     D$(1)
```

The FIELD statement identifies the file it pertains to by number, as usual. Then it lists the fields in the order that they appear on the file. For each field, it states the length and names a variable that the program will use to identify the field. All fields for a single file must be listed in one FIELD statement, separated by commas.

The total length of all fields declared by a FIELD statement must not exceed the record length established by the corresponding OPEN statement. If it does, an error occurs.

All values are transferred to and from a random-access file via the variables listed in a FIELD statement. All variables listed in a FIELD statement must be string variables. The FIELD statement effectively defines fixed lengths for each of the variables listed in it. Numeric values have to be converted to string values using special functions, a process which will be described shortly.

Using FIELD Statement Variables

Two special statements, LSET and RSET, are used to assign values to the variables defined in the FIELD statement. Here are examples:

```
5340 RSET DAT$=NTRY$
5550 LSET LCN$=BLDG$+ROOM$
```

Never use a variable listed in a FIELD statement in an INPUT statement of any kind. Never assign such a variable a value in a LET statement (with or without the command word LET present). Breaking either rule cancels the association that the FIELD statement established, so that the program can no longer use the variable to transfer a value to and from random-access file records.

The LSET and RSET statements guarantee that the variable's length will exactly match its FIELD statement definition. If the value assigned is too short, it is padded with blank spaces. The LSET statement aligns the value on the left, padding with extra blanks on the right, and the RSET statement does the opposite. If the value assigned is too long, both LSET and RSET drop characters from the right. The following example uses the RSET statement to illustrate.

```
list
10 OPEN "SAMPLE.DAT" AS #1 LEN=20
```

```
20 FIELD #1, 10 AS A$
30 RSET A$="DISK"
40 PRINT A$
run
        DISK
Ok
```

Numeric Values on Disk Files

In order to store numeric values on a random-access file, they need to be converted to numeric strings. PC BASIC has three functions ideally suited to the job.

The MKI$, MKS$, and MKD$ functions make numeric values into integer, single-precision, and double-precision string values respectively. MKI$ always returns a two-character string, MKS$ a four-character string, and MKD$ an eight-character string. For large values, they achieve a considerable savings in string length over any other conversion functions.

The MKI$, MKS$, and MKD$ functions do not convert numeric values to their ASCII character equivalents, as the other conversion functions do. Instead, they pack the values into two, four, or eight characters using the same scheme the PC uses to represent numeric values in dynamic memory. Therefore, you cannot print or display the results of an MKI$, MKS$, or MKD$ function with a PRINT statement.

The converted numeric values must still be assigned to file variables using the LSET or RSET statements, like this:

```
4700 LSET COST$=MKD$(NTRY#)
```

Numeric string values generated by the MKI$, MKS$, and MKD$ functions can be converted back to numeric values by the CVI, CVS, and CVD functions, respectively.

Writing to Random-Access Files

When a program is ready to write an entire record out to a random-access file, it must use a PUT# statement. Here is an example:

```
1550 PUT #1,ITMNR%
```

The first value in a PUT# statement specifies the file number and the second value specifies the record number. The record number is optional; if it is omitted, PC BASIC uses a record number one higher than the last record number used with the same file number.

Reading From a Random-Access File

The GET# statement reads an entire random-access record. After that, the program can use the variables named in the FIELD statement to get at the field values. Here is an example:

```
4020 GET#1, ITMNR%
```

The first value in a GET# statement is the file number and the second value is the record number. If the record number is absent, PC BASIC uses a record number one higher than the last record number used with the same file number.

End of File

Programs can read or write past the nominal end of a random-access file without a direct error. If a GET# statement specifies a record higher than any ever written by a PUT# statement to that file, PC BASIC assigns each character of every field variable a character code number of 0. (The CVI, CVS, and CVD functions all convert that to a numeric 0.) A PUT# statement that specifies a record number higher than any on the file increases the file size enough to accommodate the specified record. Any unused records between it and the former highest record will contain garbage. A GET# statement that retrieves one of those intermediate records will get garbage, which may cause errors elsewhere in the program. Therefore, programs should take steps to restrict the record numbers that will be accessed.

A random-access file has no length restrictions except the amount of disk space remaining. The LOF function tells you how much space the file is taking, to the nearest 128 bytes.

The LOC function identifies the current record number, that is, the record number last used in a GET# or PUT# statement to the specified file. Here is an example:

```
1650 IF LOC(1)=150 THEN CLOSE:END
```

The value in parentheses specifies the file number.

TRAPPING ERRORS

Using disk data files makes a program vulnerable to several errors that will stop it prematurely. For example, when a diskette fills up, the message "Disk full . . ." appears, files are closed automatically, and the program stops. Or suppose someone mistakenly puts a write-protect label on a diskette that the program needs to write on. In that case, the message "Disk Write Protected . . ." appears and the program stops.

A BASIC program can take control of more than 70 errors (not all of them disk-related, to be sure) that would otherwise disrupt program execution. The ON ERROR GOTO statement makes that possible. It stipulates a line number to which PC BASIC will branch should it detect an error later. Here is an example:

```
ON ERROR GOTO 30000
```

Most programmers place a statement like the one above in the first part of a program and put a special routine at the specified line number to handle the errors that occur. The action taken by the error-handling routine depends on the nature of the error. For a disk write-protect error, it might give the program user a choice of ending the program or fixing the problem and retrying the operation.

The error-handling routine can test the value of function ERR to determine what kind of error occurred. Errors are classified by number, and Appendix C has a list of error numbers and interpretations. Sometimes the error number alone is not enough. For example, a program that opens more than one file risks a separate write-protect error at each OPEN statement, and it may need to handle each one differently. The ERL function divulges the line number where the last error occurred, so a program can use it to differentiate between errors that have the same code.

The error-handling routine must conclude with a RESUME statement. If the program executes a STOP, END, or RETURN statement first, an error occurs. The RESUME statement has three forms. The simplest is the solitary command word, and it terminates the error-handling routine by branching back to the very statement that caused the error. Another option is the RESUME NEXT statement, which branches back to the statement after the one that caused the error. The third alternative lets you specify a line number to branch to, like this:

```
RESUME 30100
```

You certainly will not want to write an error-handling routine that attends individually to each of the more than 70 error codes. Fortunately, PC BASIC will take over error recovery if the program executes an ON ERROR GOTO 0 statement during the error-handling routine. In that case, program execution halts and the standard message appears for the error that occurred.

PC BASIC can only cope with one error at a time. If an ON ERROR GOTO statement sends a program into an error-handling routine in which a second error occurs, the second error will not be trapped, but will cause an error message to appear and the program to halt.

USING RANDOM-ACCESS DATA FILES

The two personal inventory programs described earlier in this chapter can be improved by using a random-access file. That allows immediate updating of volatile information like location and value. The file layout in Fig.

12-4 describes the file structure, and the program listed in Fig. 12-5 will create new records, review existing records, and allow changes to be made to existing records.

Improved Personal Inventory Program Analysis

The improved personal inventory program (Fig. 12-5) requires the general input subroutine (Fig. 11-4). It uses CHAIN MERGE statements to merge it, along with the improvements to it (Fig. 11-7), into the program (lines 10 and 20).

The main program starts by setting up the display screen (lines 1000 and 1010) and assigning a couple of variables (lines 1020 and 1030). Variable FILSIZ% sets the maximum number of records in file ITEM.DAT. Variable RETKEY$ contains the characters needed to display a facsimile of the symbol printed atop the ← key.

Next the program opens file ITEM.DAT, the inventory file, for random access and defines the field variables (lines 1040 and 1050). If the file is empty, the program initializes every record by setting the item number to −1 (lines 1060 through 1140). If the disk should become full in the process, that error is trapped (line 1090). An error handling routine (lines 900 through 960) reopens the file and bypasses further initialization. After all records have been initialized, the program pauses to let the user read the highest usable item number off the screen (lines 1160 through 1180).

When the inventory file is ready, the program asks the user for the first item number (lines 1200 through 1240) and retrieves the corresponding inventory record (lines 1260 and 1280). If the user makes no entry other than pressing the ← key, the program automatically retrieves the next record (lines 1270 and 1280). If the user enters the word "END" or "end," the program ends (line 1250).

If the record has never been used before, it will have an item number of −1 (thanks to the initialization of new files on lines 1060 through 1140). In that case, the program has the user enter all values before asking for changes (lines 1400 through 1440). Otherwise, it displays the values read from the disk file (lines 1460 through 1550).

With the record's current values on display, the program lets the user change any one except the item number (lines 1610 through 1720). Item number changes are prohibited to protect the integrity of the file. The user selects the entry to change with the cursor control keys, a technique developed in Chapter 11 (review Figs. 11-9 and 11-10). When the user finishes making changes, the program writes the record (line 1800) and branches back to get another item number.

Notice that the program never uses the field variables with INPUT statements, nor does it assign any of them values with LET statements.

```
10 CHAIN MERGE "11-4",20 'Merge general input subroutine
20 CHAIN MERGE "11-7",1000 'and improvements to it
890 '--Error handling routine-------------------
900 IF ERR=61 AND ERL=1120 THEN 950
910 ON ERROR GOTO 0 'Handle misc. errors
920 STOP: GOTO 910
940 ' Disk full; reopen file
950 OPEN "ITEM.DAT" AS #1 LEN=126
960 FILSIZ%=FIX(LOF(1)/126)
970 PUT #1,FILSIZ%
980 RESUME 1140
990 '++Start of main program+ + + + + + + + + + + + + + + + +
1000 CLS:KEY OFF:WIDTH 40
1010 PRINT "Personal Inventory Program--File changes"
1020 FILSIZ%=10 'Set max. no. or records for new file
1030 RETKEY$=CHR$(17)+CHR$(196)+CHR$(217) 'Facsimile of <--' key
1040 OPEN "ITEM.DAT" AS #1 LEN=126
1050 FIELD #1, 2 AS ITMNR$, 10 AS CTGRY$, 20 AS DSCR$(1), 20 AS
     DSCR$(2), 20 AS DSCR$(3), 15 AS IDNBR$, 15 AS LCN$, 8 AS ACQRD$,
     8 AS COST$, 8 AS VALU$
1060 IF LOF(1)>0 THEN 1200
1070 '--Initialize empty file----------------------------
1080 PRINT "Please stand by for file initialization"
1090 ON ERROR GOTO 900 'Trap full disk error
1100 LSET ITMNR$=MKI$(-1) 'Initialize all records to item no. -1
1110 WHILE LOC(1)<FILSIZ%
1120 PUT #1
1130 LOCATE 5,10:PRINT "Item";LOC(1);"initialized";
1140 WEND
1150 '--Wait for user to read screen----------------------
1160 LOCATE 7,1:PRINT "That is the highest usable item number"
1170 LOCATE 9,6,1:PRINT "Press space bar to continue";
1180 K$=INKEY$:IF K$<>" " THEN 1180
1190 '--Input number of record to change or enter-------
1200 CLS
1210 PRINT "Personal Inventory Program--File changes"
1220 LOCATE 2,1:PRINT "Enter item number (Type END to quit)."
1230 LOCATE 3,4:PRINT "  (Press ";RETKEY$;" alone for next item.)"
1240 INLEN%=3:INMAX#=FILSIZ%:INMIN#=0:INROW%=3:INCOL%=1: INTMPL$=
     "*":GOSUB 200
1250 IF NTRY$="end" OR NTRY$="END" THEN 2100 'End program
```

Fig. 12-5.   Personal inventory program—random access.

```
1260 IF NTRY#>0 THEN ITMNR%=NTRY#:GOTO 1280
1270 IF NTRY#=0 AND LOC(1)<FILSIZ% THEN ITMNR%=LOC(1)+1 ELSE BEEP:
     GOTO 1240
1280 GET #1,ITMNR% 'Retrieve requested record
1290 '--Display entry form--------------------------------
1300 RESTORE 7000
1310 FOR ROW%=5 TO 14
1320 READ COL%,LABEL$
1330 LOCATE ROW%,COL%:PRINT LABEL$;STRING$(13-LEN(LABEL$),".")
1340 NEXT
1370 '--Enter values (new records) or display values (existing records)---
1380 IF CVI(ITMNR$)>0 THEN  1460 'Is record not blank?
1390 '--Enter all values in  sequence---------------------
1400 LOCATE 5,22:PRINT ''(New item)''
1410 FOR N%=1 TO 10
1420 GOSUB 4000
1430 NEXT
1440 GOTO 1600 'Skip redisplaying values
1450 '--Display existing values--------------------------
1460 LOCATE 5,18:PRINT CVI(ITMNR$)
1470 LOCATE 6,18:PRINT CTGRY$
1480 LOCATE 7,18:PRINT DSCR$(1)
1490 LOCATE 8,18:PRINT DSCR$(2)
1500 LOCATE 9,18:PRINT DSCR$(3)
1510 LOCATE 10,18:PRINT IDNBR$
1520 LOCATE 11,18:PRINT LCN$
1530 LOCATE 12,18:PRINT ACQRD$
1540 LOCATE 13,18:PRINT USING  "######.## ";CVD(COST$)
1550 LOCATE 14,18:PRINT USING  "######.## ";CVD(VALU$)
1590 '--Allow changes to entries--------------------------
1600 N%=2 'Start pointer at item 2
1610 LOCATE 2,1:PRINT "To input entry pointed to, press ";CHR$(26);" key."
1620 PRINT CHR$(24);" and ";CHR$(25);" move pointer. End key exits."
1630 LOCATE N%+4,2,0:PRINT CHR$(16); 'Display pointer
1640 K$=INKEY$:IF LEN(K$)=0 THEN 1640 'Wait for keystroke
1650 PRINT CHR$(29);" "; 'Erase pointer
1660 '--Ignore meaningless keys
1670 IF LEN(K$)<>2 THEN BEEP:GOTO 1630 ELSE K%=ASC(RIGHT$(K$,1))
1680 IF K%=77 THEN GOSUB 4000:GOTO 1610 'right arrow
1690 IF K%=79 THEN 1800 'End key struck
1700 IF K%=72 AND N%>2 THEN N%=N%-1:GOTO 1630 'Up arrow
```

Fig. 12-5—Cont.   Personal inventory program—random access.

```
1710 IF K%=80 AND N%<10 THEN N%=N%+1:GOTO 1630  'Down arrow
1720 BEEP:GOTO 1630 'Meaningless key struck
1790 '--Output one record to data file--------------------
1800 PUT#1,ITMNR%
1810 GOTO 1200
2090 '--End program------------------------------------------
2100 CLS
2110 PRINT "Personal Inventory Program--Ended";TAB(39);
2120 PRINT TAB(5);TIME$;TAB(15);DATE$
2130 CLOSE #1
2140 END
3990 '==Input entry number N%============================
4000 LOCATE 2,1,0:PRINT "Type over the template.";TAB(40)
4010 LOCATE 3,1:PRINT "Press ";RETKEY$;" to end entry.';TAB(40)
4020 INMAX#=1D+20:INMIN#=-INMAX#:INROW%=N%+4:INCOL%=18:INTMPL$="*"
4050 ON N% GOTO 4100,4200,4300,4300,4300,4400,4500,4600,4700,4800
4090 '--Item number------------------------------------------
4100 LOCATE INROW%,INCOL%:PRINT ITMNR%
4110 LSET ITMNR$=MKI$(ITMNR%):RETURN
4120 PRINT SPACE$(INLEN%-LEN(NTRY$));:RETURN
4190 '--Category----------------------------------------------
4200 INLEN%=10:GOSUB 200:LSET CTGRY$=NTRY$:GOTO 4120
4290 '--Description 1,2, & 3----------------------------------
4300 INLEN%=20:GOSUB 200:LSET DSCR$(N%-2)=NTRY$:GOTO 4120
4390 '--ID number---------------------------------------------
4400 INLEN%=15:GOSUB 200:LSET IDNBR$=NTRY$:GOTO 4120
4490 '--Location----------------------------------------------
4500 INLEN%=15:GOSUB 200:LSET LCN$=NTRY$:GOTO 4120
4590 '--Date acquired-----------------------------------------
4600 INLEN%=8:GOSUB 200:LSET ACQRD$=NTRY$:GOTO 4120
4690 '--Cost--------------------------------------------------
4700 INMAX#=999999.99#:INMIN#=0:INLEN%=9:GOSUB 200:LSET COST$=MKD$(NTRY#)
4710 '--Redisplay numeric entry-------------------------------
4720 LOCATE INROW%,INCOL%:PRINT USING "######.##"; NTRY#;:RETURN
4790 '--Value-------------------------------------------------
4800 INMAX#=999999.99#:INMIN#=0:INLEN%=9:GOSUB 200:LSET VALU$=MKD$(NTRY#)
4810 GOTO 4720
6980 '---locations and labels---------------------------------
6990 ' for entry form
7000 DATA 4,Item number,4,Category,4,Description-1,4,Description-2,4,
     Description-3,4,ID number,4,Location,4,Date acquired,4,Cost,4,Value
```

Fig. 12-5—Cont.   Personal inventory program—random access.

CHANGING DISK FILE LIMITS

PC BASIC normally establishes a limit on the number of files and devices that can be open at the same time (three), and another limit on the maximum length of a random-access record (128 characters). These limits can be changed at the time PC DOS hands over control of the PC to either the Disk BASIC or Advanced BASIC interpreter.

To change the maximum number of concurrently open files and devices, suffix the PC DOS command BASIC or BASICA with a blank space, the characters ''/F:'' and the number of files and devices you need to have open simultaneously. Here is an example:

```
A>basica /f:5
```

The command above would start Advanced BASIC with an allowance for five files and devices open at the same time. The absolute maximum number is 15.

The maximum length of random-access records equals the file buffer size. You can change the file buffer size by suffixing the PC DOS command BASIC or BASICA with a blank space, the characters ''/S:'' and the buffer size you want. For example:

```
B>a:basic /s:512
```

The command above would start Disk BASIC with a file buffer size of 512 bytes (characters). The maximum file buffer size is 32767. IBM recommends 512 for best results with its diskette drives.

You may combine the effect of the two options described above by including both suffixes at the end of the BASIC or BASICA command, in either order. Here is one possibility:

```
A>basic /f:5 /s:512
```

Requisitioning additional file positions or larger file buffers has a price. Each file position appropriates dynamic memory in the amount of 190 bytes plus the size of the file buffer, which is 128 bytes unless changed as described above. Thus, increasing the number of files that can be open or increasing the file buffer size (or both) will decrease the amount of dynamic memory available for program statements and variables.

CHAPTER 13

GRAPHICS

On the PC, all three versions of BASIC make it easy to transform verbal output to graphic output. Cassette BASIC, Disk BASIC, and Advanced BASIC can all plot points and draw lines and boxes. Advanced BASIC has other graphics capabilities as well. It can draw circles, arcs, and ellipses, and can fill in any area of the screen with a solid color. The only special equipment you need is a color/graphics adapter card and some kind of color display screen. This entire chapter applies only to PC systems with that equipment.

FOREGROUND, BACKGROUND, AND BORDER

The display screen has three different regions: *border*, *background*, and *foreground*. Background, as the name implies, is the region of the screen on which everything is displayed. When you turn the PC on, the background region is the black part of the screen that can have characters on it. Text and graphic images appear in the foreground, over the top of the background. A border surrounds the background, but it is usually the same color as the background, and hence indistinguishable.

The border compensates for variations among different television sets and monitors. Television sets typically show only part of the signal they receive, losing the part around the edges of the screen. This phenomenon is called *overscan*. Some home televisions lose almost all the border, others very little, and monitors even less. Chapter 3 describes how to use the MODE command in PC DOS to widen the border on the right or left in order to compensate for a display screen with severe overscan.

TEXT AND GRAPHICS DISPLAY MODES

The PRINT and PRINT USING statements display text and special characters from the PC's set of 256 characters, which are listed in Appendix D. That is called *text mode*. The color/graphics adapter enables two more screen modes (in BASIC), and both are graphics modes. In those modes you can plot single points, draw lines and boxes, draw circles and arcs, and color the interior of delineated areas.

The PC BASIC graphics modes differ only in the number and size of the points displayed and in the number of colors allowed. *High-resolution* mode divides the screen into more points than *medium-resolution* mode. Consequently, high-resolution points are about half as wide as medium-resolution points, permitting much greater detail. High resolution is strictly black and white, but medium resolution allows up to four distinctly different colors on the screen at the same time.

Switching Screen Modes

The SCREEN statement switches between text and graphics modes. The following statement switches to medium-resolution graphics:

```
200 SCREEN 1
```

The value that follows the command word specifies the screen mode: medium resolution is 1, high resolution is 2, and text mode is 0. Therefore, the following statement switches back to text mode:

```
800 SCREEN 0
```

If the specified mode is the same as the existing mode, nothing happens. Otherwise the SCREEN statement erases the display, setting the foreground color to white and the background and border colors to black.

The COLOR Statement With Text

The COLOR statement allows you to specify different colors for foreground text, background, and border. The exact color you see varies from one monitor to the next, depending on brand name, model, and adjustment. Also, perceived color may differ from true color when certain colors are displayed together (white is particularly susceptible to such tingeing).

Colors are specified by number; Table 13-1 lists the available colors and their numbers. Here is an example:

```
210 COLOR 5,1,7
```

The first value specifies the foreground color, the second value specifies the background color, and the third value specifies the border color. The statement above makes the foreground magenta, the background blue, and the border white,

Color numbers 0 through 7 are available for foreground, background, and border, but colors 8 through 15, which are lighter shades of colors 0 through 7, are only available for the foreground and border. Some color monitors will show the same color for numbers 8 and 0, 9 and 1, 10 and 2, etc., even though the computer sends out different signals.

In text mode, the COLOR statement only affects foreground and background of characters displayed *after* it is executed. Text that is already on the screen will not change color, but text displayed later will appear in the new foreground color, against the new background color. The border color does change immediately, though. Here is an immediate mode example:

```
color 11,5,14
print "Waltz of the Toreadors"
Waltz of the Toreadors
Ok
```

In the example above, the COLOR statement changes the foreground to light cyan, the background to magenta, and the border to yellow. The COLOR statement itself is displayed in the old foreground color, over the old background color, but the PRINT statement and its output all appear in cyan on magenta.

Omit any of the numbers in a COLOR statement, and the color of the item you omitted will not change. For example, the following statement changes the background color to cyan without changing the foreground or border colors:

```
320 COLOR ,3
```

In text mode, one comma ahead of the first value, as in the example above, means the stated value sets the background color while foreground color stays the same. A COLOR statement with two commas ahead of the first value changes only the border color. The following example changes the border color to green without affecting the foreground or background color:

Table 13-1. Colors in Text Mode

Color number*	Color	Color number*†	Color
0	Black	8	Dark grey
1	Blue	9	Light blue
2	Green	10	Light green
3	Cyan	11	Light cyan
4	Red	12	Light red
5	Magenta	13	Light magenta
6	Gold (brown)	14	Yellow
7	White (grey)	15	Bright white

*Adding 16 to the foreground color number makes displayed characters blink.
†When used for background, numbers 8 through 15 produce the same colors as numbers 0 through 7.

```
8733 COLOR ,,2
```

The bottom line of the text-mode screen, line 25, displays the Soft Key definition of the ten function keys, as described in Chapter 10. The definitions always appear as black foreground letters on a white background. The KEY OFF statement erases the Soft Key definitions and changes line 25 to match the colors on the rest of the screen.

The COLOR Statement With Graphics

The COLOR statement is actually three statements in one. COLOR works one way in text mode and another way in medium-resolution graphics mode. It is altogether illegal in high-resolution graphics mode, where the foreground color is always white and the background and border colors are always black.

In medium-resolution graphics, the background color number also specifies the border color. Any of the 16 colors available in text mode foreground can be used. The background color number also determines the shade of the foreground color, light or dark. Background numbers between 0 and 7 select dark shades of both background and foreground colors and background numbers 8 through 15 select light colors for both background and foreground. But background color numbers 16 through 23 select dark background colors with light foreground colors. Table 13-2 summarizes these effects.

Medium-resolution foreground color choices are limited, and the scheme for specifying them differs markedly from the text-mode scheme. There are two sets of medium-resolution foreground hues, called *palettes*, and the COLOR statement chooses one of the two palettes. Each palette has four hues. The statements that actually do the plotting and drawing choose one of the four individual hues from the active palette. As just mentioned, the shade of the foreground color is determined by the background color number.

As you might expect, the palettes are numbered zero and one, and the hues on them are numbered from zero to three. Table 13-3 has the details. Notice on each palette that hue numbers 1, 2, and 3 are fixed, but hue number 0 is the same as the background color. Text printed on a medium-resolution screen normally appears in palette hue number 3, either gold or white.

Here is a sample medium-resolution COLOR statement:

```
1000 COLOR 1,0
```

The first number sets the background and border color, and the second number chooses the palette for the foreground hues (just the opposite of the COLOR statement in text mode). Either of the numbers may be omitted, but not both. In that case, the absent attribute remains the same.

A medium-resolution COLOR statement changes both background and foreground colors immediately and retroactively. For example, if some things were displayed in green, red, or gold with palette 0, switching to palette 1 immediately changes them to cyan, magenta, and white.

Graphics Screen Coordinates

In order to display points, lines, boxes, and so forth, the computer needs to know where they go. That means it must be able to uniquely identify each point on the screen. Imagine a piece of graph paper superimposed on the screen such that each box on the grid corresponds to one graphics point. Further imagine that the rows and columns on the graph paper are numbered. You can specify any box on the graph paper by stating its column and row numbers, which are called its *coordinates*, and that is exactly the way you identify points on the graphics screen.

Column numbers start with zero at the left edge of the screen and end at the right edge with column 319 in medium-resolution graphics, 639 in high resolution. The top row is zero, and the bottom row is 199 in both graphics modes. Before using rows 192 through 199, be sure to erase the display of Soft Key definitions from the bottom of the screen with a KEY OFF statement.

The PSET Statement

Neither the COLOR nor SCREEN statements alone create graphic images on the screen. They only condition the screen for medium- or high-resolution graphics to follow.

The PSET statement plots a single point on the graphics screen at any

Table 13-2. Medium-Resolution Background Colors

| Hue | Background color number* | | |
	Dark foreground Dark background	Light foreground Light background	Light foreground Dark background
Black	0	8	16
Blue	1	9	17
Green	2	10	18
Cyan	3	11	19
Red	4	12	20
Magenta	5	13	21
Gold	6	14	22
White	7	15	23

*The background color number affects the hue and shade of the background color and also the shade of the foreground color.

coordinates you specify. The PSET statement looks the same in either graphics mode. The following statement will plot a point at the intersection of column 45 and row 10:

```
1010 PSET (45,10)
```

A hue number is optional in the PSET statement. When it is absent in medium-resolution mode, hue 3 (gold or white) is used. If a PSET statement has no hue specification in high-resolution mode, it plots a white point.

To specify a hue in a PSET statement, add a comma and the hue number after the coordinates. In medium-resolution graphics, the hue number (0 through 3) chooses one of the four hues from the active palette (see Table 13-3). In high-resolution graphics, an odd number chooses the sole foreground color (white) and an even number chooses the sole background color (black). Here is an example:

```
1020 PSET (180,150), 1
```

In medium-resolution graphics, the statement above plots a green point or a cyan point, depending on which palette is active. In high-resolution graphics, the statement above plots a white (foreground) point.

The LINE Statement

All versions of PC BASIC have a powerful line-drawing statement, LINE. It draws straight lines, empty boxes, and solid-color boxes.

Since it takes two points to define a straight line, it stands to reason that the LINE statement must know the start and end points of a line. You can specify the coordinates of both, like this:

```
1030 LINE (50,150)-(1,10)
```

The statement above draws a straight line from the point at column 50, row 150 to the point at column 1, row 10.

The LINE statement can also specify a line hue. All it needs is a hue number following the end point coordinates. In medium-resolution graph-

Table 13-3. Medium-Resolution Foreground Hues*

| Palette number | Palette hue number | | | |
	0	1	2	3
0	Background	Green	Red	Gold
1	Background	Cyan	Magenta	White

*A COLOR statement chooses the palette; graphics statements select hues from that palette. The shade of the foreground color is determined by the background color number (see Table 13-2).

ics, the hue number chooses one of the hues from the active palette (see Table 13-3). In high-resolution graphics, an odd number chooses the foreground color and an even number chooses the background color. If the hue specification is absent, as in the example above, hue number 3 is used in medium-resolution graphics. If it is absent in high-resolution graphics, the foreground color is used.

Drawing Adjoining Lines

Suppose you want to draw a series of lines, with each line beginning where the previous line ended. You could use a series of LINE statements, like this:

```
1000 SCREEN 1 'Medium res.
1010 COLOR 0,0 'Black backgnd, palette 0
1040 LINE (60,140)-(100,90),1
1050 LINE (100,90)-(140,140),2
1060 LINE (140,140)-(100,190),1
1070 LINE (100,190)-(60,140),2
```

The four LINE statements above draw a diamond, with opposite sides the same color and adjacent sides different colors.

There is an easier way to draw adjoining lines. Every time PC BASIC plots a point or draws a line, it remembers the last point it used. The LINE statement can take advantage of this knowledge. If you omit the first coordinates from a LINE statement, it starts drawing a line at the last point it used and stops at the end point you specify. The following four LINE statements construct the same diamond as the last four LINE statements:

```
1000 SCREEN 1 'Medium res.
1010 COLOR 0,0 'Black backgnd, palette 0
1040 LINE (60,140)-(100,90),1
1050 LINE -(140,140),2
1060 LINE -(100,190),1
1070 LINE -(60,140),2
```

The first LINE statement above specifies a starting point, since the coordinates of the last point displayed are unknown. A starting point could also be established by plotting the first point with a PSET statement. Either way, the succeeding LINE statements need only specify an ending point.

In fact, if nothing has been drawn or plotted, PC BASIC will assume a starting point at the center of the screen. That is column 160, row 100 in medium resolution, or column 320, row 100 in high resolution.

Constructing Boxes

A special form of the LINE statement draws a box. All you do is add a comma and the letter B after the hue number in any LINE statement. Here is an example:

```
1100 LINE (50,70)-(70,90),2,B
```

Depending on which palette is active, the statement above outlines a red or magenta square on a medium-resolution screen. One of its corners is at column 50, row 70. The diagonally opposite corner is at column 70, row 90. Since the hue number in the statement above is even, it would draw an invisible box (in the background color) on a high-resolution screen.

When the letter B is present but the hue number is absent, hue 3 is used by default. There must still be a comma present to indicate the hue is implicit, however. The following example draws a narrow, tall rectangle in hue 3:

```
1110 LINE (150,10)-(155,190),,B
```

The letter B at the end of a LINE statement can only draw a square or a rectangle whose sides are parallel to the edges of the screen. It takes four separate LINE statements to draw other four-sided shapes.

Solid-Color Boxes

It's just as easy to create a solid-color box as an empty box. Add the letter F immediately after the letter B, like this:

```
1120 LINE (0,195)-(319,199),1,BF
```

The statement above creates a long, thin, solid bar across the bottom of the screen, using hue number 1.

Relative Coordinates

There are two ways to designate a graphics point. All examples so far have stated the actual column and row numbers of each point. This is the *absolute form* of coordinate specification. The alternative, called the *relative form*, specifies coordinates relative to the last point displayed. When the word "STEP" precedes the coordinates in a PSET or LINE statement, it means those numbers are *offsets* to the coordinates of the last point plotted. Consider these two PSET statements:

```
1200 PSET (40,23)
1210 PSET STEP (10,-3)
```

The first statement above (line 1200) uses absolute coordinates to plot a point at column 40, row 23. The second statement above (line 1210) uses relative coordinates. It plots a point at column 50, row 20, which is 10 columns to the right and 3 rows up from the previous point plotted.

You can use either the absolute or relative form to specify the coordinates of any point. If you use the relative form for the first point you display, PC BASIC uses the center of the screen as the previous point.

Mixing Text and Graphics

You can use PRINT and PRINT USING statements to display any of the PC's 256 characters in any screen mode. The characters normally appear in hue 3, which is white or gold in medium resolution (depending on the active palette) and white in high resolution. Chapter 15 describes a way to change medium-resolution character color. Medium-resolution characters are the same size as text-mode characters are when the screen width is 40. High-resolution characters are half that wide, the same as when the screen width is 80.

Character location is determined solely by LOCATE, PRINT, and PRINT USING statements the same way in all three screen modes. Graphics statements like PSET and LINE have no effect on character location. Chapter 10 has more information on displaying characters.

The text-mode coordinates used in LOCATE statements are similar in principle to the graphics mode coordinates, but there are differences. For one thing, text rows and columns are numbered starting with 1, not with 0 as in graphics mode. Also, the LOCATE statement requires rows to be specified before columns, just the opposite of graphic statement coordinates.

For purposes of character display, the screen always has 25 lines, numbered from 1 at the top to 25 at the bottom, and either 40 columns (medium resolution) or 80 columns (high resolution). Therefore one text line equals eight graphics rows, and characters are eight graphics columns wide.

Characters displayed over the top of existing graphics will erase a small rectangle around each character, eight columns wide and eight rows high. But points, lines, and boxes drawn over existing characters only obliterate the parts of the characters that they intersect.

In immediate mode, puzzling "Syntax error" messages can occur if commands are entered over graphics. That happens when there are stray text-colored graphics on the line, because PC BASIC tries to interpret them as characters. To prevent such errors, always clear the screen or at least clear the line (with the **Esc** key) before typing an immediate mode command.

USING POINTS, LINES, AND BOXES

Many programs that output a dry list of values (Fig. 13-1A) can be improved with graphic output. It may take the form of a simple dot graph (Fig. 13-1B), a line graph (Fig. 13-1C), or a bar graph (Fig. 13-1D). The graphs can use color to enhance their appearance while imparting more information.

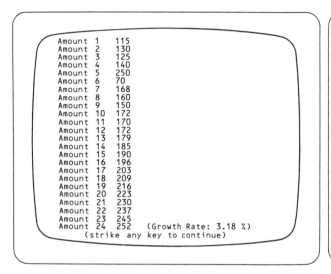

(A)   A printed list of numbers

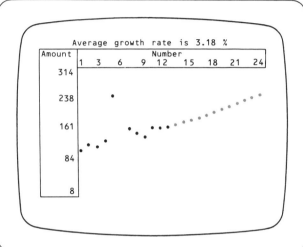

(B)   A point graph

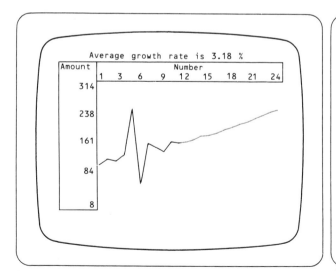

(C)   A line graph

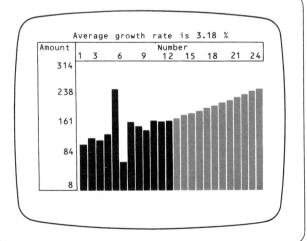

(D)   A bar graph

Fig. 13-1.   Comparing text and graphic program output.

Average Growth Rate Program Analysis

The average growth rate program (Fig. 13-2) calculates the average growth rate of a set of numbers and projects how the numbers will increase or decrease in the future. Its projections appear as a list of exact values, then as a point graph, next as a line graph, and finally as a bar graph. It employs a statistical technique called exponential regression, which can be used to project the growth of anything that increases (or decreases) exponentially over time. Typical applications include birth rate and related items like sales, income, and patronage.

The first part of the program dimensions a single-precision numeric array (line 50) and sets up the display screen for keyboard input (lines 1010 through 1250).

For brevity and simplicity, the program uses unsophisticated keyboard entry techniques, not up to the standards discussed in Chapter 11. The program user must divide the analysis period into past and future (lines 1200 and 1210), and the total number of past and future amounts cannot exceed 24 (line 1220). After that, the program user must enter the known amounts (lines 1260 through 1340).

During the entry phase, the program accumulates some figures it needs for the exponential regression (lines 1300 through 1340). The final steps in the exponential regression occur right after the entry phase (lines 1400 through 1420). Next, the program projects future figures (lines 1500 through 1520).

Lines 1600 through 1690 display the exact amount of each past and future figure. The program waits for its user to read the screen and press a key before it continues (line 1690).

Because there are no bounds on the values entered or projected, the program must scale them to fit in the space available on the screen (lines 2000 through 2080). To do that, it must find the highest and lowest figures (lines 2000 through 2060). Then it can divide the graph height, 168 rows, by the sum of the highest and lowest figures (line 2080), resulting in a vertical scaling factor.

To prepare for graphing, the program sets medium-resolution graphics mode and chooses the background color and foreground palette (lines 2200 and 2210). Then it displays the graph headings (lines 2220 through 2320). Notice how it uses LINE statements to draw boxes around the horizontal and vertical scales (lines 2310 and 2320).

A simple PRINT statement (line 2240) displays the horizontal scale, but displaying the vertical scale is more complicated. The program computes five selected amounts that span the range of known and projected values, by applying the vertical scaling factor to rows 4, 44, 84, 124, and 164 of the graph area (lines 2260 through 2290). Those rows correspond to the

```
  50 DIM AMT(24)
1010 CLS:KEY OFF:WIDTH 40
1100 PRINT
1110 PRINT "    This program uses an exponential"
1120 PRINT "regression technique to analyze past"
1130 PRINT "amounts and make future projections."
1140 PRINT "You specify past amounts and the number"
1150 PRINT "of past and future amounts. The total"
1160 PRINT "number of amounts cannot exceed 24."
1170 PRINT
1200 INPUT "How many past amounts";PAST%
1210 INPUT "How many amounts to project";FUTR%
1220 IF PAST%+FUTR%>24 THEN PRINT:PRINT "Only 24 amounts total,
     please! ":GOTO 1170
1230 PRINT
1240 PRINT "Now enter past amounts:"
1250 PRINT
1260 FOR NBR%=1 TO PAST%
1270 PRINT "Amount";NBR%;
1280 INPUT AMT(NBR%)
1290 '   Accumulate intermediate exponential regression values
1300 X=NBR%-1:Y=LOG(AMT(NBR%))
1310 I1 = I1 + X:I2 = I2 + Y
1320 I3 = I3 + X∧2:I4 = I4 + Y∧2
1330 I5 = I5 + X*Y
1340 NEXT NBR%
1390 '--Calculate coefficients of exponential equations---
1400 B=(PAST%*I5-I2*I1)/(PAST%*I3-I1∧2)
1410 A=(I2-B*I1)/PAST%
1420 RATE=CINT((EXP(B)-1)*10000!)/100
1490 '--Project future amounts----------------------------
1500 FOR NBR%=PAST%+1 TO PAST%+FUTR%
1510 AMT(NBR%)=INT(EXP(A)*EXP(B*(NBR%-1))+.5)
1520 NEXT NBR%
1590 '--Display exact amounts----------------------------
1600 CLS
1610 FOR NBR%=1 TO PAST%+FUTR%
1630 PRINT
1640 PRINT "Amount";NBR%;TAB(11);AMT(NBR%);
1650 NEXT NBR%
```

Fig. 13-2.   Average growth rate program.

```
1660 PRINT TAB(18);"(Growth Rate:";RATE;"%)";
1690 LOCATE 25,6:PRINT "(strike any key to continue)";:A$=
     INPUT$(1)
1990 '--Compute vertical scaling factor-------------------
2000 MIN=AMT(1)
2010 MAX=AMT(1)
2020 '  Find max and min amounts
2030 FOR NBR%=1 TO PAST%+FUTR%
2040 IF AMT(NBR%)>MAX THEN MAX=AMT(NBR%)
2050 IF AMT(NBR%)<MIN THEN MIN=AMT(NBR%)
2060 NEXT NBR%
2070 ' Scale so both max & min amounts will fit inside graph area
2080 SCALE=168/(MAX+MIN)
2190 '--Display graph form---------------------------------
2200 CLS:SCREEN 1 'Med res (clears screen too)
2210 COLOR 23,0 'Lt. grey (white) backgnd, green/red/yellow palette
2220 PRINT TAB(6);"Average growth rate is";RATE;"%"
2230 PRINT "Amount";TAB(22);"Number"
2240 PRINT TAB(8);"1  3   6   9   12   15  18   21  24";
2250 ' Display vertical scale
2260 FOR CTR%=0 TO 4
2270 LOCATE 24-CTR%*5,1 'At lines 4, 9, 14, 19, & 24
2280 PRINT USING " ###### ";(40*CTR%+4)/SCALE;'Display amount
2290 NEXT CTR%
2300 ' Box the legends
2310 LINE (51,7)-(319,23),3,B
2320 LINE (0,7)-(51,191),3,B
2390 '--Display point graph--------------------------------
2400 FOR NBR%=1 TO PAST%+FUTR%
2410 IF NBR%<FUTR% THEN HUE=2 ELSE HUE=1 'Choose point color
2420 PSET (NBR%*11+45,191-CINT(SCALE*AMT(NBR%))),HUE
2430 NEXT NBR%
2490 '--Display line graph---------------------------------
2500 A$=INPUT$(1) 'Wait for keystroke
2510 HUE=2 'Hue for past
2520 PSET (56,191-CINT(SCALE*AMT(1))),HUE
2530 FOR NBR%=2 TO PAST%+FUTR%
2540 IF NBR%>PAST% THEN HUE=1 'Change hue for projections
2550 LINE -(NBR%*11+45,191-CINT(SCALE*AMT(NBR%))),HUE
```

Fig. 13-2 –Cont.   Average growth rate program.

```
2560 NEXT NBR%
2590 '--Display bar graph---------------------------------
2600 A$=INPUT$(1) 'Wait for keystroke
2610 HUE=2 'Hue for past
2620 LINE (52,24)-(319,191),0,BF 'Erase graph area
2630 FOR NBR%=1 TO PAST%+FUTR%
2640 IF NBR%>PAST% THEN HUE=1 'Change hue for projections
2650 LINE (NBR%*11+45,191)-(NBR%*11+54,191-CINT(SCALE*AMT(NBR%))),HUE,BF
2660 NEXT NBR%
2690 '--End Program----------------------------------------
2700 A$=INPUT$(1) 'Wait for keystroke
2710 SCREEN 0
2720 END
```

Fig. 13-2–Cont.   Average growth rate program.

midpoints of lines 24, 19, 14, 9, and 4, whereon the selected values are displayed. (Note that the graph area occupies 168 rows on the screen, between rows 24 and 191.)

The program displays a point graph by using the PSET statement (lines 2400 through 2430). Variable HUE is used to change point color, red for known values and green for projections. The column coordinate of each point is calculated by multiplying a horizontal spacing factor, 11, times the point number, 1 to 24, and adding the product to 45, which is the left edge of the graph area. The row coordinate is calculated by multiplying the vertical scaling factor times the known or projected amount, and subtracting the product from 191, which is the bottom row of the graph area.

When the program user presses any key, the dot graph is replaced by a line graph (lines 2500 through 2560). A PSET statement plots the first point (line 2520). A LINE statement draws line segments between remaining points (line 2550). Column and row coordinates are calculated as before, and variable HUE again determines the color of the point.

Finally, the program displays the bar graph (lines 2600 through 2660). First it erases the graph area by displaying a solid box in the background color (line 2620). Then it constructs a solid-color rectangle for each past and future amount (lines 2630 through 2660). The width of each box is the same, but the height varies according to the magnitude of the amount. Variable HUE determines the color of the box.

CIRCLES AND SOLID COLORS

Straight lines seem to pervade typical computer graphics, because it is usually easy to plot points, draw lines, and construct boxes in BASIC.

Advanced BASIC transcends all that with the CIRCLE statement, which makes drawing circles, arcs, and ellipses fast and easy.

Another Advanced BASIC statement, PAINT, works especially well with CIRCLE. It fills areas of the screen with solid colors, making it just as easy to create disks as it is to create hollow circles.

The CIRCLE Statement

Before Advanced BASIC can draw a circle, it needs to know where the circle will go on the display screen, how big to make the circle, and what color to draw the circle in. Finally, since CIRCLE is a general statement which draws partial circles or whole ones, Advanced BASIC needs to know which part of the circle to draw.

The following sample statement draws a complete circle in the middle of a medium-resolution screen:

```
CIRCLE (160,100),50,1,0,6.2831
```

The first two numbers specify the coordinates of the center of the circle, namely column 160 and row 100. The third number, 50, determines the size of the circle. The fourth number tells which color to draw in. The last two numbers specify which part of the circle to draw.

Standard column and row numbers specify the center of the circle. A circle's radius determines its size, and one unit of radius equals the width of one column. Therefore a circle with a radius of 6 has a diameter of 12 columns. Of course columns and rows are not the same size, nor is the screen square—it is wider than it is tall—but the CIRCLE statement compensates automatically for these facts. In medium resolution, six columns equal five rows, and in high resolution, 12 columns equal five rows. For example, a medium-resolution circle with a diameter of 12 columns also has a diameter of ten rows.

Medium-resolution circles can be drawn in any hue available on the active palette, with the current background color number determining the color shade (review Tables 13-2 and 13-3). In high resolution, an odd color number draws a white circle, and an even color number draws a circle in the background color. Number 0, the background hue, is useful for erasing. For example, the following program draws two circles, one cyan and one white, then it waits for someone to press any key on the keyboard. When that happens, the program erases the white circle by drawing over it with the background hue.

```
10 SCREEN 1 'med. res. graphics
20 CLS
30 CIRCLE (200,120),25,1,0,6.2831  'cyan
40 CIRCLE (110,140),25,3,0,6.2831  'white
```

```
50 A$ = INPUT$(1) 'Wait for keystroke
60 CIRCLE (110,140),25,0,0,6.2831 'backgnd
```

The color specification in a CIRCLE statement is optional. The following high-resolution example shows the color number missing:

```
10 CIRCLE (320,100),100, ,0,6.2831
```

Notice that the comma for the color specification remains. When the color specification is absent, Advanced BASIC draws a circle in the standard foreground color. That is color number 3 (white or gold) in medium resolution. In high resolution, color number 1 (white) is the default color.

Drawing Arcs

The CIRCLE statement can draw just part of a circle. How does Advanced BASIC know which arc to draw? The answer relies on a convention of geometry that says every complete circle contains 360 degrees. Think of a compass; it has 360 degrees. Geometry does not number the degrees of a circle the same as a compass, however. It starts with 0 at 3 o'clock and proceeds counterclockwise, with 90 degrees at 12 o'clock, 180 degrees at 9 o'clock, 270 degrees at 6 o'clock, and back around to 360 degrees at 3 o'clock (Fig. 13-3A).

To further complicate matters, Advanced BASIC measures circles not in degrees, but in *radians* (Fig. 13-3B). Radians relate to the mathematical constant π, which is about 3.14159. One-half circle, 180 degrees, is the same as π radians. A full circle is 360 degrees, or 2π (about 6.2831) radians. Therefore to convert from degrees to radians, multiply by 0.0174532.

To specify an arc, state the point on the circle where it starts and the point where it ends. State both points in radians. So far, examples of the CIRCLE statement specified the arc starting at 0 and ending at 6.2831 radians, in other words the whole circle. The following statement specifies just half a circle:

```
10 CIRCLE (160,100),50,1,0,3.1416
```

One ambiguity remains: the two points that specify an arc actually specify *two* arcs. Draw counterclockwise from the start point and one arc appears, but draw clockwise and a different arc appears. To resolve the ambiguity, Advanced BASIC draws counterclockwise if the first arc endpoint is less than the second, but it draws clockwise if the first arc endpoint is greater than the second (Fig. 13-4).

Drawing Rays

In addition to drawing arcs, the CIRCLE statement can draw a ray from

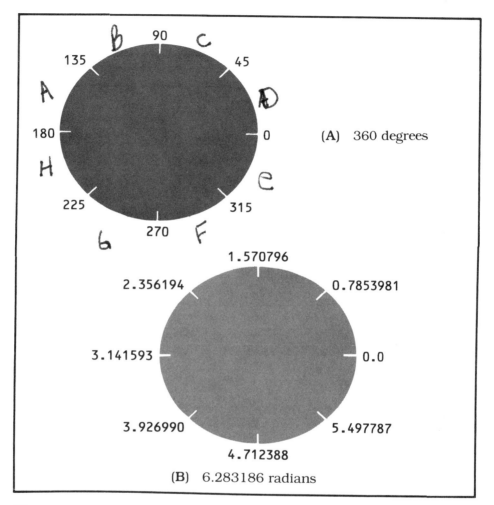

Fig. 13-3. **Measuring a circle: 360 degrees equal 6.283186 radians.**

the center of the arc to either arc endpoint. A negative endpoint in a CIR-CLE statement generates a ray to that endpoint. The minus sign does not affect the arc itself. The following example draws a ray from coordinates (40,100) to the arc's second endpoint:

```
1230 CIRCLE (40,100),30, ,3.1416,-4.7124
```

The endpoint -0 is not treated as a negative endpoint, and no ray will be drawn to it. To circumvent this limitation, use -0.001 instead of -0.

When both endpoints are negative, both rays are drawn, creating a pie-shaped wedge. Here is an example:

```
1350 CIRCLE (240,100),30,2,-3.1416,-4.7124
```

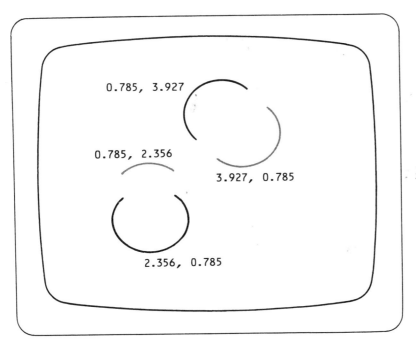

Fig. 13-4.   Endpoints of sample arcs.

Drawing Ellipses

The CIRCLE statement can also draw ellipses. To do so, it needs to know the *aspect ratio* of the ellipse to be drawn, which is the relationship between its height and width. Here is an example:

```
1410 CIRCLE (270,100),50,1,0,6.2831,5/3
```

The extra number at the end of the statement above specifies the aspect ratio. The easiest way to understand the aspect ratio is to think of it as a fraction, with a separate numerator and denominator. The numerator tells how many rows the CIRCLE statement should consider equivalent to the number of columns specified by the denominator. In medium resolution, an aspect ratio of 5/6 yields a circle, an aspect ratio of 1/3 (or 2/6) produces a short, wide ellipse, and an aspect ratio of 5/3 (or 10/6) yields a tall, narrow ellipse (Fig. 13-5). In high resolution, an aspect ratio of 5/12 yields a circle.

Decimal fractions make perfectly acceptable aspect ratios too. For example, the ratio 5/6 is the same as the decimal fraction .8333333. It so happens that when the aspect ratio has a value less than 1, Advanced BASIC draws ellipses with the same width and varies the height, but when the aspect ratio is greater than 1, the height stays the same and the width varies (Fig. 13-6).

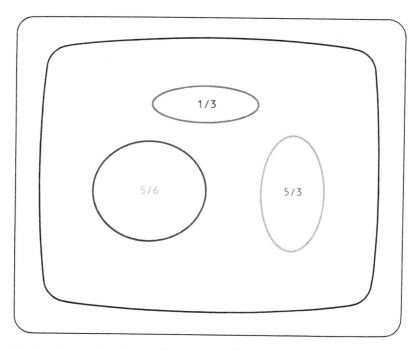

Fig. 13-5. Aspect ratios of some medium-resolution ellipses.

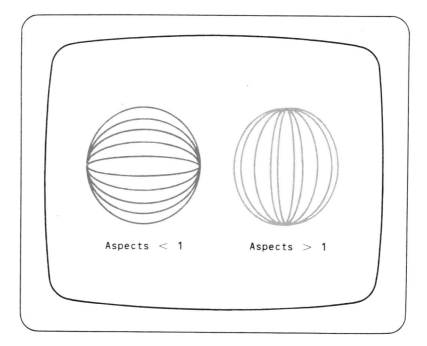

Fig. 13-6. Effect of aspect ratio value on ellipses.

The PAINT Statement

The Advanced BASIC graphics statement PAINT fills in a selected area on the screen with one of the graphics mode hues. Here is an example:

```
20 PAINT (150,100),1,3
```

The statement above tells the computer to start at point (150,100) and paint the screen hue 1 in all directions, and to not stop painting in any direction until it encounters hue 3. That means there must be some shape outlined in foreground hue 3 surrounding point (150,100).

The fill color and outline color can be different or the same, but the entire region to be filled must be bordered by a single color, or the PAINT statement will not work as expected. The region borders can be constructed of any combination of points, lines, boxes, circles, arcs, and ellipses. If there are gaps in the outline color, the fill color will leak out and paint the rest of the screen. This feature of the PAINT statement makes it possible to paint the entire background with a foreground color. The following statements do that with foreground color 1 and then hollow a circle out of it.

```
10 SCREEN 1 'med. res. graphics
20 CLS
30 PAINT (0,0),1,1 'Paint whole background
40 CIRCLE (50,150),20,0,0,6.2831 'outline shape
50 PAINT (50,150),0,0 'fill with backgnd color
```

The PAINT statement uses the run-time stack, so it is conceivable that the "Out of memory . . ." error can occur while filling a shape with color. It is more likely if the PAINT statement is part of a deeply nested FOR/NEXT loop or subroutine, or if the shape being filled is extremely complicated. Chapter 15 tells you how to increase the size of the run-time stack.

USING CIRCLES AND SOLIDS

There are many practical uses of the CIRCLE and PAINT statements. For example, circles depict proportions well. If a circle of one size represents, say, 20, a circle twice as large as the first will visually represent 40, and a circle half as large will represent 10 (Fig. 13-7). Of course the classic way to depict proportional shares of a whole is with a pie chart, which certainly relies on a circle drawing capability (Fig. 13-8).

Proportional Circles Program Analysis

The proportional circles program (Fig. 13-9) will divide a whole amount into as many as six parts and display a proportionally sized circle for each part. Fig. 13-8 shows program output for inputs of 20, 40, 3, 7, 10, and 8.

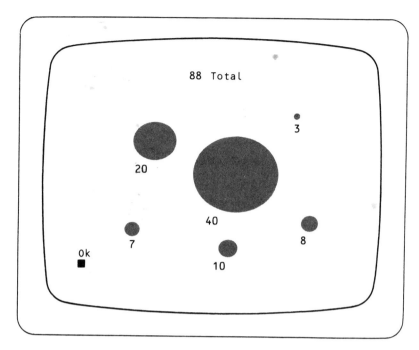

Fig. 13-7. Using circles to depict proportions.

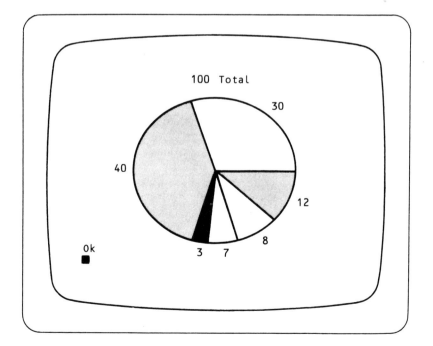

Fig. 13-8. A pie chart.

```
10 '--Column and row coordinates for circles-------------
20 DATA 85,60,175,95,245,35
30 DATA 60,150,165,170,260,145
40 KEY OFF
50 CLS
60 '--Input 6 amounts-----------------------------------
70 FOR J=1 TO 6
80 PRINT "Amount for part";J;
90 INPUT PART(J)
100 TOTAL=TOTAL+PART(J) 'Accum. running total
110 NEXT J
120 '--Set up screen-----------------------------------
130 SCREEN 1 'Med. res.
140 CLS
150 LOCATE 1,15
160 PRINT TOTAL;"Total"
170 '--Display circles---------------------------------
180 FOR J=1 TO 6
190 IF PART(J)=0 THEN GOTO 260 'Skip 0 amounts
200 READ C,R 'Get circle center
210 RAD=100*PART(J)/TOTAL 'Compute circle size
220 LOCATE (R+RAD)/8+2,(C-RAD)/8 'Position and
230 PRINT PART(J); 'display amount
240 CIRCLE (C,R),RAD,2,0,6.2831 'then outline circle
250 PAINT (C,R),1,2 'and fill it in
260 NEXT J
270 LOCATE 22
280 END
```

Fig. 13-9. Proportional circles program.

The program is fairly unsophisticated, so it will not work for all input combinations.

Program lines 20 and 30 hold the column and row coordinates for each of the six circles that may be output; the first circle is at (85,60), the second is at (175,95), and so on.

The first thing the program does is set up the screen for keyboard input (lines 40 and 50). Next, the program user must enter the amounts to be apportioned (lines 70 through 110). Any amount can be 0. While this is going on, the program keeps a running total of amounts entered (line 100). After finishing the input, the program sets up the screen for medium-resolution graphics, and displays a screen title (lines 130 through 160).

Finally, the program draws the proportionally sized circles (lines 180 to 260). If any of the six amounts is 0, the program skips it (line 190). For nonzero amounts, the program gets circle coordinates from the data statements (line 200). Next, it computes the size of the circle according to the ratio of the partial amount to the total amount (line 210). Then, in a position near where it will display the circle, the program displays the partial amount (lines 220 and 230). After that, it draws a circle (line 240) and fills it with color (line 250).

After displaying all circles, the program moves the cursor to the bottom of the screen (line 270) in anticipation of the "Ok" message at the end of the program.

Pie Chart Program Analysis

The pie chart program (Fig. 13-10) constructs a pie chart with up to 25 wedges. The program user must enter the number of wedges and the size of each wedge. Fig. 13-9 shows program output for six wedges: 30, 40, 3, 7, 8, and 12. The program displays the wedge size near the center of the appropriate arc.

The program begins by allocating space for 25 wedges—the practical maximum (line 10). Next it sets up the display screen for keyboard input in medium-resolution mode (lines 20 through 40). Then it inputs the number of wedges (lines 60 and 70) and the size of each wedge (lines 80 through 120). During the input phase, the program keeps a running total of wedge sizes (line 110).

When input is finished, the program clears the display screen and displays a title (lines 140 through 160). It starts the first wedge at 0 radians (line 170) and sets the length of each wedge radius at 90 (line 180).

Lines 200 through 280 display the wedges. For each wedge, the program computes the endpoint and midpoint in radians (lines 210 and 220). Then near the midpoint, it displays the wedge size (lines 230 and 240). After that, the program outlines the wedge (line 250). Negative start and end points in the CIRCLE statement draw the wedge radii, and subtracting .001 from the start point keeps it nonzero. Line 260 fills the wedge with color, starting near the wedge center. The next wedge starts where the current wedge ends (line 270).

After displaying the pie chart, the program moves the cursor to the bottom of the screen (line 290) in anticipation of the "Ok" message at the end of the program.

THE ADVANCED BASIC GRAPHICS LANGUAGE

In Advanced BASIC, the DRAW statement employs a special graphics lan-

```
10 DIM PART(25)
20 KEY OFF
30 SCREEN 1
40 CLS
50 '--Input all amounts----------------------------------
60 PRINT "How many parts";
70 INPUT N
80 FOR J=1 TO N
90 PRINT "Size of part";J;
100 INPUT PART(J)
110 TOTAL=TOTAL+PART(J) 'Keep a running total
120 NEXT J
130 '--Prepare to display pie chart----------------------
140 CLS
150 LOCATE 1,15
160 PRINT TOTAL;"Total";
170 STARTPT=0 'Start point of 1st wedge
180 RAD=90 'radius of circle
190 '--Display all wedges--------------------------------
200 FOR J=1 TO N
210 ENDPT=6.283185*PART(J)/TOTAL+STARTPT 'Compute share of pie
220 MIDPT=(STARTPT+ENDPT)/2 'Midpoint of wedge arc
230 LOCATE (100-SIN(MIDPT)*(RAD-8))/8,(160+COS(MIDPT)*(RAD+16))/8
240 PRINT PART(J); 'Display the amount of this wedge
250 CIRCLE (160,100),RAD,3,-STARTPT-.001,-ENDPT 'Outline the wedge and
260 PAINT (160+COS(MIDPT)*RAD*.75,100-SIN(MIDPT)*RAD*.75),
    J MOD 4,3 'Fill it in
270 STARTPT=ENDPT 'Next wedge starts where this one ended
280 NEXT J
290 LOCATE 22
300 END
```

Fig. 13-10. Pie chart program.

guage to draw combinations of straight lines and points. Starting from the
last point illuminated on the screen, you can draw a line of any length in
any one of eight directions. From there, you can draw another line, again
of any length, and again in any of the eight directions. You can keep adding lines like that almost indefinitely. Each line can be any of the four colors available on the active palette, or it can be invisible. You can also draw
a line to any point on the screen, using absolute or relative coordinates.
You can shrink or enlarge your drawing, and you can rotate it 90, 180, or
270 degrees.

The Graphics Subcommands

The graphics language that makes all this possible consists of 15 one-letter subcommands. To construct a drawing, you make up a string value that contains the appropriate sequence of subcommands. With most of the subcommands, you must also specify an amount: how far to draw, which color number to use, how much to enlarge the drawing, things like that. For example, the subcommand R draws a line to the right. The following program will draw a line from the center to the right margin of the medium-resolution screen:

```
10 SCREEN 1
20 DRAW "R159"
```

In the DRAW statement above, the subcommand R159 means "Draw a line, starting where you are, 159 columns to the right." Since PC BASIC always starts at the center of the screen right after a SCREEN 1 statement, it draws a line from coordinates (160,100) to (319,100).

Nine of the one-letter subcommands both draw lines and control movement, and the other six control special effects. Table 13-4 lists all 15 graphics subcommands, and Fig. 13-11 shows which direction each of the line drawing/movement subcommands goes.

Combining Graphics Subcommands

A single DRAW statement can construct a complex object, if its command string consists of several graphics subcommands, in the correct order. The following example will construct a square in the middle of the medium-resolution screen:

```
40 DRAW "BM130,125U50R60D50L60" 'square
```

In the DRAW statement above, the subcommand B prefixes the subcommand M130,125 and turns it into a pure move command—no line is drawn. So starting at coordinates (130,125), the next subcommand, U50, draws a vertical line 50 rows high. Following that, R60 draws a line 60 columns to the right, D50 draws down 50 rows, and L60 draws left 60 columns, arriving back at coordinates (130,125). The disparity between the number of columns and rows drawn accounts for the fact that, on the medium-resolution screen, six rows are equal in length to five columns.

Specifiying Amounts

Amounts can be specified by numeric integer constants suffixed to the subcommand letter, as illustrated in the last two examples, or by numeric variables. Array elements are acceptable, but functions and expressions

Table 13-4. DRAW Statement Subcommands

Sub-command	Effect	Meaning of n^a, h, v, k^a, $s\$$
	Move and draw[b]	
Un	Up	n rows[c]
Dn	Down	n rows[c]
Rn	Right	n columns[c]
Ln	Left	n columns[c]
En	Diagonally up and right	n = diagonal distance[d]
Fn	Diagonally down and right	n = diagonal distance[d]
Gn	Diagonally down and left	n = diagonal distance[d]
Hn	Diagonally up and left	n = diagonal distance[d]
Mh,v	To specified point	h,v = absolute coordinates
M$+h,+v$	To specified point	$+h,+v$ = relative coordinates
	Special effects	
B	Do not draw on the next move	N/A
N	Return to current point after next move	N/A
Ak	Rotate all subsequent moving and drawing counterclockwise[e]	k = rotation angle $\quad 0 = 0°\qquad 2 = 180°$ $\quad 1 = 90°\qquad 3 = 270°$
Sk	Scale subsequent distances up or down[e]	k = magnification factor $\quad 1 = \frac{1}{4}x \qquad 4 = 1x$ $\quad 8 = 2x \qquad 36 = 9x$ $\qquad$ etc.
Ck	Select color	k = hue: 0 or 1 in high-res $\quad 0,1,2,3$ = from medium res palette
X$s\$$;	Execute subcommands from another string	$s\$$ = a string variable that contains more subcommands

[a]For all subcommands except M and X, values can be either integer constants or numeric variables with integer values. To use a variable, prefix its name with an = character and suffix its name with a semicolon, like this: R=COL; (R is a subcommand, COL is a variable name).

[b]A relative movement subcommand that would go off the edge of the screen stops when it reaches the edge.

[c]Five units of vertical distance are equivalent to six units of horizontal distance. For example, to draw a square 5 rows tall, make it 6 columns wide. Note, however, that the diagonal movement subcommands will not connect opposite corners of such a square.

[d]One unit of diagonal distance covers the same screen area as 1.4142135 vertical units (rows). Thus a diagonal of length 100 will exactly connect two opposite corners of a rectangle whose sides are 100 rows by 100 columns.

[e]The rotation and scale subcommands do not affect an M subcommand that uses absolute coordinates.

are not. However, values for the M subcommand must be specified by integer constants; variables will not work. To use a variable in a DRAW statement command string, you must prefix its name with a = character and suffix it with a semicolon, like this:

```
100 DRAW "u=VERT;"
```

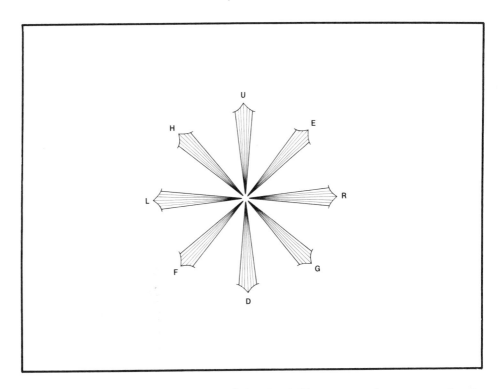

Fig. 13-11.   Directional effect of the DRAW statement movement subcommands.

In the example, the letter u is the subcommand and VERT is the variable name. Notice that letters in a command string can be any combination of upper- and lower-case.

If the value specified with one of the draw/move subcommands other than M would draw off the screen, PC BASIC stops at the edge of the display area. No error message occurs unless the value is negative or exceeds 32767. However, the values used with subcommands A (rotation angle) and C (color) must be between 0 and 3, and the amount used with the subcommand S (scale factor) must be between 0 and 255, or an error message appears.

The Special Effects Subcommands

The program listed in Fig. 13-12 constructs the geometric design shown in Fig. 13-13. The program draws the same simple hexagon over and over, rotating it with the A subcommand, changing its color with the C subcommand, and changing its size with the S subcommand. In the process, it also demonstrates how to execute a command string from within another command string with the X subcommand.

```
10 CLS:KEY OFF
20 SCREEN 1 'Medium res
30 COLOR 16,0 'Black bkgnd, brite fgnd
40 HX$="u25e15r30d25g15l30" '1 hexagon
50 '--Display everything in 10 sizes---------------------
60 FOR SCALE=1 TO 10
70 S$="s"+STR$(SCALE) 'scale factor
80 '--Compute color to use for each size-----------------
90 C$="c"+STR$(SCALE MOD 3+1) 'color number
100 '--Display shape at all 4 angles of rotation--------
110 FOR ROTATE=0 TO 3
120 R$="a"+STR$(ROTATE) 'rotation angle
130 SHAPE$="xS$;xC$;xR$;xHX$;" 'Assemble command string
140 DRAW SHAPE$ 'display 1 shape
150 NEXT ROTATE
160 NEXT SCALE
170 A$=INPUT$(1) 'Wait for keystroke to end
180 END
```

Fig. 13-12. DRAW command demonstration program.

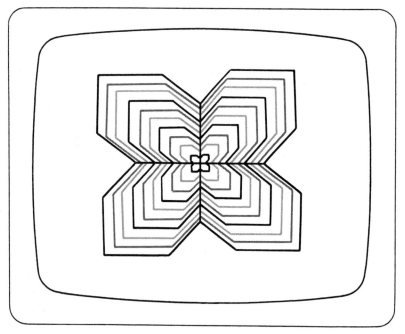

Fig. 13-13. Geometric shape composed of hexagons (program listed in Fig. 13-12).

The program begins by setting up the medium-resolution display screen (lines 10 through 30). Then it defines the command string that will display one hexagon (line 40). Following that are two nested FOR/NEXT loops, which will vary the scale, color, and rotation of the hexagons that are drawn.

The outer loop (lines 60 through 160) sets both the size and the color. Scale factor 4 produces an image in its true size, so this program draws reduced hexagons with scale factors 1 through 3, and enlarged ones with scale factors 5 through 10 (line 60). The color number is computed by applying the MOD operation to the scale factor, reducing it to a value of 0, 1, or 2 (line 90). Adding 1 to that avoids use of color number 0, which would draw invisibly against the background.

The inner loop (lines 110 through 150) changes the rotation angle. The hexagon is redisplayed at each angle, using the color and scale factors set in the outer loop. Rotation factors 0, 1, 2, and 3 correspond to rotation angles of 0, 90, 180, and 270 degrees, going counterclockwise. When rotating 90 or 270 degrees, Advanced BASIC adjusts the vertical and horizontal distances to maintain the object's proportions.

The DRAW statement itself is inside the inner loop (line 140). Its command string, SHAPE$, is composed of four other command strings: S$, the scale factor; C$, the color number; R$, the rotation angle; and HX$, the subcommands that draw one hexagon.

ANIMATION

Film animation is really a series of still pictures, each of which varies slightly from the one before it. When shown in rapid succession, the individual pictures blend together, creating the illusion of continual motion. To create the film, a movie camera photographs each individual picture, which may be created by hand drawing or other techniques. To see the animation, a movie projector must show the film on a screen.

Computer animation can be done with camera and film too. You can draw the still pictures on the screen with PSET, LINE, CIRCLE, PAINT, and DRAW statements, and photograph each in turn with a movie camera. But the computer adds another dimension to animation, because the display screen itself can be animated, eliminating the camera, film, and projector.

To move an object across the display screen, you must first erase it and then redisplay it at its new location. Continuous movement must be done a bit at a time or it will look like the object disappeared one place and reappeared somewhere else. All that is easy enough to program using just a simple loop and the graphics statements presented so far. But to avoid jerky motion, each small move must occur quickly. That feat is difficult or impossible using the regular graphics statements. Fortunately, Advanced BASIC has two additional graphics statements, GET and PUT, that make live action possible.

You can use animation for amusement. Even a single object can be entertaining as it moves around on the screen, perhaps changing size or pace. Animation has its practical uses too, like moving pointers on charts or graphs, or peeling off layer after layer of an illustrated object to reveal its inner workings.

The GET and PUT Statements

The GET statement reads the colors of all points inside a rectangular area of the display screen and stores them in a numeric array. The PUT statement writes the colors back onto the screen. You might think of the GET statement as a camera, the numeric array as a slide, and the PUT statement as a slide projector. The PUT statement can display an image fast enough to animate small objects on the screen.

Defining the Screen Area To Capture

The rectangular area of the screen that the GET statement captures can be of any size and at any location. For example, the following statements draw the image of an explosion (Fig. 13-14) in the middle of the screen:

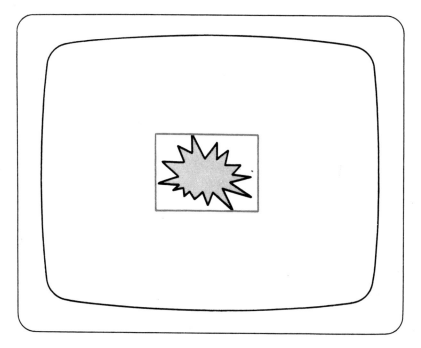

Fig. 13-14. The image of an explosion (see text for program listing).

```
10 '--Dark blue background, and ---------
20 ' light green/red/gold palette
30 CLS:KEY OFF:SCREEN 1:COLOR 17,0
40 '--Outline explosion image-------------
50 DRAW "c2bm190,82m178,91m178,73m163,91
   m148,65m148,85m133,79m139,94m112,94
   m133,109m106,118m133,118m127,124m139,121
   m139,130m145,124m151,133m160,124m166,139
   m172,124m196,145m184,121m223,133m193,115
   m217,109m196,106m205,97m187,97m190,82 "
60 '--Fill with gold----------------------
70 PAINT (160,100),3,2
80 '--Show the screen area occupied-------
100 LINE (105,65)-(225,145),1,B
```

You designate the shape, size, and location of the rectangular area that the GET statement is to read by stating two of its corners, as in a LINE statement with the B option. The LINE statement above, which boxes in the explosion image, outlines the region that the image actually occupies. That rectangular portion, whose corners are (105,65) and (225,145), is all that a GET statement need read in order to capture the explosion image.

Figuring the Array Size

You must specify a numeric array that is large enough to hold the screen data the GET statement will read. A simple program (Fig. 13-15) will calculate the minimum number of elements required for an integer, single-precision, or double-precision array. The program asks you to enter the coordinates you plan to use in the GET statement and specify which graphics mode will be in effect. For example, using the coordinates of the

```
10 CLS
20 INPUT "Medium resolution (Y/N)"; R$
30 IF R$="Y" OR R$="y" THEN BR=2: GOTO 60
40 INPUT "High resolution (Y/N)"; R$
50 IF R$="Y" OR R$="y" THEN BR=1 ELSE GOTO 10
60 INPUT "1st column,row: ",H1,V1
70 INPUT "2nd column,row: ",H2,V2
80 BYTES=4+INT(((ABS(H1-H2)+1)*BR+7)/8)*(ABS(V1-V2)+1)
90 PRINT "--Minimum array dimensions--"
100 PRINT "INTEGER%(";CINT(BYTES/2)-1;")"
110 PRINT " SINGLE!(";CINT(BYTES/4)-1;")"
120 PRINT " DOUBLE#(";CINT(BYTES/8)-1;")"
130 PRINT "(";BYTES;" bytes required)"
```

Fig. 13-15. Calculating GET statement array requirements.

box that the last example draws around the explosion image as inputs, the program calculates that a single-precision array would need at least 628 elements.

The following statements dimension an array suitable for capturing the explosion image drawn by the previous example:

```
90  DIM XPLODE(628)
100 GET (105,65)-(225,145),XPLODE
```

Notice that the GET statement uses only the array *name*—no parentheses or indexes.

Displaying the Captured Image

The PUT statement reproduces the entire rectangular area captured by a GET statement, and will put it anywhere on the screen. You specify the coordinates at which you want the upper left-hand corner of the rectangle, and the name of the numeric array that holds the screen data. The following example redisplays the explosion image (Fig. 13-14) twice, both in new locations:

```
110 '--Redisplay image twice-----------
120 PUT (15,25),XPLODE
130 PUT (199,0),XPLODE
```

To erase the image just displayed by a PUT statement like one of those above, just repeat the same PUT statement, like this:

```
150 '--Erase all 3 images-------------
160 PUT (105,65),XPLODE '1st original
170 PUT (15,25),XPLODE 'Then both
180 PUT (199,0),XPLODE ' copies
```

Moving Objects

The following steps will move an object whose image is captured in a numeric array:

- Display it initially with a PUT statement (like the one above);
- Calculate its new coordinates;
- Erase it with a PUT statement at the old coordinates;
- Redisplay it with a PUT statement at the new coordinates;
- Repeat from the second step.

The following statements use the steps outlined above to flash explosion images in several screen positions:

```
190 '--Flash random explosions---------
210 NEWCOL=0:NEWROW=119 'Start position
220 PUT (NEWCOL,NEWROW),XPLODE 'Image on
230 FOR DUP=1 TO 10
240 OLDCOL=NEWCOL:OLDROW=NEWROW
250 NEWCOL=RND*199:NEWROW=RND*119
260 FOR T%=1 TO 2100/10:NEXT 'Pause
270 PUT (OLDCOL,OLDROW),XPLODE 'Image off
280 PUT (NEWCOL,NEWROW),XPLODE 'Image on
300 NEXT DUP
```

By executing an empty FOR/NEXT loop (line 260), the program segment above waits about 1/10 second before erasing and redisplaying the explosion image. Experiments show that PC BASIC will execute such a loop about 2100 times per second.

The program segment above also uses the RND function to calculate the image's new position (line 250). That function returns a random decimal fraction between 0 and 1, so multiplying its value times 199 or 119 calculates a value between 0 and 199 or 0 and 119, respectively. The RND function will produce the same series of numbers each time the program is run. To get a truly random set of numbers each time the program is run, add the following statement:

```
200 RANDOMIZE VAL(RIGHT$(TIME$,2))
```

A RANDOMIZE statement like the one above selects the set of random numbers that subsequent RND functions will draw from. The value specified determines which set to use. Every integer between -32768 and 32767 will choose a different set. The example above bases its choice on the time, as kept by the internal clock and reported by the TIME$ function. The TIME$ function, available only in Disk BASIC and Advanced BASIC, reports 24-hour time as an eight-character string value like "08:30:11". The example above only uses the last two digits, namely the seconds, which will always be a number between 0 and 59.

PUT Statement Options

A plain PUT statement interacts with whatever is already displayed in the region it uses. Previous examples used that fact to erase an image by displaying it over itself, leaving the background intact. There are actually five different ways the PUT statement can interact with the existing images on the display screen, and you choose one by suffixing the PUT statement with one of five words: PSET, PRESET, AND, OR, or XOR. Here is an example:

```
280 PUT (NEWCOL,NEWROW),XPLODE,XOR
```

It turns out that a PUT statement with an XOR suffix, like the one above, works exactly the same way as a plain PUT statement with no suffix. The AND, XOR, and OR suffixes each blend array and screen colors according to different rules, which are spelled out in Table 13-5. For example, the AND operation would blend a cyan point (color 1) with a white point (color 3) and get a cyan point (color 1), the OR suffix would blend cyan and white and get white, while the XOR suffix would get magenta from cyan and white.

The PSET suffix does not blend array and screen colors, it simply plots every point exactly as it was captured by a GET statement, without regard to what is already on the screen. The PRESET suffix does the same thing as PSET, except it plots a negative image, where colors 0 and 3 are negatives of each other, as are colors 1 and 2.

An Animation Example

The program listed in Fig. 13-16 animates ten objects on the display screen: nine dots and a wedge. Fig. 13-17 illustrates the action with selected still pictures. First, the dots march on the screen in a line and wave back and forth like a ribbon in a breeze. Soon the wedge enters at the right edge of the screen and chatters by opening and shutting rapidly at its apex. Then it advances at high speed towards the line of dots. It rams into them, but they resist. Finally, it breaks through the line, shooting one of the dots towards the other end of the screen. The wedge chatters again, shrinks to fit through the opening in the line of dots, and rushes up to the lone dot. Then the wedge opens all the way up, surrounds the dot, and

Table 13-5. PUT Statement Color-Blending Suffixes*

Array color	AND Screen color				OR Screen color				XOR Screen color			
	0	1	2	3	0	1	2	3	0	1	2	3
0	0	0	0	0	0	1	2	3	0	1	2	3
1	0	1	0	1	1	1	3	3	1	0	3	2
2	0	0	2	2	2	3	2	3	2	3	0	1
3	0	1	2	3	3	3	3	3	3	2	1	0

*There are two other suffixes. PSET plots exactly as captured. PRESET plots a negative image (colors 0 and 3 are negatives; so are 1 and 2).

```
9 '--Dimension GET & PUT graphic arrays------------------
10 DIM DOT(37),WEDG1(82),WEDG2(82),WEDG3(82),WEDG4(82),WEDG5(82)
20 DOT.HITE=21
30 DIM NDP(8,25) 'Holds next horizontal dot positions
90 '--Construct the players----------------------------
100 CLS:KEY OFF:SCREEN 1:COLOR 0,1
110 CIRCLE (160,100),10,1,0,6.283001
120 PAINT (160,100),1,1
130 GET (148,90)-(172,110),DOT
190 '--A closed wedge----------------
200 CLS:DRAW "C2BM142,100M+30,-20M+0,+40M-30,-20"
210 PAINT (160,100),2,2
220 GET (142,80)-(172,120),WEDG1
290 '--A partially open wedge---------
300 ANGL$="M-30,-10M+30,-10" 'DRAW commands
310 CLS:DRAW "C2BM172,120;XANGL$;XANGL$;M+0,+40;"
320 PAINT (171,101),2,2:PAINT (171,99),2,2
330 GET (142,80)-(172,120),WEDG2
390 '--A wide open wedge-------------
400 CLS:DRAW "C2BM142,80M+30,+0M+0,+40M-30,+0"
410 GET (142,80)-(172,120),WEDG3
490 '--A short wedge-----------------
500 CLS:DRAW "C2BM142,100M+30,-10M+0,+20M-30,-10"
510 PAINT (160,100),2,2
520 GET (142,80)-(172,120),WEDG4
590 '--A wedge & dot combo-----------
600 CLS:PUT (142,80),WEDG1:PUT (148,90),DOT
610 GET (142,80)-(172,120),WEDG5
990 '--Get horizontal coordinates for dots in each different frame---
1000 CLS:FOR FRAME=0 TO 25:FOR K%=0 TO 8
1010 READ NDP(K%,FRAME)
1020 NEXT K%,FRAME
1190 '--Dots march on screen------------------------------
1200 GOSUB 4900 'Dots enter
1290 '--Dots wave 5 times-----------------------------
1300 FOR DUP=1 TO 5:FOR FRAME=1 TO 2
1310 GOSUB 4000 'Move dots
1320 NEXT FRAME,DUP
1390 '--Wedge enters----------------------------------
1400 OLDCOL=285:NEWCOL=OLDCOL:ROW=3.5*DOT.HITE
```

Fig. 13-16. Sample screen animation program.

```
1410 PUT (OLDCOL,ROW),WEDG1
1420 FOR DUP=1 TO 2
1430 GOSUB 10000:GOSUB 4600 'Wedge chatters after med. delay
1440 NEXT DUP
1450 GOSUB 10000 'Medium delay
1490 '--Wedge approaches dots-----------------------------
1500 FOR NEWCOL=OLDCOL-15 TO NDP(4,2)+24 STEP -15
1510 GOSUB 4500 'Move wedge
1520 NEXT
1590 '--Dots twice resist battering-----------------------
1600 NEWCOL=OLDCOL 'Start with current wedge pos.
1610 FOR DUP=1 TO 2
1620 FOR FRAME=3 TO 10 '3 steps forward, 4 back, 1 forward
1630 IF FRAME<6 OR FRAME=10 THEN NEWCOL=NEWCOL-5 ELSE NEWCOL=NEWCOL+5
1640 GOSUB 4000:GOSUB 4500 'Move dots, then wedge
1650 NEXT FRAME, DUP
1790 '--Wedge plows through--------------------------------
1800 FOR FRAME=11 TO 18
1810 NEWCOL=NEWCOL-5
1820 GOSUB 4000:GOSUB 4500 'Dots spread out and wedge advances
1830 NEXT FRAME
1840 GOSUB 10000 'Medium delay
1850 GOSUB 4600 'Wedge chatters
1860 PUT(OLDCOL,ROW),WEDG1 'Wedge
1870 PUT(OLDCOL,ROW),WEDG4 ' shrinks
1890 '--Shrunken wedge advances on lone dot--------------
1900 FOR NEWCOL=OLDCOL TO 65 STEP -5
1910 PUT (OLDCOL,ROW),WEDG4
1920 PUT (NEWCOL,ROW),WEDG4
1930 OLDCOL=NEWCOL
1940 NEXT NEWCOL
1950 PUT (OLDCOL,ROW),WEDG4 'Wedge resumes
1960 PUT (OLDCOL,ROW),WEDG1 ' normal size
1970 GOSUB 10000 'Medium delay
1980 PUT (OLDCOL,ROW),WEDG1 'Erase wedge image
2090 '--Wedge surrounds lone dot---------------------------
2100 GOSUB 4700 'Wedge opens part way
2110 PUT (OLDCOL,ROW),WEDG3 'Wedge opens  wide
2120 FOR NEWCOL=OLDCOL TO 35 STEP -5 'Surrounds dot
2130 PUT (OLDCOL,ROW),WEDG3
```

Fig. 13-16–Cont.   Sample screen animation program.

```
2140 PUT (NEWCOL,ROW),WEDG3
2150 OLDCOL=NEWCOL
2160 NEXT NEWCOL
2170 PUT (OLDCOL,ROW),WEDG3 'Erase open wedge
2190 '--Wedge closes----------------------------------------
2200 GOSUB 4700 'Wedge closes part way
2210 PUT (OLDCOL,ROW),WEDG1 'Fully closed
2290 '--Dot line straightens-------------------------------
2300 FOR FRAME=19 TO 25
2310 GOSUB 4000 'Move dots
2320 NEXT FRAME
2390 '--Wedge leaves, full---------------------------------
2400 FOR NEWCOL=OLDCOL TO 0 STEP -3
2410 PUT (OLDCOL,ROW),WEDG5
2420 PUT (NEWCOL,ROW),WEDG5
2430 OLDCOL=NEWCOL
2440 NEXT NEWCOL
2450 PUT (OLDCOL,ROW),WEDG5 'Erase wedge
2460 GOSUB 10000:GOSUB 10000 'Two medium delays
2490 '--Captured dot replaced and dots march off----------
2500 PUT (140,4*DOT.HITE),DOT 'Replace captured dot
2510 GOSUB 10000:GOSUB 10000 'Two medium delays
2520 GOSUB 4900 'Dots leave
3000 END
3990 '==Move all dots=============================
4000 FOR K%=0 TO 8
4010 IF NDP(K%,FRAME-1)<>NDP(K%,FRAME) THEN PUT (NDP(K%,FRAME-1),
     K%*DOT.HITE),DOT:PUT(NDP(K%,FRAME),K%*DOT.HITE),DOT
4020 NEXT K%:RETURN
4490 '==Move wedge=============================
4500 PUT (OLDCOL,ROW),WEDG1
4510 PUT (NEWCOL,ROW),WEDG1
4520 OLDCOL=NEWCOL
4530 RETURN
4590 '==Wedge chatters=========================
4600 FOR K%=1 TO 5
4610 PUT (OLDCOL,ROW),WEDG1
4620 GOSUB 4700 'Wedge opens part way
4630 PUT (OLDCOL,ROW),WEDG1 'Restore normal wedge
4640 NEXT K%:RETURN
```

Fig. 13-16—Cont.   Sample screen animation program.

```
4690 '==Wedge opens part way=====================
4700 PUT (OLDCOL,ROW),WEDG2
4710 PUT (OLDCOL,ROW),WEDG2
4720 RETURN
4890 '==Dots march on or off screen===============
4900 FOR K%=0 TO 8
4910 PUT (NDP(K%,0),K%*DOT.HITE),DOT
4920 GOSUB 10100 'Short delay
4930 NEXT K%:RETURN
9990 '==Medium timing delay=====================
10000 FOR T%=1 TO 1250*1.5:NEXT:RETURN
10090 '==Short timing delay=====================
10100 FOR T%=1 TO 1250/8:NEXT:RETURN
10990 '--Horizontal dot coordinates---------------------
20000 DATA 140,140,140,140,140,140,140,140,140 :REM starting positions
20010 DATA 130,130,130,130,130,130,130,130,130 :REM wave back and forth
20020 DATA 140,140,140,140,140,140,140,140,140
20030 DATA 140,140,140,140,135,140,140,140,140 :REM resist wedge
20040 DATA 140,140,140,135,130,135,140,140,140
20050 DATA 140,140,135,130,125,130,135,140,140
20060 DATA 140,140,140,135,130,135,140,140,140
20070 DATA 140,140,140,140,135,140,140,140,140
20080 DATA 140,140,140,140,140,140,140,140,140
20090 DATA 140,140,140,140,145,140,140,140.140
20100 DATA 140,140,140,140,140,140,140,140,140
20110 DATA 140,140,140,140,135,140,140,140,140 :REM wedge plows through
20120 DATA 140,140,140,135,130,135,140,140,140
20130 DATA 140,140,135,130,125,130,135,140,140
20140 DATA 140,135,130,125,110,125,130,135,140
20150 DATA 140,135,125,115,090,115,125,135,140
20160 DATA 140,135,125,105,065,105,125,135,140
20170 DATA 140,135,125,105,050,105,125,135,140
20180 DATA 140,135,125,105,041,105,125,135,140
20190 DATA 140,135,125,115,041,115,125,135,140 :REM straighten out
20200 DATA 140,135,130,125,041,125,130,135,140 :REM remaining dots
20210 DATA 140,140,135,130,041,130,135,140,140
20220 DATA 140,140,140,135,041,135,140,140,140
20230 DATA 140,140,140,140,041,140,140,140,140
20240 DATA 140,140,140,145,041,145,140,140,140
20250 DATA 140,140,140,140,041,140,140,140,140
```

Fig. 13-16—Cont.   Sample screen animation program.

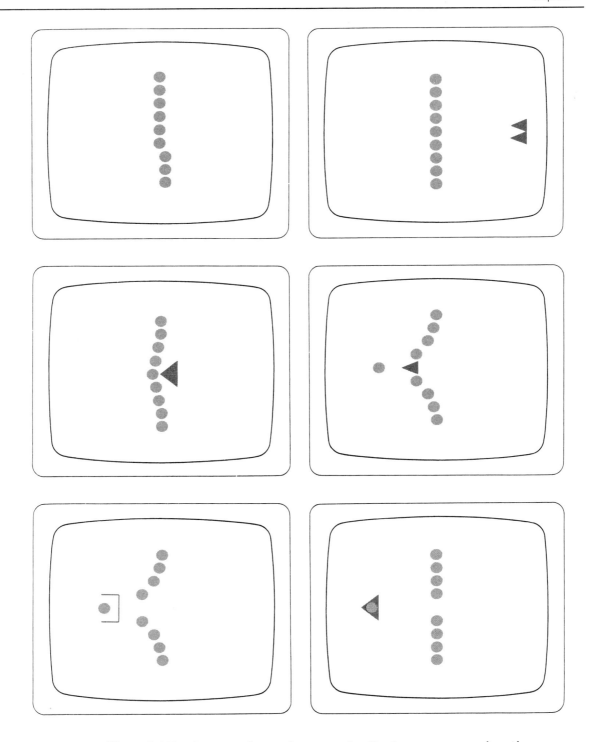

Fig. 13-17. Scenes from the sample display screen animation program (listed in Fig. 13-16).

closes again. The dots resume their line. The wedge, with its captive dot, leaves the screen. The captured dot is replaced in the line, and the dots march off the screen.

This short subject requires a total of six players (Fig. 13-18): one dot and five variations of the wedge. There is a normal wedge, half-open and fully open wedges used to create the illusion of an opening and shutting wedge, a shrunken wedge to slip through the line of dots, and a wedge with a captured dot enclosed. Before the action starts, each player flashes on the screen as the program displays it and captures it in an array.

The program comments explain how the program works. Notice how the DRAW statements that construct the various wedges use relative coordinates (lines 200, 310, 400, and 500), and in one case, X subcommands to include a separate command string (lines 300 and 310). The program uses an array to determine the horizontal position of every dot any time they move. It reads the array values from a DATA statement table of values (lines 20000 through 20250). There are other ways to determine the position of a player; the wedge position is recalculated before every move, for example.

If you run the program, you will notice great variations in the speed at which the players move. The line of dots seems to wave faster than it

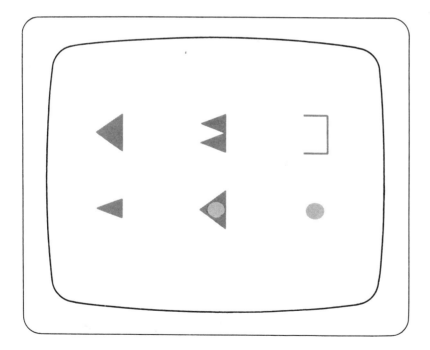

Fig. 13-18. Players used in the sample screen animation program (see Figs. 13-16 and 13-17).

bends under the pressure of the wedge because each movement during the waving cycle covers twice the distance of a movement in the bending cycle. For example, the fifth dot waves between columns 140 and 130 (lines 20010 and 20020), but it starts to yield by moving from column 140 to 135 (lines 20020 and 20030). Wedge speed varies mostly for another reason. The wedge moves fast when it is the only player moving (for example, lines 1500 through 1520), but when the dots move at the same time, it slows way down (for example, lines 1610 through 1650). With ten objects moving, it takes a while to get around to each one a second time.

CHAPTER 14

SOUND

The PC can generate sounds and music through its built-in speaker using either of two statements, SOUND or PLAY. Both statements give you control over the frequency and duration of a tone, but neither statement can control loudness. Tones produced are always pure; there is no direct way to distort them for sound effects.

GENERATING TONES

The SOUND statement generates a tone of any frequency between 37 and 32767 hertz (cycles per second), lasting for any duration from a split second to a half hour. Here is an example:

```
SOUND 523.25, 18.2
```

The example above generates a tone that has a frequency of 523.25 hertz, which is the note middle C. Fig. 14-1 illustrates the frequencies of the natural notes spanning two octaves below middle C and two octaves above it.

The second number in a SOUND statement determines the duration of the tone. Duration is measured in *clock ticks*, and there are 18.2 ticks per second. Table 14-1 compares selected clock tick values with typical music tempos and their equivalent number of beats per minute.

PC BASIC does not wait for a SOUND statement to finish before going on to the next statement. The following example demonstrates:

```
10 CLS:WIDTH 40
20 SOUND 440, 27.3
30 FOR K=1 TO 40
```

```
40 LOCATE RND(1)*23+1,RND(1)*39+1
50 PRINT CHR$(14);
60 NEXT K
70 LOCATE 24,1
```

After clearing the screen, the program above generates the note A below middle C for a second and a half. While it holds the note, PC BASIC executes the rest of the program, which displays musical note characters at random locations on the screen. In fact, the program finishes before the note stops.

PC BASIC will not overlap execution of two SOUND statements, however. If a second SOUND statement occurs before the end of a tone from a prior SOUND statement, the PC waits until the first tone finishes. For example, if the following line were added to the previous example, the note it generates (D above middle C) would not occur until after the earlier note lasted its 1½ seconds:

```
80 SOUND 587.33, 9.1
```

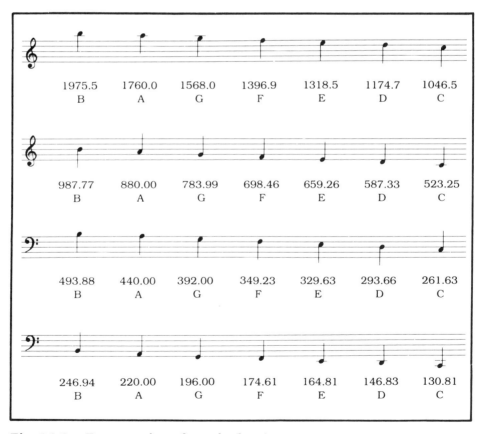

Fig. 14-1. Frequencies of musical notes.

Table 14-1. Musical Tempos

Clock ticks	Tempo	Beats per minute
↑		↑
27.30	Larghissimo	40
↕	Largo	↕
18.20		60
↑	Larghetto	↑
	Grave	
	Lento	
16.55		66
↑	Adagio	↑
	Adagietto	
14.37		76
↑	Andante	↑
	Andantino	
10.11		108
↑	Moderato	↑
	Allegretto	
9.10		120
↑	Allegro.	↑
	Vivace	
6.50		168
↕	Presto	↕
5.25		208
↓	Prestissimo	↓

You can turn sound off at any time by executing a SOUND statement with a duration of zero, like this:

```
sound 1760,32767
Ok
sound 100,0
Ok
```

Tones above 25,000 hertz are inaudible; in fact most people cannot hear tones above 15,000 hertz. Therefore a SOUND statement that specifies a high frequency will generate periods of silence.

Sound Effects

You can use the SOUND statement to create some acceptable sound effects. Unfortunately, there are no rules or guidelines that apply; all you can do is experiment. Fig. 14-2 lists some program lines that you can use as a starting point.

MUSIC

While it is possible to play music using the SOUND statement, the requisite translation of notes to multidigit numbers is awkward at best. In

```
10  REM '--Random noise----------------
20  SOUND RND(1)*300+440,RND(1)*RND(1)
30  GOTO 20


10  '--Bouncing----------------------
20  FOR K=60 TO 1 STEP -2
30  SOUND 246.94-K/2,K/20
40  SOUND 32767,K/15
50  NEXT K


10  '--Falling------------------------
20  FOR K=2000 TO 550 STEP -10
30  SOUND K,K/4000
40  NEXT K


10  '--Siren--------------------------
20  FOR L=650 TO -650 STEP -4
30  SOUND 780-ABS(L),.3
40  L=L-2/650
50  NEXT L
60  GOTO 20


10  '--Hi-lo alarm--------------------
20  SOUND 987.7,5
30  SOUND 329.63,5
40  GOTO 20


10  '--Motor--------------------------
20  FOR L=50 TO 60 STEP 10
30  SOUND L,.002
40  NEXT L
50  GOTO 20
```

Fig. 14-2. Sample sound effects programs.

Advanced BASIC, you can use the PLAY statement instead. It has a special music language that makes it easy to program tunes. The music language consists of 19 subcommands, which are listed in Table 14-2. To play a tune, you make up a string value that contains the appropriate sequence of subcommands, as explained in the following paragraphs.

Table 14-2. PLAY Statement Subcommands

Subcommand	Interpretation
note	Play a named note (C, D, E, F, G, A, or B) in the current octave, either sharp (suffix + or #), flat (suffix -), or natural (letter alone)
O*oct*	Set octave number, 0 to 6 (middle C is octave 3)
N*nbr*	Play a note by number, 0 to 84 (0 means rest)
L*len*	Set the length of all later notes, from a whole note (*len* = 1) to a 64th note (*len* = 64); Optionally, *len* alone may suffix a single note to only affect that note
P*len*	Pause (rest); *len* as described for the L subcommand
dots	Each period that suffixes a note or pause subcommand holds the note or pause 1½ times normal
T*beat*	Set the tempo in beats per minute, 32 to 255
MF	Music foreground, program waits
MB	Music background, program continues
MN	Music normal, not legato or staccato
ML	Music legato
MS	Music staccato
X*s$*;	Execute subcommands from another string

Naming Notes

There are two ways to specify notes in a PLAY statement subcommand string. You can name the note by letter, like this:

```
100 PLAY "C D E F G A B"
```

The example above plays a seven-note scale, starting with the C above middle C.

For sharp notes, suffix the name of the note with a # or + character. For flat notes, use the - character as a suffix. Sharps and flats that have no corresponding black key on a piano are not allowed, namely B-sharp, E-sharp, C-flat, and F-flat.

To change octaves, use the O subcommand. The PLAY command has seven octaves, three below middle C numbered 0 through 2, and four above it numbered 4 to 7. The following example plays all the notes, including half steps, in the octave starting with middle C:

```
110 PLAY "O3 C C# D D# E F F# G G# A
      A# B"
```

Altogether, there are 84 notes in the seven available octaves (Fig. 14-3). Instead of designating them by octave and name, you can designate them by number, using the N subcommand. The following example generates the same scale as the last example:

```
PLAY "N37 N38 N39 N40 N41 N42 N43 N44
      N45 N46 N47 N48"
```

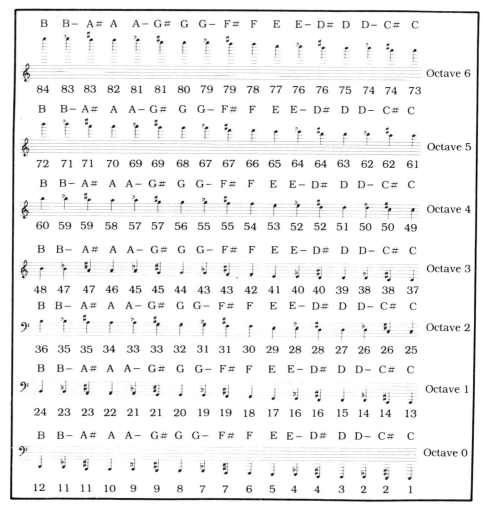

Fig. 14-3. Notes available in the PLAY statement. (Numbers shown below notes are for the N subcommand.)

Note Length

Notes in the examples so far have had the length of a quarter note. To change the length of the note, suffix it with a number, like this:

```
PLAY "O3 C1 C2 C4 C8 C16 C32 C64"
```

The length of the note is equal to one divided by the number that follows the note. Thus a suffix of 1 designates a whole note, a 2 designates a half note, and so on. The example above plays seven middle C notes, the first one a whole note, the next a half note, then comes a quarter note, after that a sixteenth note, and the last two are thirty-second and sixty-fourth notes (Fig. 14-4).

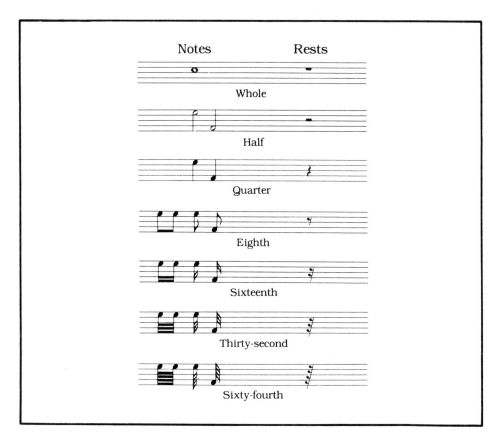

Fig. 14-4. Note and rest lengths.

You can use the L subcommand to establish a note length that will be used by default. Just suffix it with a number as described in the preceding paragraph. The following example plays a descending scale of eighth notes:

```
PLAY  "02 L8 C B A G F E D"
```

To play a dotted note, suffix it with a period. You can use more than one period after a note; each period increases the note's length by 50 percent. Here is an example of a dotted half note and a dotted eighth note:

```
PLAY  "C2. G8."
```

Pauses (Rests)

The P subcommand establishes pauses (rests), with the length determined by a number the same as for the L subcommand (Fig. 14-4). Here is an example:

```
PLAY  "03 C P1 C P2 C P4 C P8 C P16 C"
```

Tempo

The tempo of a musical composition (the rate of speed at which it is played), is indicated by notations like *allegro*, *andante*, and so forth, or by metronome timing. The T subcommand sets the tempo using metronome timing. Table 14-1 compares tempo notations like *allegro* and *andante* with metronome timing.

Music Foreground or Background

Normally, Advanced BASIC will not proceed to the next note in a tune until the current note finishes playing. That is called *music foreground* mode. The MB subcommand tells Advanced BASIC to process up to 32 notes and store them in a memory buffer, and to play music from the buffer while it goes ahead with program execution. That is called *music background* mode. So for short tunes with 32 notes and rests or less, it is possible to have the computer do two things at once: play a tune and keep executing the remainder of the program.

Style: Staccato, Legato, Normal

The PLAY statement can play notes staccato, with distinct breaks between them; it can play notes legato, with no breaks between them; or it can play notes normally, with just enough pause between them to make them distinct. The MS subcommand produces a staccato performance by only holding each note for $\frac{3}{4}$ of its nominal length, and resting for the remaining $\frac{1}{4}$ beat. The ML subcommand creates a legato performance by holding each note for the full length, so that succeeding notes seem to run together. Subcommand MN produces a normal performance by playing notes $\frac{7}{8}$ of their nominal lengths, resting for the remaining $\frac{1}{8}$ beat.

Playing Music

The PLAY statement does a credible job performing simple tunes, especially those written for keyboard instruments like the piano or organ. It is limited, however, to playing just one part. Two suitable compositions by Johann Sebastian Bach, the "Minuet" and the "Minuet in D Minor" from his *Anna Magdalena Notebook*, are shown in Figs. 14-5 and 14-6. Programs that play them are listed in Figs. 14-7 and 14-8. To make comparing the programs with the music easier, the name of each note is printed underneath it on the musical score. The following paragraphs briefly analyze how the programs work and how the musical scores were translated into subcommands.

Both programs work the same way. They store the PLAY statement subcommands in DATA statements starting at line 1010, and read the sub-

Fig. 14-5. "Minuet" from *Anna Magdalena Notebook*, by **J.S. Bach.**

Fig. 14-6. "Minuet in D minor" from *Anna Magdalena Notebook*, by J.S. Bach.

```
10 DIM TUNE$(4)
20 CLS:WIDTH 40:KEY OFF
30 LOCATE 11,17:PRINT "Minuet"
40 LOCATE 12,15:PRINT "J.S. Bach"
90 REM '--Read music from data----------------------------
100 FOR MEASURE=1 TO 32
110 READ NOTES$
120 TUNE$(MEASURE\8)=TUNE$(MEASURE\8)+NOTES$
130 NEXT MEASURE
190 '--Play the tune---------------------------------------
200 PLAY "xTUNE$(0); xTUNE$(1); xTUNE$(2); xTUNE$(3); xTUNE$(4);"
1000 '--Music, measure by measure-------------------------
1010 DATA T110 L8 MS D4 MN O3 G A B O4 C
1020 DATA D4 O3 MS G4 MN G4
1030 DATA O4 MS E4 MN C D E F#
1040 DATA G4 O3 MS G4 MN G4
1050 DATA MS O4 C4 MN D C O3 B A
1060 DATA MS B4 MN O4 C O3 B A G
1070 DATA MS F#4 MN G A B G
1080 DATA B4 A2
1090 DATA O4 MS D4 MN O3 G A B O4 C
1100 DATA D4 O3 MS G4 G4
1110 DATA O4 E4 MN C D E F#
1120 DATA G4 O3 MS G4 G4
1130 DATA O4 C4 MN D C O3 B A
1140 DATA B4 O4 C O3 B A G
1150 DATA A4 B A G F#
1160 DATA G2.
1170 DATA O4 B4 G A B G
1180 DATA A4 D E F# D
1190 DATA G4 E F# G D
1200 DATA C#4 O3 B O4 C# O3 A4
1210 DATA A B O4 C# D E F#
1220 DATA MS G4 MN F#4 E4
1230 DATA MS F#4 O3 A4 O4 C#4
1240 DATA MN D2.
1250 DATA D4 O3 G F# G4
1260 DATA O4 E4 O3 G F# G4
1270 DATA O4 D4 C4 O3 B4
1280 DATA A G F# G A4
1290 DATA D E F# G A B
1300 DATA O4 C4 O3 B4 A4
1310 DATA B O4 D O3 G4 F#4
1320 DATA G2.
```

Fig. 14-7.   Program to play Bach Minuet (see Fig. 14-5).

```
10 DIM TUNE$(4)
20 CLS:WIDTH 40:KEY OFF
30 LOCATE 11,12:PRINT "Minuet in D minor"
40 LOCATE 12,17:PRINT "J.S. Bach' '
90 REM '--Read music from data--------------------------
100 FOR MEASURE=1 TO 32
110 READ NOTES$
120 TUNE$(MEASURE\8)=TUNE$(MEASURE\8)+NOTES$
130 NEXT MEASURE
190 '--Play the tune----------------------------------
200 PLAY "xTUNE$(0); xTUNE$(1); xTUNE$(2); xTUNE$(3); xTUNE$(4);"
1000 '--Music, measure by measure--------------------
1010 DATA T90 ML L8 O3 A4 O4 F E D C#
1020 DATA D4 O3 A4 B-4
1030 DATA O3 C# E G B- A G
1040 DATA F4 E F D4
1050 DATA F4 B- A O4 D C
1060 DATA F4 E D C O3 B-
1070 DATA A B-16 O4 C16 O3 F4 E4
1080 DATA F2.
1090 DATA A4 O4 F E D C#
1100 DATA D4 O3 A4 B-4
1110 DATA C# E G B- A G
1120 DATA F4 E F D4
1130 DATA F4 B- A O4 D C
1140 DATA F4 E D C O3 B-
1150 DATA A B-16 O4 C16 O3 F4 E4
1160 DATA F2.
1170 DATA MS O4 A4 O3 F ML O4 A G F
1180 DATA E16 F16 G C2
1190 DATA MS F4 O3 D ML O4 F E D
1200 DATA C#16 D16 E O3 A2
1210 DATA A B O4 C# D E F
1220 DATA G E C# B- A G
1230 DATA F16 E16 D E4 C#4
1240 DATA D2.
1250 DATA MS A4 O3 F ML O4 A G F
1260 DATA E16 F16 G C2
1270 DATA MS F4 O3 D ML O4 F E D
1280 DATA C#16 D16 E O3 A2
1290 DATA A B O4 C# D E F
1300 DATA G E C# B- A G
1310 DATA F16 E16 D E4 C#4
1320 DATA D2.
```

Fig. 14-8.   Program to play Bach Minuet in D minor (see Fig. 14-6).

command strings into string array TUNE$ one measure at a time. Then, playing the tune stored in the array is simply a matter of using an X subcommand to incorporate each array element in turn.

The score for the "Minuet" specifies a tempo of *moderato* (Fig. 14-5), which Table 14-1 says equals 108 to 120 beats per minute. The T subcommand in the first measure (Fig. 14-7, line 1010) sets the tempo at 110. It also establishes the default note length as an eighth note. The dot over the first note in the first measure means it is to be played staccato, so the MS subcommand designates that. The note itself is a D in octave 4 (the default octave), and it is a quarter note, so the subcommand D4 plays it. The next subcommand, MN, sets normal performance style, since the remainder of the notes in the measure are not marked staccato. The next note is in octave 3, and the O3 subcommand stipulates that. The G, A, and B subcommands play the appropriate eighth notes. The last note in the measure is C in octave 4, played by subcommands O4 and C. Each of the other 31 measures in the composition is similarly translated to a single DATA statement (lines 1020 to 1320).

The tempo in the second composition (Fig. 14-6) is *andante*. The first subcommand (Fig. 14-8, line 1010) sets the tempo at 90 beats per minute, which is within the range indicated by Table 14-1. The ML subcommand then establishes a legato performance, as directed by the musical score. The rest of the DATA statements translate the composition into subcommands in a straightforward way.

CHAPTER 15

DIRECT ACCESS AND CONTROL

Compared to BASIC on other computers, PC BASIC is remarkably complete. It gives you access to most of the features of the system. Still, the PC has a few features and options that no BASIC statement or function will specifically control, things like determining the state of the **Num Lock** key, or switching between the monochrome adapter and the color/graphics adapter when both are present. There are also occasions when BASIC is too slow at using the PC features that it can control. Display screen animation is one example. And in addition, Disk BASIC and Advanced BASIC programs can only make use of about 92,000 bytes of dynamic memory (Cassette BASIC, only about 65,000), even if the system has more available. Assembly language programs are not limited like that, so they can be much larger on systems that have lots of memory.

To circumvent these limitations, PC BASIC includes several statements and functions that give you direct access to the system memory. This chapter explains how to use those statements and functions, and illustrates their use with half a dozen examples. The chapter concludes with a general discussion of machine language and assembly language programming, but it does not teach you how to devise machine language programs.

Use the statements and functions explained in this chapter with caution. They all bypass the normal safeguards BASIC maintains and let you change anything in dynamic memory, including the BASIC interpreter, PC DOS, and the BASIC program and variables. Change the wrong area of memory, and you can disrupt things to the point where you must reset the computer with **Ctrl|Alt|Del**. You may even have to turn the system unit completely off, wait a few seconds, and turn it back on again in order to regain control.

DIRECT MEMORY REFERENCE

The PC uses its memory in many different ways. In order to run even a simple BASIC program, it must allocate a segment of memory to the BASIC program lines and another segment to the BASIC variables. Other segments go to the BASIC interpreter, workspace for the interpreter, the contents of the display screen, and the run-time stack, not to mention the disk operating system program.

Each memory cell contains a value between 0 and 255. The value may represent things as diverse as a character code, a BASIC command token, the status of a piece of PC equipment, or a machine language instruction. When you start manipulating memory directly, you are the one who must decide how to interpret the value in a particular memory cell.

Most of the time, BASIC programmers do not need to worry about how memory is organized or what the value in a particular memory cell is. But for those features and options of the PC system that BASIC cannot monitor or control in any other way, the DEF SEG and POKE statements, along with the PEEK function, permit access to single memory cells. In addition, an option of the CLEAR command lets you control the size of the run-time stack.

Memory Addressing

Each individual memory cell in the PC is identified by a number, called its *address*. The PC can have up to 1,048,576 memory cells (that is, 1,024K bytes), whose addresses range from 0 to 1048575. Dynamic memory uses some of those addresses, read-only memory uses other addresses, and on most PC systems, part of the addresses are vacant. The vacant addresses occur on systems that have less memory than the maximum allowed.

Because of the way the PC's 8088 microprocessor works, you cannot specify a PC memory address just by stating a number between 0 and 1048575. First, you must define a base address, called a *segment address*, and then you may state an offset relative to that base address. To compute the actual address, the PC multiplies the segment address by 16 and adds the offset. For example, if the segment address is 64 (hexadecimal 40) and the offset is 23 (hexadecimal 17), the actual address is 64*16+23=1047 (hexadecimal 417).

There are no restrictions placed on the segment address or the offset, except that each must be between 0 and 65535. Therefore, there are many combinations of segment address and offset that yield the same actual address. For example, if the segment address is 0 and the offset is 1047 (hexadecimal 417), the actual address is 0*16+1047=1047 (hexadecimal 417), exactly the same as the address calculated in the last paragraph.

PC memory addresses are customarily written in the form *segment:offset*, and the segment address and offset numbers are usually stated in hexadecimal. For example, address 1047 (hexadecimal 417) might be written 0:417 or 40:17. Several useful addresses are offsets from the beginning of the BASIC workspace, whose segment address varies depending on which version of BASIC you are using. Those addresses are written DS:*offset*.

Defining the Memory Segment Address

The DEF SEG statement defines the memory segment address, in other words, the *segment* part of a *segment:offset* address. The following example uses a hexadecimal number to specify the segment address:

```
100 DEF SEG=&H40
```

PC BASIC multiplies the specified value by 16 and uses the product as a base address for all subsequent direct memory reference statements and functions like PEEK, POKE, BLOAD, BSAVE, CALL, and DEF USR (all described later in this chapter). The value must be between 0 and 65535.

The memory segment address portion of the DEF SEG statement is optional. If absent, PC BASIC automatically supplies the base address of the BASIC workspace area. This form of the DEF SEG statement specifies the first part of a DS:*segment* address, and looks like this:

```
1310 DEF SEG 'Use BASIC workspace segment
          address
```

When the BASIC interpreter first gets control of the system, it sets the segment address to the base address of the BASIC workspace. Later, DEF SEG statements may change it to any location. RUN and other statements will not reset the segment address to the BASIC workspace area; only restarting the interpreter or executing a plain DEF SEG statement will do that.

Examining Memory

The PEEK function lets you examine the contents of any memory cell. It is a function, not a statement, and must be used in that context. Here is an example:

```
200 DEF SEG=0:LW=PEEK(&H4A) 'Determine
          line width
```

The value in parentheses specifies the offset into the current segment, and must be between 0 and 65535 (hexadecimal FFFF). This is the *offset* part of a *segment:offset* address.

The PEEK function merely reports the numeric value between 0 and 255 that is stored in the memory cell it examines. You must interpret that value as a character code, a BASIC command token, a line number, part of a multibyte numeric value, etc. Sometimes you can determine the correct interpretation by the context, but if you are unsure, stick to examining memory cells whose use you know, like those described later in this chapter.

Changing Memory Contents

You can change the contents of any dynamic memory cell with a POKE statement. It has no effect on read-only memory or on vacant memory addresses. Here is an example:

```
225 DEF SEG=0:POKE &H41A,PEEK(&H41C) 'Clear
    keyboard
```

The first value in a POKE statement, which must be between 0 and 65535 (hexadecimal FFFF), specifies an offset into the current segment. This is the *offset* part of a *segment:offset* address. The second value listed is placed in the specified memory cell, and it must be between 0 and 255 (hexadecimal FF).

SOME USEFUL MEMORY ADDRESSES

Table 15-1 lists some interesting memory addresses that you can use PEEK functions and POKE statements with, and several of those addresses are described in more detail in the paragraphs below. These descriptions fulfill the promises of earlier chapters by telling you how to circumvent some specific regular system features.

Changing Medium-Resolution Character Color

Text and other characters displayed on the medium-resolution graphics screen normally appear in color 3, which is white or gold depending on the active palette (review Table 13-3). A compound statement like the one below will change the color of characters displayed after it is executed:

```
1300 DEF SEG:POKE &H4E,HUE
```

In the example above, variable HUE must have a value of 1, 2, or 3 in order to choose one of the foreground hues from the active palette. Making HUE 0 causes all characters to display in the background color, rendering them invisible. That eliminates display screen echoing of keystrokes, which effectively blocks keyboard input. If the program does not restore character visibility with another POKE statement, you will not be able to enter immediate mode commands without resetting the system.

Table 15-1. Some Useful Memory Addresses

Use	Offset		Bytes
	Hexadecimal	Decimal	
DEF SEG			
Current BASIC line number	&H02E	46	2 *
Line number of last BASIC error	&H347	839	2 *
Offset to start of BASIC program text	&H030	48	2 *
Offset to start of BASIC variables	&H358	856	2 *
BASIC keyboard buffer control†	&H06A	106	1
Medium-resolution text color†	&H04E	78	1
DEF SEG = 0			
Adapter card selection†	&H410	1040	1
Keyboard status†	&H417	1047	1
Pointer to head of system kybd buffer†	&H41A	1050	2
Pointer to tail of system kybd buffer	&H41C	1052	2
System keyboard buffer	&H41E	1054	16
Current screen mode	&H449	1097	1
Screen width (columns)	&H44A	1098	2

*It takes two consecutive memory cells to store values which, like a line number, may be greater than 255. In that case, the total value equals the value in the first cell plus 256 times the value in the second cell.
†See text for details.

Selecting the Video Adapter Card

A PC that has both the monochrome adapter and color/graphics adapter cannot use both at the same time. Whenever you turn on or reset the PC, it selects a video adapter based on the system configuration switches (see pages 5-13 to 5-15 in the "Options" section of the IBM manual *Guide to Operations*). You can choose either adapter under program control by changing the contents of memory address 0:410. The following two programs illustrate this:

```
10 '--Switch to 40-col color --------
20 DEF SEG=0:POKE &H410,(PEEK(&H410) AND
   &HCF) OR &H10
30 SCREEN 1:SCREEN 0:WIDTH 40 '40-col. text
40 LOCATE ,,1,6,7 'cursor shape

10 '--Switch to 80-col monochrome---
20 DEF SEG=0:POKE &H410,PEEK(&H410) OR &H30
30 SCREEN 0:WIDTH 80 '80-col. text mode
40 LOCATE ,,1,12,13 'cursor shape
```

The same memory cell will tell you which monitor adapter is active, like this:

```
10 '--Check for color/graphics adapter--------
20 DEF SEG=0
30 IF (PEEK(&H410) AND &H30)<>&H30 THEN 100
40 PRINT "This program requires the
   color/graphics adapter."
50 END
100 REM continue graphics program here
```

Determining Screen Width

You can design a program with the ability to use both 40- and 80-column display lines, depending on the capabilities of the monitor. Memory address 0:4A will tell you the currently selected line width. Here is an example:

```
200 DEF SEG=0:LW=PEEK(&H4A) 'Determine
    screen width
```

Determining Keyboard Modes

There is no way to tell just by looking at the keyboard whether the **Caps Lock** key has locked the keyboard in capitals mode, and there is also no way to tell whether the **Num Lock** key has put the keypad in numeric mode or nonnumeric mode. Examining memory address 0:417 discloses both facts. The following program shows how:

```
10 DEF SEG=0
20 '--Check Shift Lock key--------------------
30 LOCATE 25,39:IF (PEEK(&H417) AND &H40)=&H40
   THEN PRINT CHR$(24); ELSE PRINT CHR$(25);
40 '--Check Num Lock key--------------------
50 LOCATE 25,38:IF (PEEK(&H417) AND &H20)=&H20
   THEN PRINT "#" ; ELSE PRINT CHR$(219);
```

The program above displays characters on line 25 of the screen to announce the keyboard modes. If capitals mode is in effect, the character ↑ appears in column 39; otherwise the character ↓ appears there. If the keypad is in numeric mode, the program displays the character # in column 38; in nonnumeric mode a solid square appears there.

You can use the same memory address to set the keyboard modes too, like this:

```
10 DEF SEG=0
20 POKE &H417,(PEEK(&H417) OR &H40) 'upper-case
20 POKE &H417,(PEEK(&H417) AND &HBF) 'lower-case
30 POKE &H417,(PEEK(&H417) OR &H20) 'numeric
30 POKE &H417,(PEEK(&H417) AND &HDF) 'nonnumeric
```

Choose one of the two line 20's and one of the two line 30's to set the keyboard as you like. You may also wish to display characters that announce the keyboard mode like the previous example did.

Ignoring Stray Keystrokes

The PC maintains a 15-character *keyboard buffer* so that you can type at full speed even when it has to divert its attention momentarily away from keyboard entry, as it does during disk access, for example. A program can clear the keyboard buffer just before requesting keyboard input, effectively ignoring any stray keystrokes typed since it last requested keyboard input. Setting memory address 0:41A equal to the contents of memory address 0:41C has that affect. The following example could add this feature to the general input subroutine (Fig. 11-4):

```
225 DEF SEG=0:POKE &H41A,PEEK(&H41C) 'Clr kybd
```

PC BASIC has its own keyboard buffer which keeps track of all the characters that result from a single keystroke. Soft key definitions, for example, can generate several characters with a single keystroke. You can clear extra characters from the BASIC keyboard buffer with a program like this:

```
235 DEF SEG:POKE &H6A,0 'Clear BASIC kybd bfr
```

Enlarging the Run-Time Stack

PC BASIC uses the run-time stack to keep track of nested FOR/NEXT loops, nested subroutine calls (including recursive subroutines), and complex PAINT statements. If a program nests too deeply or tries to fill too complex a shape with color, the run-time stack may run out of memory, resulting in the "Out of memory . . ." error. You can forestall this error by increasing the stack size with a variation of the CLEAR statement. It looks like this:

```
10 CLEAR ,,2048 'Set stack size
```

The value specifies the number of memory cells to reserve for the run-time stack. The standard number is 512 bytes or one-eighth of the dynamic memory available to BASIC, whichever is smaller. The CLEAR statement also erases all variables and arrays, without touching the program lines, as described in Chapter 8.

MACHINE LANGUAGE PROGRAMMING

In forsaking machine language for BASIC, you sacrifice some program execution speed for the convenience and expediency of a more natural, problem-oriented language. For most programming applications, the slight degradation of performance is not noticeable, but in areas like computer animation, program execution speed can be critical, and a BASIC program may not be fast enough. PC BASIC gives you the best of both worlds. You can use BASIC for parts of the program that are not speed sensitive, and then use a CALL statement or USR function in the BASIC program to branch to a machine language program for the parts of the program that require maximum execution speed.

No one writes programs directly in machine language for the PC. Instead they use assembly language, which is a symbolic version of machine language. Its instructions consist of easy-to-remember combinations of letters, yet each one can be exactly translated into a single machine language instruction.

In order to program efficiently in assembly language, you need to know how to use several service programs. These include an *editor* for typing in the program, an *assembler* for translating the program to machine language, a *linker* for creating a memory image from the machine language program, and a *debugger* for assistance in testing and troubleshooting the program.

Clearly, assembly language programming is a lengthy and complex topic, one this book cannot possibly cover. For more information, you may wish to consult the following books:

- *IBM Personal Computer Disk Operating System, 2nd ed.*, part number 6024001. Chapters 4, 5, and 6 describe how to use the IBM editor, linker, and debugger programs.

- *IBM Personal Computer BASIC, 2nd ed.*, part number 6025010. Appendix C explains how to incorporate machine language programs within BASIC programs.

- *IBM Personal Computer MACRO Assembler*, part number 6024002. Describes how to use the IBM assembler program.

- Rector, Russell and George Alexy, *The 8086 Book: includes the 8088*, Osborne/McGraw-Hill, Berkeley, CA, 1980. Chapters 1 through 6 describe assembly language programming for the PC's microprocessor, the Intel 8088.

- Willin, David, *8088 Assembly Language Programming: The IBM PC*, Howard W. Sams & Co., Indianapolis, Indiana, 1983. Describes how to program the PC in assembly language.

APPENDIXES

Subfiles

BASIC SUMMARY

This appendix contains a summary of all BASIC commands, statements, and intrinsic functions. There is also a list of mathematical functions that can be derived from the intrinsic functions. The descriptions in this appendix apply to versions 1.05 and 1.10 of the Disk and Advanced BASIC interpreters, and to version 1.0 of the Cassette BASIC interpreter. Each command, statement, and function specifies which dialects of BASIC it is available in: Advanced, Disk and Advanced, or all three (Advanced, Disk, and Cassette). For in-depth information on the commands, statements, and functions listed here, consult the Index of this book or Chapter 4 of *IBM Personal Computer BASIC, 2nd ed.*

When entering the commands listed here, type all characters printed in **BOLDFACE** exactly as shown, except you may use any combination of capital and small letters. Where you see *italics*, substitute an actual word, constant, variable, array element, expression, or whatever else may be appropriate. Anything enclosed in square brackets ([]) is optional, but if you include it, do not type the brackets themselves. You can repeat any item that is followed by an ellipsis (. . .); do not type the ellipsis itself. Be sure to include all punctuation marks (except square brackets and ellipses), including commas, colons, slashes, hyphens, periods, equal signs, and number signs.

COMMANDS

The commands listed here are most common in immediate mode, but three commands—NAME, TRON, and TROFF—are occasionally useful in programmed mode too. Several multiple keystrokes are also commands of sorts.

- **Ctrl|Scroll Lock** interrupts processing and leaves the PC in immediate mode.
- **Ctrl|Alt|Del** ends BASIC and resets the PC.
- △|**PrtSc** copies the text on the screen onto the printer (device LPT1:).

■ **Ctrl|Num Lock** puts the display screen in a state of suspended animation.

AUTO [*first line number*] [,[*increment*]]
Sets automatic line numbering mode. **Ctrl|Scroll Lock** reverts to manual line numbering. (All)

BLOAD *file name*[,[*offset*]]
Retrieves a memory image from the named file and puts it in memory at its original address unless the *offset* specifies another address (see DEF SEG). (All)

BSAVE *file name, offset, length*
Saves a memory image on the named file. The image starts in memory at the specified *offset* address (see DEF SEG) and has the stated *length*. (All)

CLEAR [,[*program memory*]][,*stack memory*]]
Assigns 0 to all numeric variables and array elements, and assigns null values to all string variables and array elements. Optionally specifies the amount of program memory available (for program lines, variables, and interpreter workspace) and the amount of dynamic memory reserved for the run-time stack. (All)

CONT
Continues program execution at the next statement after a halt. (All)

DELETE *first line*[-*last line*]
Deletes the specified program lines. (All)

EDIT *line number*
Displays the specified line for editing. (All)

FILES [*file name*]
Displays those file names from the disk directory that match the named file (generic names are Ok). (Disk and Advanced)

LIST [*first line*][-[*last line*]][, *file/device name*]
Displays all or part of the program lines in memory. Optionally prints lines on a named file or device. (All)

LLIST [*first line*][-[*last line*]]
Prints all or part of the program lines in memory on the printer (device LPT1:). (All)

LOAD *file name*[,**R**]
Loads a program from the named file, erasing any existing program lines, and optionally runs the loaded program. (All)

MERGE *file name*
  Merges program lines from the named file with those in memory. (All)

NAME *old name* **AS** *new name*
  Renames a disk file. (Disk and Advanced)

NEW
  Deletes all program lines, variables, and arrays from memory. (All)

RENUM [[*first new line*][,[*first old line*][,*increment*]]
  Renumbers program lines. (All)

RESET
  Closes all open files and devices. (Disk and Advanced)

RUN [*line number*]
  Executes the program in memory, optionally starting at a specified line number. (All)

RUN *file name*[,**R**]
  Loads and runs the program in the named file, erasing any existing program lines. Optionally leaves files open. (All)

SAVE *file name*[,*option*]
  Saves the program in memory on the named file using a compressed format, unless *option* is A, for ASCII coded characters, or P, which prevents subsequent listing of the program. (All)

SYSTEM
  Transfers control to PC DOS. (Disk and Advanced)

TRON
  Turns on program trace mode. (All)

TROFF
  Turns off program trace mode. (All)

STATEMENTS

The statements listed here are most common in programmed mode, but most can be used in immediate mode too. The two exceptions are DATA and DEF FN.

BEEP
  Beeps the internal speaker. (All)

CALL *numeric variable* [(*variable*[,*variable*,]. . .)]
  Transfers control to the machine language program located at the offset address specified by the *numeric variable* (see DEF SEG). Passes the memory address of each optional *variable* listed to the machine language pro-

gram via the microprocessor's stack. (All)

CHAIN [MERGE] *file name*[,[*line expression*][,[**ALL**]] [,**DELETE** *first line,last line*]]

Loads and runs the program in the named file, erasing any existing program lines unless the MERGE option is present. Optionally starts program execution at the line number specified by the *line expression*. Clears all variables (except those listed in previous COMMON statements), unless the ALL option is present. Optionally deletes a range of line numbers before merging incoming program lines. (Disk and Advanced)

CIRCLE (*col,row*),*radius*[,[*hue*][,[*arc start,arc stop*][,[*aspect*]]]]

Draws a circle, an ellipse, or an arc with its center at (*col,row*) and a radius measuring *radius* columns. Draws in text color unless the optional *hue* selects another: 0 or 1 in high resolution, 0 through 3 from the medium-resolution palette (see Table 13-3). Optionally draws an arc from *arc start* to *arc stop* (both measured in radians, 0 to 6.2831) instead of a whole circle, and a negative value draws a ray from the arc endpoint to the center of the circle. Optionally draws an ellipse with height/width ratio specified by *aspect* (5/6 is a circle in medium resolution, 5/12 in high resolution). (Advanced)

CLOSE [#][*file/device number*][,[#][*file/device number*]]. . .

Closes the files and devices identified by the *file/device numbers*. If none is specified, closes all files and devices. (All)

CLS

Clears the display screen. (All)

COLOR [*foreground*][,[*background*][,*border*]]

Determines colors on the text-mode screen. Table 13-3 lists colors. (All)

COLOR [*background/border*][,*palette*]

Specifies one of 16 *background/border* colors for the medium-resolution screen. Selects the medium-resolution *palette* (0 or 1) for foreground hues. Tables 13-2 and 13-3 list colors and hues. (All)

COM (*adapter*) *action*

The *action* can be OFF, ON, or STOP. It determines whether the statement disables (OFF), enables (ON), or suspends (STOP) serial communications on *adapter* number 1 or 2 (see ON COM-GOSUB). (Advanced)

COMMON *variable*[,*variable*,]. . .

Names variables and whole arrays whose values will be retained during a subsequent CHAIN statement. Specify an array variable by suffixing the array name with the characters ( ). (Disk and Advanced)

DATA *constant,[constant,]. . .*

Adds string and number *constants* to the program's list of values for READ statements. (All)

DATE$ = *string value*

Sets the system calendar. (Disk and Advanced)

DEF FN*name[(dummy[,dummy]. . .)]* = *definition*

Names and defines a string or numeric function. Each optional *dummy* is a variable name that can appear in the *definition* expression. Dummy variables are replaced by actual values supplied each time the function is used (see function FN). (All)

DEF SEG[= *address*]

Define the current segment *address*, which is multiplied internally by 16 and added to offset addresses to compute actual addresses in BLOAD, BSAVE, CALL, and POKE statements as well as PEEK and USR functions. If the *address* is absent, uses the segment address of the BASIC workspace. (All)

DEF*type letter[-letter][,letter[-letter]]. . .*

Defines the *type* for variables whose names begin with letters listed. The *type* must be INT for integer, SNG for single precision, DBL for double precison, or STR for string. (All)

DEF USR[*number*] = *offset*

Defines the *offset* address of a numbered machine language subroutine that is called by a USR function. The *number* must be a digit between 0 and 9. (All)

DIM *array name(index[,index]. . .)* [*,array name(index[,index]. . .)]. . .*

Allocates memory space for arrays. Each *index* expression specifies a maximum subscript number (see OPTION BASE). (All)

DRAW *subcommand string*

Draws a shape as directed by the *subcommand string*. Table 13-4 lists subcommands. (Advanced)

END

Halts the program, closes all files and devices, and returns to immediate mode. (All)

ERASE *array name[,array name]. . .*

Eliminates named arrays. (All)

ERROR *code*

Generates the stipulated error *code* (see ON ERROR GOTO). (All)

FIELD [#]*file number, length* **AS** *string variable [,length* **AS** *string*

variable]. . .
Defines fields in a random-access file. (Disk and Advanced)

FOR *counter variable* = *first value* **TO** *last value*[[**STEP** *increment value*]
Marks the start of a FOR / NEXT loop. (All)

GET [#]*file number*[,*record number*]
Retrieves a record from a random-access file. Uses the next available record number unless the *record number* specifies another. (Disk and Advanced)

GET (*col1,row1*)-(*col2,row2*),*array name*
Uses the named array to capture the color of every point bounded by the rectangle with the specified opposite corner points. (Advanced)

GOSUB *line number*
Branches to a subroutine at the *line number* (see RETURN). (All)

GOTO *line number*
Branches to the *line number*. (All)

IF *condition* **THEN** *statement*[:*statement*]. . . [**ELSE** *statement*[:*statement*]. . .]
Conditionally executes one or more statements. If the *condition* is true, the first set of *statements* is executed, otherwise the second set of *statements* is executed. If the *condition* is false and there is no ELSE clause, execution falls through to the next program line. (All)

IF *condition* **THEN GOTO** *line number* [**ELSE** *statement*[:*statement*]. . .]
Conditionally executes one or more statements. If the *condition* is true, branches to the *line number*, otherwise the second set of *statements* is executed. If the *condition* is false and there is no ELSE clause, execution falls through to the next program line. (All)

INPUT [;][“*cue*”; or “*cue*”,] *variable*[,*variable*]. . .
Assigns values entered on the keyboard to each named *variable*. To prompt entry, displays a question mark, and optionally displays a *cue*. A comma after the *cue* suppresses the prompting question mark; a semicolon there permits it. A semicolon after INPUT suppresses the carriage return that normally occurs when the ◄─┘ key is pressed to end entry. (All)

INPUT #*file number*,*variable*[,*variable*]. . .
Assigns values retrieved from the designated file or device to each named *variable* in turn. Recognizes carriage returns, line advances, and commas as value separators, as well as blanks between numeric values. (All)

KEY *number,string value*
Activates the specified function key (*number* 1 to 10) as a Soft Key and

assigns it the *string value* as a definition. If the *string value* is null, the function key is deactivated as a Soft Key. (All)

KEY *action*

The *action* must be OFF, ON, or LIST. It either displays the first six characters of the Soft Key definitions on screen line 25 (ON), erases them (OFF), or displays all 15 characters on the main part of the screen (LIST). (All)

KEY (*numeric value*) *action*

The *action* can be OFF, ON, or STOP. It determines whether the statement disables (OFF), enables (ON), or suspends (STOP) trapping of the designated function key or cursor control key (*numeric values* between 1 and 14). (Advanced)

KILL *file name*

Deletes the named disk file. (Disk and Advanced)

[**LET**] *variable* = *expression*

Assigns the value of the *expression* to the *variable*. (All)

LINE [(*col1,row1*)]-(*col2,row2*)[,[*hue*][,**B**[**F**]]]

Draws a line or box on the display screen. Optionally fills the box with color. Draws in text color unless *hue* selects another: 0 or 1 in high resolution, 0 through 3 from the medium-resolution palette (see Table 13-3). (All)

LINE INPUT[;]["*cue*";] *string variable*

Accepts all characters typed on the keyboard until the next ◄─┘ key, then assigns them all to the *string variable*. Does not display a prompting question mark unless it is part of the optional *cue*. A semicolon after INPUT suppresses the carriage return that normally occurs when the ◄─┘ key is pressed to end entry. (All)

LINE INPUT #*file number,string variable*

Accepts all characters received from the designated file up to the next carriage return character that is followed by a line advance character. Assigns all accepted characters to the *string variable*. (All)

LOCATE [*row*][,[*col*][,[*visible*][,[*first*][,*last*]]]]

Moves the cursor to the specified location (using text row mode and column numbering). The value of *visible* determines cursor visibility; 0 for invisible and 1 for visible. Values of *first* and *last* determine the cursor size and shape. (All)

LPRINT [**USING** *template*;] *list of values*[;]

Prints on the main system printer (device LPT1:), but otherwise works the same as a PRINT statement. (All)

LSET *field variable* = *string value*

Assigns the *string value* to the named *field variable* in a random-access file buffer. Aligns the value on the left, filling unused spaces on the right with blanks. Will also left-align a value in a regular string variable. (Disk and Advanced)

MID$(*string variable,first character[,number of characters]*) = *string value*

Replaces the part of the *string variable* that starts at the *first character* with the *string value*. Optionally limits the *number of characters* used from the *string value*. (All)

MOTOR *state*

Starts (*state*<>0) or stops (*state*=0) tape movement on a tape recorder. (All)

NEXT [*counter variable*][*,counter variable*]. . .

Marks the end of one or more FOR/NEXT loops. (All)

ON COM (*adapter*) **GOSUB** *line number*

Establishes the *line number* of the subroutine to branch to when serial communications activity on *adapter* 1 or 2 is trapped (see COM-ON). (Advanced)

ON ERROR GOTO *line number*

Establishes the *line number* to branch to when an error is trapped (see RESUME). (All)

ON *expression* **GOSUB** *line number[,line number]*. . .

Branches to a subroutine at one of the *line numbers* listed, depending on the value of the *expression* (see RETURN). (All)

ON *expression* **GOTO** *line number[,line number]*. . .

Branches to one of the *line numbers* listed, depending on the value of the *expression*. (All)

ON KEY (*numeric value*) **GOSUB** *line number*

Establishes the *line number* of the subroutine to branch to when a function key or cursor control key (*numeric value* between 1 and 14) is trapped (see KEY-ON). (Advanced)

ON PEN GOSUB *line number*

Establishes the *line number* of the subroutine to branch to when light pen activity is trapped (see PEN ON). (Advanced)

ON STRIG (*numeric value*) **GOSUB** *line number*

Establishes the line number of the subroutine to branch to when game control trigger activity (*numeric values* 0, 2, 4, or 6) is trapped (see STRIG ON). (Advanced)

OPEN *file/device name* [**FOR** *mode*] **AS** [#]*file/device number*
  [**LEN** = *record length*]
  Assigns the *file/device number* to the named file or device and identifies
the access *mode* that will be used. Selects sequential access when *mode* is
INPUT, OUTPUT or APPEND. Selects random access when the FOR clause
is absent. Optionally stipulates random-access *record length*. (All)

OPEN *mode,*[#]*file/device number,file/device name*[,*record length*]
  Alternate version of the OPEN statement above. Here the choices for
mode are O for sequential output, I for sequential input, or R for random
access. (All)

OPEN "**COM***adapter:protocol*" **AS** [#]*device number* [**LEN** = *buffer
  length*]
  Assigns the *file/device number* to serial communications *adapter* 1 or
2. Optionally determines communications *protocol*. Table A-1 lists *protocol* options. (Disk and Advanced)

OPTION BASE *lowest index*
  Stipulates the *lowest index* in all arrays, 0 or 1 (see DIM). (All)

OUT *port,byte value*
  Writes the *byte value* to the designated machine output *port*. (All)

PAINT (*col,row*)[,*fill*[,*boundary*]]
  Starting at the designated point, fills the screen in all directions with the
specified *fill* color, but not past the specified *boundary* color. Uses text
color unless the optional *fill* or *boundary* colors select others: 0 or 1 in
high resolution, 0 through 3 from the medium-resolution palette (see Table
13-3). (Advanced)

PEN *action*
  The *action* must be OFF or ON, and it determines whether the PEN function can be used (ON for yes, OFF for no). In Advanced BASIC, *action* can
also be STOP, and it either enables (ON), disables (OFF), or suspends
(STOP) trapping of light pen activity. (All)

PLAY *subcommand string*
  Plays a tune through the internal speaker, as directed by the *subcommand string*. Table 14-2 lists subcommands. (Advanced)

POKE *offset,byte value*
  Stores the *byte value* at the *offset* address (see DEF SEG). (All)

PRESET (*col,row*)[,*hue*]
  Plots one point on the display screen. Uses background color unless the
hue selects another: 0 or 1 in high resolution, 0 through 3 from the
medium-resolution palette (see Table 13-3). (All)

PRINT [*list of values*][;]

Displays the listed values, if any, on the screen. Displays carriage return and line advance characters after the last value unless the terminal semicolon is present. Semicolons that separate values on the list have no effect on character positions, but commas can separate values on the list and each will advance the cursor to the next print zone. (All)

PRINT [#*file/device number*,] [**USING** *template*;] *list of values*

Displays the listed values on the screen, unless the *file/device number* specifies another device or file. Optionally formats output according to the *template* (see Table 10-1 for template characters). Semicolons that separate values on the list have no effect on character positions. But when the USING clause is absent, commas can separate values on the list and each will advance to the next print zone. A terminal semicolon suppresses the carriage return that otherwise occurs after printing the last value. (All)

PSET (*col,row*)[,*hue*]

Plots one point on the display screen. Uses text color unless the *hue* selects another: 0 or 1 in high resolution, 0 through 3 from the medium-resolution palette (see Table 13-3). (All)

PUT #*file number*[,*record number*]

Stores a record on a random-access file. Uses the next available record number unless the *record number* specifies another. (Disk and Advanced)

PUT (*col,row*),*array name*[,*blend*]

Displays the colors of all points in a rectangular region of the screen. Starts displaying the upper left-hand corner of the rectangle at the designated coordinates. The named array contains all the point colors. Optionally blends the array colors with existing screen colors. Table 13-5 lists *blend* options. (Advanced)

RANDOMIZE *integer value*

Selects the set of random numbers specified by the *integer value* (see function RND). (All)

READ *variable*[,*variable*]. . .

Assigns values to the named variables from the list established by DATA statements. (All)

REM [*remark*]

Designates that all characters that follow on the same line are program comments, and are not to be executed. (All)

RESTORE [*line number*]

Resets the pointer for the list of DATA statement values to the first DATA statement in the program, or optionally to the designated *line number*. (All)

RESUME [*option*]

Resumes program execution after an error was trapped by an ON ERROR GOTO statement. If the *option* is 0 or absent, execution resumes at the statement that caused the error. If the *option* is a line number, execution resumes there. If the *option* is the word 'NEXT', execution resumes at the next statement after the one that caused the error. (All)

RETURN [*line number*]

Returns from a subroutine to the statement following the most recent GOSUB (or ON-GOSUB) statement. Advanced BASIC can return to a designated *line number*. (All)

RSET *field variable = string value*

Assigns the *string value* to the named *field variable* in a random-access file. Aligns the value on the right, filling unused spaces on the left with blanks. Will also right-align a value in a regular string variable. (Disk and Advanced)

SCREEN [*mode*][,[*burst*][,[*active page*][,*visible page*]]]

Selects display screen *mode* (0 = text, 1 = medium resolution, 2 = high resolution). Optionally inhibits color images (if *burst* = 0 in text mode or <>0 in medium resolution). In text mode, can also select the *active page* for output statements like PRINT and the *visible page* that is displayed (either page can be 0 to 3 for width 80, 0 to 7 for width 40). (All)

SOUND *frequency,duration*

Generates a tone of the designated *frequency* (37 to 32767 hertz) of a specified *duration* (measured in clock ticks, at 18.2 ticks per second). A *duration* of zero stops sound. In Advanced BASIC, SOUND is affected by some PLAY statement subcommands. (All)

STOP

Stops program execution, displays a "Break. . ." message, and returns to immediate mode. (All)

STRIG *action*

The *action* must be OFF or ON, and it determines whether the STRIG function can be used (ON for yes, OFF for no). (All)

STRIG (*numeric value*) *action*

The *action* can be OFF, ON, or STOP. It determines whether the statement disables (OFF), enables (ON), or suspends (STOP) trapping of the designated game control trigger (*numeric values*: 0 for trigger A1, 2 for trigger B1, 4 for trigger A2, and 6 for trigger B2). (Advanced)

SWAP *variable,variable*

Exchanges the values of the two named variables. (All)

TIME$ = *string value*

Sets the system clock. (Disk and Advanced)

WAIT$ *port,mask[,select]*

Suspends program execution and monitors an input port. Program execution resumes when the result of the following expression is nonzero:

port XOR *select* AND *mask*

If *select* is absent, 0 is used. (All)

WEND

Branches back to the preceding WHILE statement. (All)

WHILE *condition*

If the specified *condition* is true, execution proceeds with the next statement. Otherwise, execution branches to the statement that follows the next WEND statement. (All)

WIDTH [*device number,*]*width*

Sets the *width* of the display screen or of another device designated by the *device number*. (All)

WIDTH *device name,width*

Prepares for a *width* change on the named device, but defers the change until the device is later opened. (All)

WRITE [#*file number,*]*list of values*

Displays the listed values, displays a comma between each of them, and displays quotation marks around string values. Optionally writes the values the same way to a sequential file designated by the *file number*. (All)

FUNCTIONS

All functions are listed here in alphabetical order. Most functions have one or more operands, which may be constants, variables, array elements, other functions, or expressions, unless stated otherwise. Some functions restrict the range of operand values as noted. Numeric functions compute single-precision values unless stated otherwise.

ABS(*numeric value*)

Computes the absolute value of the *numeric value*. (All)

ASC(*string value*)

Determines the character code number of the first character in the *string value*. (All)

ATN(*numeric value*)

Calculates the arctangent of the *numeric value*. (All)

CDBL(*numeric value*)
Converts the *numeric value* to a double-precison value. (All)

CHR$(*code*)
Determines the character whose *code* number is specified (see Appendix D). (All)

CINT(*numeric value*)
Rounds the *numeric value* to the nearest integer. (All)

COS(*numeric value*)
Calculates the cosine of the *numeric value*. (All)

CSNG(*numeric value*)
Rounds the *numeric value* to a single-precision value. (All)

CSRLIN
Reports which screen row the text cursor is on. (All)

CVD(*string value*)
Converts an eight-character *string value* to a double-precision value (inverse of MKD$). (Disk and Advanced)

CVI(*string value*)
Converts a two-character *string value* to an integer value (inverse of MKI$). (Disk and Advanced)

CVS(*string value*)
Converts a four-character *string value* to a single-precision value (inverse of MKS$). (Disk and Advanced)

DATE$
Reports the system date. (Disk and Advanced)

EOF(*file number*)
Reports whether the end of the designated data file has been reached. Returns a value of True (− 1) or False (0). (All)

ERL
Reports the line number where the last error was detected. (All)

ERR
Reports the code of the last error detected (see Appendix C). (All)

EXP(*numeric value*)
Raises the constant *e* (2.718282) to the power of the *numeric value*. (All)

FIX(*numeric value*)
Truncates the *numeric value* to an integer value. (All)

FNname[(*value*[,*value*]. . .)]

Invokes the named function as defined by a corresponding DEF FN statement, which also determines the number and type of *values* required.

FRE(*string value* or *numeric value*)
Reports the amount of free memory. The *string value* or *numeric value* is not used, except the presence of any *string value* forces the reorganization of the string storage area of memory. (All)

HEX$(*numeric value*)
Converts the *numeric value* to its hexadecimal equivalent. (All)

INKEY$
Reports which key is currently depressed on the keyboard. A null value means the keyboard is inactive. A one-character value is the character that corresponds to the keystroke. A two-character value means the keystroke has no corresponding character and must be interpreted as an extended code (see Appendix D). (All)

INP(*port*)
Reports the value of the designated machine *port*. (All)

INPUT$(*number*[,[#]*file / device number*])
Reads the specified *number* of characters from the keyboard unless the *file / device number* designates another device or file. (All)

INSTR([*start*],*source,pattern*)
Searches the *source* string for the first occurrence of the *pattern* string, starting with the first character in the *source* unless a different *start* character is specified. (All)

INT(*numeric value*)
Computes the largest integer less than or equal to the the *numeric value*. (All)

LEFT$(*string value,length*)
Extracts a substring of the specified *length* from the leftmost characters of the *string value*. (All)

LEN(*string value*)
Determines the number of characters in the *string value*. (All)

LOC(*file number*)
Determines the current position in the specified file. (Disk and Advanced)

LOF(*file number*)
Reports the length of the specified file. (Disk and Advanced)

LOG(*numeric value*)
Calculates the natural logarithm of the *numeric value*. (All)

LPOS(*numeric value*)

Reports the position of the last character in the printer buffer. The *numeric value* is required but not used in Cassette BASIC. In Disk and Advanced BASIC, the *numeric value* designates which printer to check (0=LPT1:, 1=LPT1:, 2=LPT2:, and 3=LPT3:). (All)

MID$(*string value,first character,[length]*)

Extracts the part of the *string value* that starts with the designated *first character*. Optionally limits the *length* of the substring extracted. (All)

MKD$(*numeric value*)

Converts the *numeric value* to a double-precision number and makes it an eight-character string value (inverse of CVD). (Disk and Advanced)

MKI$(*numeric value*)

Rounds the *numeric value* to an integer and makes it a two-character string value (inverse of CVI). (Disk and Advanced)

MKS$(*numeric value*)

Rounds the *numeric value* to a single-precision number and makes it a four-character string value (inverse of CVS). (Disk and Advanced)

OCT$(*numeric value*)

Converts the *numeric value* to its octal equivalent. (All)

PEEK(*offset*)

Reports the value of the memory cell at the specified *offset* from the current segment address (see statement DEF SEG). (All)

PEN(*numeric value*)

Reports light pen activity. Table A-2 describes the effects of different *numeric values*. The PEN function will not work unless a PEN ON statement has occurred. (All)

POINT(*col,row*)

Determines the color at the specified graphics screen coordinates. (All)

POS(*numeric value*)

Reports which screen column the text cursor is on; the *numeric value* is required but not used. (All)

RIGHT$(*string value,length*)

Extract a substring of the specified *length* from the rightmost characters of the *string value*. (All)

RND[(*numeric value*)]

Computes a random number between zero and one. If the *numeric value* is zero, the previous random number is repeated. If the *numeric value* is positive or absent, the next number from the current list is used. If the numeric value is negative, it specifies a new list of numbers and the first number on that list is used (see statement RANDOMIZE). (All)

SCREEN(*row,col*[,*option*])
Determines the code number of the character displayed at the specified location (using text mode row and column numbering). The *option* is valid only in text mode. If it has a True value (nonzero), SCREEN reports the color attributes at the specified location instead of the code number of the character there. Use the expressions below to decipher the color attributes. (All)

  color attributes = SCREEN(*row,col,* − 1)
  foreground color = *color attributes* MOD 16
  background color = ((*color attributes* - *foreground color*)/ 16) MOD 128
  blinking character if (*color attributes*>127) is True (− 1)

SGN(*numeric value*)
Returns + 1 if the *numeric value* is positive, − 1 if it is negative, and 0 if it is zero. (All)

SIN(*numeric value*)
Calculates the sine of the *numeric value*. (All)

SPACE$(*number*)
Generates the designated *number* of blank spaces. (All)

SPC(*number*)
Skips ahead the designated *number* of columns on the print line. Valid only with PRINT and LPRINT statements. (All)

SQR(*numeric value*)
Calculates the square root of the *numeric value*.

STICK(*numeric value*)
Reports the positions of two joysticks or other game controls. Actually checks the control positions only when the *numeric value* is zero, but other values report individual coordinates too; Table A-3 lists meaningful values. (All)

STRIG(*numeric value*)
Determines the status of the game control triggers (buttons). Table A-4 shows how the *numeric value* determines which trigger is checked. The STRIG function will not work unless an STRIG ON statement has occurred. (All)

STRING$(*length, string value or code*)
Generates a string of the designated *length*. Its characters are all the same as the first character of the *string value* or have the specified *code* number, whichever is present. (All)

STR$(*numeric value*)

Converts the *numeric value* to a string of characters. (All)

TAB(*column*)

Advances to the designated *column* on the print line. Valid only with PRINT and LPRINT statements. (All)

TAN(*numeric value*)

Calculates the tangent of the *numeric value*. (All)

TIME$

Reports the system time. (Disk and Advanced)

USR[*number*](*string variable* or *numeric value*)

Transfers control to a numbered machine language program located at the address defined by a DEF USR statement. Passes either the *numeric value* or the memory address of the *string variable*, whichever is present, to the machine language program. (All)

VAL(*string value*)

Converts the *string value* to its numeric equivalent. (All)

VARPTR(*variable*)

Determines the memory address of the value of the *variable*. (All)

VARPTR(#*file number*)

Determines the memory address of the BASIC file control block for the designated file. (All)

VARPTR$(*variable*)

Determines the *variable* type and its memory address. Converts those values to a three-character string. (Disk and Advanced)

DERIVED FUNCTIONS

The intrinsic transcendental functions can be combined to calculate other transcendental functions (listed below). The equations that follow define the derivations in terms of n, which can be any numeric constant, variable, array element, function, or expression. Any values of n that would cause error messages are noted.

$\text{ARCCOS}(n) = 1.570796 - \text{ATN}(n/\text{SQR}(1-n*n))$

Inverse cosine of n, when $\text{ABS}(n) < 1$.

$\text{ARCCOT}(n) = 1.570796 - \text{ATN}(n)$

Inverse cotangent of n.

$\text{ARCCOSH}(n) = \text{LOG}(n + \text{SQR}(n*n-1))$

Inverse hyperbolic cosine of n, when $n >= 1$.

ARCCOTH(n) = LOG((n + 1)/(n − 1))/2
  Inverse hyperbolic cotangent of n, when ABS(n)>1.
ARCCSC(n) = ATN(1/SQR(n*n − 1)) + (SGN(n) − 1)*1.570796
  Inverse cosecant of n, when ABS(n)>1.
ARCCSCH(n) = LOG((SGN(n)*SQR(n*n + 1) + 1)/n)
  Inverse hyperbolic cosecant of n, when n>0.
ARCSEC(n) = ATN((SQR(n*n − 1)) + (SGN(n) − 1)*1.570796
  Inverse secant of n, when ABS(n)> = 1.
ARCSECH(n) = LOG((SQR(1 − n*n) + 1)/n)
  Inverse hyperbolic secant of n, when 0<n< = 1.
ARCSIN(n) = ATN(n/SQR(1 − n*n))
  Inverse sine of n, when ABS(n)<1.
ARCSINH(n) = LOG(n + SQR(n*n + 1))
  Inverse hyperbolic sine of n.
ARCTANH(n) = LOG((1 + n)/(1 − n))/2
  Inverse hyperbolic tangent of n, when ABS(n)<1.
COSH(n) = (EXP(n) + EXP(−n))/2
  Hyperbolic cosine of n.
COT(n) = 1/TAN(n)
  Cotangent of n, when n<>0.
COTH(n) = EXP(−n)/(EXP(n) − EXP(−n))*2 + 1
  Hyperbolic cotangent of n, when n<>0.
CSC(n) = 1/SIN(n)
  Cosecant of n, when n<>0.
CSCH(n) = 2/(EXP(n) − EXP(−n))
  Hyperbolic cosecant of n, when n<>0.
LOG$_a$(n) = LOG(n)/ LOG(a)
  Base a logarithm of n, when a>0 and n>0.
LOG$_{10}$(n) = LOG(n)/2.302585
  Common logarithm (base 10) of n, when n>0.
SEC(n) = 1/COS(n)
  Secant of n, when n<>1.570796.
SECH(n) = 2/(EXP(n) + EXP(−n))
  Hyperbolic secant of n.
SINH(n) = (EXP(n) − EXP(−n))/2
  Hyperbolic sine of n.
TANH(n) = (EXP(−n) − EXP(n))/EXP(−n)) + EXP(n))
  Hyperbolic tangent of n.

Table A-1. Serial Communications Protocol Options*

Option	Meaning
baud	Data transmission rate: 75, 110, 150, 300, 600, 1200, 1800, 2400, 4800, 9600
,*parity*	S for space (0 bit), M for mark (1 bit), O for odd, E for even, N for none
,*word*	Size of data word in bits: 4, 5, 6, 7, or 8
,*stop*	Number of stop bits: 1 or 2
,RS	Suppress the request-to-send (RTS) signal
,CS*ms*	Wait *ms* milliseconds for clear-to-send (CTS) signal
,DS*ms*	Wait *ms* milliseconds for data set ready (DSR) signal
,CD*ms*	Wait *ms* milliseconds for carrier detect (CD) signal
,LF	Forces output of a line advance character after every carriage return character

*Use these options in OPEN ''COM statements; specify in the order listed here.

Table A-2. PEN Function Operand

Numeric value	Meaning
0	Pen down since last poll*
1	Last active graphics column
2	Last active graphics row
3	Pen switch on*
4	Last valid graphics column
5	Last valid graphics row
6	Last active text row
7	Last active text column
8	Last valid text row
9	Last valid text column

*Both PEN(0) and PEN(3) return True (−1) or False (0) values.

Table A-3. STICK Function Operand

Numeric value	Meaning
0	Horizontal coordinate, control A
1	Vertical coordinate, control A
2	Horizontal coordinate, control B
3	Vertical coordinate, control B

Table A-4. STRIG Function Operand

Numeric value*	Meaning†
0	Trigger A1 pressed since last STRIG(0)
1	Trigger A1 now pressed
2	Trigger B1 pressed since last STRIG(2)
3	Trigger B1 now pressed
4	Trigger A2 pressed since last STRIG(4)
5	Trigger A2 now pressed
6	Trigger B2 pressed since last STRIG(6)
7	Trigger B2 now pressed

*Values 4 through 7 valid only in Advanced BASIC.
†The STRIG function always returns a True (− 1) or False (0) value.

PC DOS SUMMARY

This appendix contains a summary of all standard PC DOS (version 1.10) commands, listed in alphabetic order. For in-depth information on the commands listed here, refer to Chapters 3 and 5 of this book, or to Chapter 3 of *IBM Personal Computer Disk Operating System, 2nd ed.*

Since there are ways to create custom commands (see Chapter 5), your system may have additional commands not listed here. For example, many Winchester disk drives use their own commands for disk formatting and copying.

When entering the commands listed here, type all characters printed in **BOLDFACE** exactly as shown, except you may use any combination of capital and small letters. Substitute actual values for terms printed in *italics*. Anything enclosed in square brackets ([ ]) is optional, but do not type the brackets themselves. You can repeat any item that is followed by an ellipsis (. . .). Be sure to include all punctuation marks (except square brackets and ellipses), including commas, colons, slashes, equal signs, and plus signs.

drive:
Logs the designated *drive* as the one to use by default in commands where a drive specification is omitted.

[*drive:*]*file* [*options*]
Executes the command or batch *file*. The *options* vary depending on the requirements of the command or batch *file*.

CHKDSK [*drive:*]
Checks a disk's files for integrity and displays a report on disk and memory usage.

COMP [*drive:*]*file* [*drive:*][*file*]
Compares the contents of the two named files and reports the locations of dissimilarities discovered.

COPY [*drive:*]*source*[*option*] [+ [*drive:*]*concatenation*[*option*]]
[*drive:*][*target*][*option*] [/**V**]

Copies the *source* file to the *target* file, optionally adding on the *concatenation* file. Verifies the copy operation if the /V is present. The *option* can be /A or /B. The /A means a source file is copied up to the first end-of-file character (code number 26) and a target file has that character added at the end. The /B means the entire source file is copied and no special character is added to the end of the target file.

DATE [*date*]

Sets the system date. If the *date* is absent, PC DOS requests it.

DIR [*drive:*][*file*] [/**P**][/**W**]

Lists all or part of the files on a disk directory.

DISKCOMP [*drive:*] [*drive:*] [/**1**]

Compares two diskettes and reports any discrepancies. The /1 forces a single-sided compare.

DISKCOPY [*source:*] [*target:*] [/**1**]

Copies the diskette in the *source* drive onto the diskette in the *target* drive. Performs a single-drive copy if only one drive (or none) is specified. The /1 forces a single-sided copy.

ERASE [*drive:*]*file*

Erases the named file from a disk directory.

EXE2BIN [*drive:*]*file* [*drive:*][*file*]

Converts a type EXE file to a type COM file.

FORMAT [*drive:*] [/**S**][/**1**]

Initializes a diskette for the PC DOS recording format, earmarks bad areas on the diskette, and sets up a blank directory. The /S option makes the formatted diskette a system disk by writing selected PC DOS programs on it. The /1 forces a single-sided format.

MODE LPT:*number*[*width*][,*height*]

Can set the line *width* (1 to 132 characters) and line *height* (1/6 or 1/8 inch) for printer *number* 1, 2, or 3. The line height setting only works with some printer models.

MODE [*width*][,*direction*][,**T**]

Can set the screen *width* (40 or 80 characters). Can also shift the displayed area on the screen the designated direction (R for right, L for left), with a test pattern (T present) or without it (T absent).

MODE COM*adapter:**baud*[,*parity*[,*word*[,*stop*[,**P**]]]]

Determines serial communications protocol to be used with *adapter* number 1 or 2. Data transmission speeds can be 110, 150, 300, 600, 1200, 2400, 4800, or 9600 *baud*. The *parity* can be even (E), odd (O), or none (N). The *word* length can be 7 or 8 bits. There can be 1 or 2 *stop* bits.

MODE LPT*number*: = COM*adapter*

Redirects output for printer *number* 1, 2, or 3 to serial communications *adapter* number 1 or 2.

PAUSE [*remark*]

Suspends processing to display the word "PAUSE" along with the optional *remark* and the message 'Strike any key when ready. . . ", and waits for a keystroke.

REM [*remark*]

Displays the word "REM" along with the optional *remark*.

RENAME [*drive:*]*old new*

Changes a file's *old* name to a *new* name.

SYS *drive:*

Copies the PC DOS program files needed to make a disk a system disk, but only if the designated *drive* contains a disk formatted with the /S option.

TIME [*time*]

Sets the system time. If the *time* is absent, PC DOS requests it.

TYPE [*drive:*]*file*

Displays the contents of the specified *file*, interpreting everything on the file as an ASCII character code (see Appendix D).

ERROR MESSAGE SUMMARY

This appendix contains a summary of all PC BASIC error messages, listed in alphabetic order. Each entry refers to the error number reported by function ERL. That number also cross-refers to the list of amplified error messages in Appendix A of *IBM Personal Computer BASIC, 2nd. ed.*

Message	Number
Advanced feature	73
Bad file mode	54
Bad file name	64
Bad file number	52
Bad record number	63
Can't continue	17
Communication buffer overflow	69
Device Fault	25
Device I/O error	57
Device Timeout	24
Device Unavailable	68
Direct statement in file	66
Disk full	61
Disk Media Error	72
Disk not Ready	71
Disk Write Protect	70
Division by zero	11
Duplicate definition	10
FIELD overflow	50
File already exists	58
File already open	55
File not found	53
FOR without NEXT	26
Illegal direct	12
Illegal function call	5
Input past end	62
Internal error	51
Line buffer overflow	23
Missing operand	22
NEXT without FOR	1
No RESUME	19

Message	Number
Out of data	4
Out of memory	7
Out of paper	27
Out of string space	14
Overflow	6
RESUME without error	20
RETURN without GOSUB	3
String formula too complex	16
String too long	15
Subscript out of range	9
Syntax error	2
Too many files	67
Type mismatch	13
Undefined line number	8
Undefined user function	18
Unprintable error	—
WEND without WHILE	30
WHILE without WEND	29

CHARACTERS, CODES, AND KEYSTROKES

Table D-1 correlates the 256 characters available on the display screen with their code numbers. Codes 128 through 256 are not available in Cassette BASIC.

You can generate characters with codes between 32 and 126 by typing on the keyboard as you would on an ordinary typewriter. For example, press the A key to generate the letter A. You can also generate a character by holding down the **Alt** key while you type in the character's code on the numeric keypad, as described in Chapter 7. That technique does not work with codes 0 through 31 nor code 127 when typing commands in immediate mode or when responding to INPUT or LINE INPUT statements. It does work in response to INPUT$ and INKEY$ functions, however. Of course, the CHR$ function can generate any available character.

On most printers, codes 0 through 32 are control codes and produce no printed output themselves. Control code interpretation varies from one printer to another with all but a few of the codes, and those are listed in Table 10-3. The interpretation of codes above 127 varies greatly among different printers. And on printers with interchangeable type wheels (daisywheels or thimbles), even codes 32 through 127 may be different from the ASCII standard shown in Table D-1.

Table D-2 lists the extended codes that are generated chiefly by multiple keystrokes involving the **Alt**, ⇧, and **Ctrl** keys. They have no corresponding characters and are detectable only with the INKEY$ function, as described in Chapter 11.

Table D-1.   Screen Characters and Codes

Decimal code	Character	Decimal code	Character	Decimal code	Character
000	(null)	047	/	094	∧
001	☺	048	0	095	—
002	●	049	1	096	`
003	♥ *	050	2	097	a
004	♦	051	3	098	b
005	♣	052	4	099	c
006	♠	053	5	100	d
007	(beep)	054	6	101	e
008	(backspace)	055	7	102	f
009	(tab)	056	8	103	g
010	(line advance)	057	9	104	h
011	(cursor home)	058	:	105	i
012	(clear screen)	059	;	106	j
013	(carriage return)	060	<	107	k
014	♫	061	=	108	l
015	☼	062	>	109	m
016	►	063	?	110	n
017	◄	064	@	111	o
018	↕	065	A	112	p
019	‼	066	B	113	q
020	¶	067	C	114	r
021	§	068	D	115	s
022	▬	069	E	116	t
023	↨	070	F	117	u
024	↑	071	G	118	v
025	↓	072	H	119	w
026	→	073	I	120	x
027	←	074	J	121	y
028	(cursor right)	075	K	122	z
029	(cursor right)	076	L	123	{
030	(cursor up)	077	M	124	|
031	(cursor down)	078	N	125	}
032	(space)	079	O	126	~
033	!	080	P	127	⌂
034	"	081	Q	128	Ç
035	#	082	R	129	ü
036	$	083	S	130	é
037	%	084	T	131	â
038	&	085	U	132	ä
039	'	086	V	133	à
040	(	087	W	134	å
041	)	088	X	135	ç
042	*	089	Y	136	ê
043	+	090	Z	137	ë
044	,	091	[	138	è
045	-	092	\	139	ï
046	.	093	]	140	î

Table D-1.—Cont.   Screen Characters and Codes

Decimal code	Character	Decimal code	Character	Decimal code	Character
141	ì	180	⊣	219	■
142	Ä	181	╡	220	▬
143	Å	182	╢	221	▌
144	É	183	╖	222	▐
145	æ	184	╕	223	▀
146	Æ	185	╣	224	α
147	ê	186	║	225	β
148	ö	187	╗	226	Γ
149	ò	188	╝	227	π
150	û	189	╜	228	Σ
151	ù	190	╛	229	σ
152	ÿ	191	┐	230	µ
153	Ö	192	└	231	τ
154	Ü	193	┴	232	Φ
155	¢	194	┬	233	⊖
156	£	195	├	234	Ω
157	¥	196	─	235	δ
158	Pt	197	+	236	∞
159	ƒ	198	╞	237	∅
160	á	199	╟	238	∈
161	í	200	╚	239	∩
162	ó	201	╔	240	≡
163	ú	202	╩	241	±
164	ñ	203	╦	242	≥
165	Ñ	204	╠	243	≤
166	a̲	205	═	244	⌠
167	o̲	206	╬	245	⌡
168	¿	207	╧	246	÷
169	⌐	208	╨	247	≈
170	¬	209	╤	248	°
171	½	210	╥	249	•
172	¼	211	╙	250	·
173	¡	212	╘	251	√
174	«	213	╒	252	ⁿ
175	»	214	╓	253	²
176	░	215	╫	254	■
177	▒	216	╪	255	(blank 'FF')
178	▓	217	┘		
179	│	218	┌		

*Typing character code 3 directly (with the **Alt** key) causes a break similar to **Ctrl|Scroll Lock**, but CHR$(3) always generates the listed character.

†On most printers, character code 12 advances the paper to the top of the next page.

Table D-2. Extended Keyboard Codes

Decimal code	Keystroke	Decimal code	Keystroke
3	(null character)		
15	⟵|	85	⇧|F2
16	Alt|Q	86	⇧|F3
17	Alt|W	87	⇧|F4
18	Alt|E	88	⇧|F5
19	Alt|R	89	⇧|F6
20	Alt|T	90	⇧|F7
21	Alt|Y	91	⇧|F8
22	Alt|U	92	⇧|F9
23	Alt|I	93	⇧|F10
24	Alt|O	94	Ctrl|F1
25	Alt|P	95	Ctrl|F2
30	Alt|A	96	Ctrl|F3
31	Alt|S	97	Ctrl|F4
32	Alt|D	98	Ctrl|F5
33	Alt|F	99	Ctrl|F6
34	Alt|G	100	Ctrl|F7
35	Alt|H	101	Ctrl|F8
36	Alt|J	102	Ctrl|F9
37	Alt|K	103	Ctrl|F10
38	Alt|L	104	Alt|F1
44	Alt|Z	105	Alt|F2
45	Alt|X	106	Alt|F3
46	Alt|C	107	Alt|F4
47	Alt|V	108	Alt|F5
48	Alt|B	109	Alt|F6
49	Alt|N	110	Alt|F7
50	Alt|M	111	Alt|F8
59	F1 *	112	Alt|F9
60	F2 *	113	Alt|F10
61	F3 *	114	Ctrl|PrtSc
62	F4 *	115	Ctrl|⟵ (previous word)
63	F5 *	116	Ctrl|⟶ (next word)
64	F6 *	117	Ctrl|End
65	F7 *	118	Ctrl|PgDn
66	F8 *	119	Ctrl|Home
67	F9 *	120	Alt|1
68	F10 *	121	Alt|2
71	Home	122	Alt|3
72	↑	123	Alt|4
73	PgUp	124	Alt|5
75	⟵	125	Alt|6
77	⟶	126	Alt|7
79	End	127	Alt|8
80	↓	128	Alt|9
81	PgDn	129	Alt|0
82	Ins	130	Alt|−
83	Del	131	Alt|=
84	⇧|F1	132	Ctrl|PgUp

*When disabled as soft key

INDEX

END, 98, 290
End key, 20, 62
  in PC DOS, 71
End-of-page subroutine, 177
Enter key; *See* Return key
Entry cues, INPUT, 126
Entry; *See* Data entry
EOF, 209
EOR, 298
Equivalence, logical, 136-137
EQV, 136-137
ERASE
  BASIC arrays, 120-121, 290
  PC DOS files, 52, 307
ERL, 298
ERR, 298
ERROR, 290
Errors
  announcing during data entry, 196-197
  BASIC, 95-96
  branching out of subroutines, 155-156
  checking for after file copy, 69
  checking for after INPUT, 126-127
  coloring graphics shapes, 242
  correcting during data entry, 197-199
  correcting transcription, 60-65
  cursor positioning, 167
  DATA and READ compatibility, 123-124
  data file field delimiter, 207
  detecting during data entry, 194-196
  diskette duplicating, 45
  diskette formatting, 42, 43
  displaying file contents, 69
  expression, 133
  file concatenation, 68
  GOTO, 145-146
  immediate mode on graphics screen, 231
  LEFT$, 139
  messages, 95-96, 309-310
  MID$, 139
  numbers, 309-310
  numeric string comparisons, 142
  ON-GOTO, 147
  relational expressions, 135-136
  RIGHT$, 139
  self-starting software, 56
  starting BAS software, 58
  starting PC DOS, 32, 33
  SWAP, 127
  trapping, 216-217
  typographical, 23
  with arrays, 120, 121
Esc key, 19, 23, 62

Esc key—cont
  AUTO, 105
  INPUT, 125
  PC DOS, 39, 73, 80
Exclamation point, variable type suffix, 115-117
EXE software, starting, 57
EXE2BIN, 307
EXP, 298
Expansion slots, 7
Explosion image display program, 253
Explosion image movement program, 255
Exponentiation, 133-134
Expressions
  converting values in, 133-134
  DRAW subcommands, 247-249
  evaluating, 132-133
  function-defining, 140
  logical,
  numeric, 133-134
  relational, 134-136, 147-148
  string, 134
  uses of, 132
Extended keyboard codes, 190, 311, 314
Extension, file name, 35, 36

F

F1 key
  checking transcription with, 60
  in PC DOS, 72, 73-76, 80
F2 key, in PC DOS, 72, 76-80
F3 key, in PC DOS, 72, 75-80
F4 key, in PC DOS, 72, 78-80
F5 key, in PC DOS, 72, 80
F6 key
  checking transcription with, 61
  in PC DOS, 72, 81
F7 key, in PC DOS, 72
False, logical expressions, 136-137
FIELD, 214, 290-291
Fields, data file, 200
File buffers, 203
File names
  changing, 52-53
  extensions, 34, 35, 36
  generic, 35, 41, 51, 68, 108
  in directory, 37
  rules for, 34
File numbers; *See also* Device numbers
  assigning, 203-204
  reassigning, 204
FILES, 108, 287
Files; *See also* Random access; Sequential
  access